The Nepal New Constitution and Madhesi Movement

The Nepal New Constitution and Madhesi Movement

Dr. Krishna Kumari
Prashant Kr. Jha

PRASHANT PUBLISHING HOUSE
DELHI-110094

Published by :
Prashant Publishing House
C-34, 28 Foota Road, Gali-3,
West Karwal Nagar, Delhi-110094
Phone : 011-22963970, Mob. : 9810396373
e-mail.: prashantpublishinghouse@gmail.com

The Nepal New Constitution and Madhesi Movement

First Published 2016

ISBN 978-93-80565-66-8

PRINTED IN INDIA
Published by Mr. R.K. Jha M/s Prashant Publishing House and Published at H.S. Offset House Press, Delhi.

Contents

Preface

The book explicates a liberal democratic constitution as the bedrock for accomplishing the nation building process. In this context, the federal republican design of the 2015 Constitution and its implementation explain the possible paths and leeway of nation building in Nepal. Despite being one of the main driving forces of the 2015 Constitution, from the very beginning of its derivation, federalism is facing arcane challenges.

The Interim Constitution provides for a Constituent Assembly, which was charged with writing Nepal's permanent constitution. Under the terms of the Interim Constitution, the new constitution was to be promulgated by May 28, 2010, but the Constituent Assembly postponed the promulgation by a year because of disagreements. On May 25, 2011, the Supreme Court of Nepal ruled that the 2010 extension of the Interim Constitution was not right. Since May 29, 2011 the Constituent Assembly repeatedly extended the Interim Constitution.

On May 28, 2012, the Constituent Assembly was dissolved after it failed to finish the constitution after the latest extension, ending four years of constitution drafting and leaving the country in a legal vacuum. New elections were held on November 19, 2013 to the Second and political leaders pledged to draft a new constitution within a year.

The new assembly expressly committed that the new constitution would be promulgated on January 22, 2015. However, due to continued differences on key issues including system of governance, judicial system and federation issues like number, name and areas of the states to be carved, the constitution could not be finalized and promulgated in time.

The recent turmoil in Madhes (or the Terai plains bordering India) was a stark reflection of the challenges confronting the restructuring process in Nepal. It was also a reminder to the current interim government that the problems in Nepal are not yet over and that there are serious socio-economic and political issues that need to be addressed.

The Madhesi uprising in January was marked by bans, protests, and violence in some major areas of Nepal's terai resulting in the death of over thirty people. This has in several ways changed the interim government's approach to and the management of Nepal's political restructuring and peace process. It has also raised many questions. Why was the violence so potent? Who was responsible? How will it affect the restructuring process? And so on.

These questions are palpable in the context of Nepal's fragile political restructuring process that is underway. While exploring answers to these questions, however, there is a proclivity to misinterpret the Madhesi issue. Some (mis) conceptions that have come about in the wake of the uprising are not only erroneous but also dangerous. All the matter is just compiled and edited in nature. Taken from the various sources which are in public domain.

The most important task of constitution-making is the building of consensus, and developing a framework for coexistence and cooperation among communities, based on social justice, values and national identity. There is an earnest desire among the peoples of Nepal that their political leaders should come to a consensus and take the peace process forward and not squander this historic opportunity.

—*Editor*

1

Nepal from Monarchy to Democratic Constitution

Much of the citizens of Nepal's capital are in a celebratory mood upon the promulgation of the nation's first constitution drafted by a democratically elected Constituent Assembly (CA). After a decade-long Maoist insurgency, the abolishment of the monarchy, and the declaration of a republic in 2008 followed by seven years of shameless and anti-climatic thumb-twiddling by the CA the actualization of a constitution is reason for balloons and fireworks lighting up Kathmandu's nightscape Nepal is governed according to the Constitution of Nepal, which came into effect on September 20, 2015, replacing the Interim Constitution of 2007. The Constitution was drafted by the Second Constituent Assembly following the failure of the First Constituent Assembly to produce a constitution in its mandated period.

The Interim Constitution provides for a Constituent Assembly, which was charged with writing Nepal's permanent constitution. Under the terms of the Interim Constitution, the new constitution was to be promulgated by May 28, 2010, but the Constituent Assembly postponed the promulgation by a year because of disagreements. On May 25, 2011, the Supreme Court of Nepal ruled that the 2010 extension of the Interim Constitution was not right. Since May 29, 2011 the Constituent Assembly repeatedly extended the Interim Constitution.

On May 28, 2012, the Constituent Assembly was dissolved after it failed to finish the constitution after the latest extension, ending four years of constitution drafting and leaving the country in a legal vacuum. New elections were held on November 19, 2013 to the Second and political leaders pledged to draft a new constitution within a year.

The new assembly expressly committed that the new constitution would be promulgated on January 22, 2015. However, due to continued differences on key issues including system of governance, judicial system and federation issues like number, name and areas of the states to be carved, the constitution could not be finalized and promulgated in time.

But the mood in southern Nepal is a different tale.Strong opposition from minority groups, particularly the Madhesis and Tharus, who inhabit the southern plains along the Indian border, remain dissatisfied recently to the point of violent outrage over what they define as centuries of marginalization and discrimination from the Kathmandu centric political power base. In the last few weeks, over 40 people including police have either been bludgeoned to death, butchered, shot or set on fire.

With the promulgation of Constitution, They have been protesting since August 15, 2015, even before constitution was drafted which took on fire after promulgation setting constitution on fire and forming human chain. During the protest more than 45 people were killed at point blank distance. They are demanding equal rights in all areas including high official positions.

On November 2, Nepalese police moved in to clear out the protesters in Birgunj. Despite police actions, the protesters managed to return and continue the blockade. Protesters attacked a Nepalese police station with petrol bombs and stones. In retaliation, the police opened fire, kill one person, Ashish Kumar Ram, who was later identified as an Indian citizen, which raised concerns over involvement of Indians in the Madhesh protests.

Six Nepalese police officers were injured in the attack and more than 25 protesters and civilians were injured. Since then, a curfew has been imposed in Birgunj.

The dialogue in Beijing is also considering specialised military training exchanges in the defence academies in the two countries.

The unrest is largely over the contentious manner in which the country has been carved up into seven federal states, which, according to much of the southern population, discriminates against them. They want more states and representation equal to their population an ethnic based model of federalism rather than the voted in geographical model that favors the continuation of the old ruling elites.

Due to an open border treaty between Nepal and India, citizens of both countries can move freely, work, and live across borders without passports, making tracking the movement of people difficult. Indian encroachment had long been an issue straining Nepal-India relations. Madheshis share strong socio-cultural ties to the neighbouring Indian states of Bihar and Uttar Pradesh.

India had expressed concerns over the violent protests, and had asked Nepal to take Madhesi interests into consideration. The government of Nepal and the Nepalese media portrayed Madhesi movements as subversively backed by Indian infiltrators, and as an assault on their sovereignty, furthermore, Nepal's feel it is ultimately an attempt to absorb Nepal into India in whole or in part, citing the case of Nepali dominated Sikkim..

The same day, in which the fuel blockade began, India had demanded specific changes to the new Nepali constitution. While the Indian Government denied this claim The Indian Express reporter stood by his/her original report restating that "these amendments / changes were communicated by New Delhi to

Kathmandu". In an Economic Times reporting, Indian Sash Astra Seema Bal (SSB) personnel "confirmed that at least till the third week of September, they had orders from above to intercept fuel shipments to Nepal". Nepali social media took to immediate protest against the alleged Indian interference with the hash tag Back off India as well as street agitation. When news of the blockage of shipments reached the government, Kathmandu sent additional military forces to the border. Despite the suppression of the bandh, supplies had been blocked on the Indian side.

Some Maoist leaders of various parties claimed India had infiltrated the Madhesh with Indians protesters, and Madheshi leaders have refuted the infiltration allegations, stating that the Madheshis should not be mistaken for Biharis or other Indians.

In 1948, the Government of Nepal Act was enacted. Since the mid-nineteenth century, the country had been a monarchy where the prime ministers, from the Rana dynasty, had sweeping control over the affairs of the state. The 1948 document introduced limited democratic elements, but the experiment was not successful due to the misgivings of the Rana rulers to give away power.

The Interim Government of Nepal Act 1951 was promulgated after the Revolution of 1951 that the end of the Rana period. This text strengthened the authority of the king, and introduced relevant reforms such as the creation of the Supreme Court and the inclusion of fundamental rights and socio-economic goals to be pursued by the state.

The CONSTITUTION OF THE KINGDOM OF NEPAL, 1959 followed the previously mentioned interim text. Interestingly, despite the establishment of a bicameral parliament, the king continued to hold important powers such as the prerogative to appoint half of the members of the Senate and the suspension of parliament under certain circumstances.

The democratic experiment was short-lived, as in 1962 a new constitution came in to eliminate political parties, and to introduce the so-called panchayat system. In this model, panchayats were councils organized at the local level, presumably to ensure the representation of citizens. However, the king exercised much stronger authority than in the 1959 regime. and could modify the constitution or suspend it in case of emergency.

In 1990, the first Jana Andolan, Popular Revolt, brought multi-party democracy back to Nepal. The CONSTITUTION OF THE KINGDOM OF NEPAL(1990) lifted the ban on political parties, described a democratic representative system where the authority of the king was curtailed, and enshrined fundamental rights. Although the 1990 constitution substantially increased the democratic character of the state in comparison with the

Panchayat Regime, critiques have argued that this text did not adequately represent all sectors of society, even though Nepal is a multi-cultural country where diverse social groups coexist Again following the second janaandolan an interim constitution was promulgated in 2005.

MADHESI'S: HISTORICAL BACKGROUND

In Nepal, people have normally been identified as Nepali or Pahadi, the hill origin people, and Madheshi, the non-Nepali speaking people originating from the plains living mostly in Tarai region. Pahadi and Madheshi are socio-culturally, ethnically and linguistically two distinct ethnic communities and each of these two broad ethnic groups is composed of indigenous Janjati, Hindu caste hierarchy including Dalits, the socially deprived community, and Muslims. In the English language, we use three distinct words, namely Nepal, as a country, Nepali people speaking Nepali language as their mother tongue or their first language, and Nepalese, the citizen of Nepal. Whereas in Nepali language we use only two words e.g. Nepal and Nepali, the later indicates both people speaking Nepali and citizen of Nepal. In the preamble of the present Interim Constitution, "Nepali people" has been mentioned but not the "people from Nepal". It confuses Madheshi people. An Indian Nepali is granted the status of Nepali in Nepal but not a Madheshi who is being asked if he is a Nepali. Naturally, this frustrates a Madheshi and they feel their identity being threatened in their own country. After the Andolan I we could have coined the word 'Nepalbasi" for any person who is a citizen of Nepal; it could have helped bringing Madheshi and Nepali people together.

In this chapter, Khas indicates people speaking Nepali language as their mother tongue, Nepali specifies people speaking Nepali language as their mother tongue or their first language, and Nepalbasi as the people from Nepal. Madheshi people feel proud of calling themselves as Nepalbasi or Nepalese but not Nepali.

The Tarai region is otherwise known as Madhesh. Maybe move that section here. According to the 2001 census, the total population of Nepali and Madheshi community in Nepal was estimated to be about 68% and 32% respectively. This skewed ratio has been questioned by many Madheshi scholars and politicians as widely manipulated and they have very often raised voices for a fresh census before the Constituent Assembly election.

In 2001, 48.4% of the country's total population of 23.2 million lived in 20 Tarai districts. Just over 95% of the Madheshi population live in Tarai districts whereas Nepali people live in all the 75 districts of the country; currently, about 36% of the population living in Tarai districts are Nepali which is mostly due to planned migration of hill origin people in 1960s and 1970s and also due to restructuring of Tarai districts in 1963 which included large areas of mid mountains and Siwaliks, about 34%, however, these areas are sparsely populated. About 96% of the Muslim people live in Tarai.

Since the unification of Nepal in 1768 and more so after the Sugauli Treaty of 1815 and 1860 with British India, the Madheshi community has been considered as a minority group being secluded from all forms of planned socio-political and economic initiatives as well as governance, state opportunities and education. Till the 1940s, Madheshi people were required an entry paper to visit Kathmandu, the capital of their own country, Nepal.

They have been discriminated against for decades and they have almost lost "the sense of belongingness to Nepal". Madheshi people collectively suffered and had to bear systematic discriminatory treatment because of their socio-cultural and ethnic background by the rulers who have been mostly from the Nepali community. Very recently in early 2007, a large number of the Madheshi obtained citizenship rights.

In reality, Nepal has become to a greater extent an "Unequal Society" in which the Khas community having Nepali language as their mother tongue have prospered while many other communities including Madheshi have not. Social, economic and political exclusion of Madheshi, Janjati, Dalits and women has been fostering unequal society for an intolerable period of time.

Madheshi nationalism surfaced following the 1990 democratic movement, which restored a democratic system in the country after nearly 30 years. The democratic constitution could not do justice to Madheshi people and the political systems between 1990 and early 2006 did not, in practice, adopt the concept of power sharing and proportional representation in governance, opportunity in state organs, decision-making, policy planning process, nor in all other forms of planned socio-economic development. Madheshi people have seldom been allowed to be in the right place at the right time for their voices to be heard or considered. Ironically, the key players in the governing parties during this period e.g. Nepali Congress and UML were elected from Tarai districts by Madheshi people. The representation of Madheshi people in the national legislature in 1999 was merely 17%, and again, most of these Madheshi parliamentarians till the February 2007 showed 'sleeping syndrome' seldom raising the issues, concerns and the aspiration of Madheshi people who elected them as their representatives; in practice they were considered second class politicians in their respective parties. They probably feared threats of expulsion from the party for demonstrating rebellious tendencies such as raising serious Madheshi issues. Some of them even preferred to benefit personally by obeying their Nepali leaders instead.

The Madheshi people have awakened and they want to exercise their natural rights like other Nepali people, like other citizens of Nepal . They do not want to remain a forcibly secluded community any more. Since 1993, a few Madheshi scholars started writing and publishing articles on Madheshi community and national integration. Since 2006, many Nepalese scholars living in Nepal or abroad have analysed the causes of socio-political and economic exclusion, their impacts, current status and issues, and measures to mitigate adverse impacts.

Some of the researchers elaborated the glorious culture and history as well as the strengths of Madhesh and the Madheshi people; several kingdoms in Madhesh were established and perished with time, abandoned and turned to forests. However, the ancient history of Madhesh and the culture of Madheshi people were practically discarded while writing the history of Nepal by Nepali people.

The Anglo-Nepalese war (1814-1815) and the resulting Treaty of Sugauli (1815) and the subsequent Treaty (1860) with British

India substantially reduced the size of Madhesh in Nepal ; Madhesh nation was divided between Nepal and India . Madhesh remained an internal colony of Khas rulers from 1768 to 1951, but the oppression and suppression continued till 2006 by Nepali people ruling the country through various political parties.

The contribution made by Madheshi people during the 1990 democratic movement called Andolan I was conveniently ignored by the Nepali politicians and many of them do not even know that the first women martyrs in the history of Nepal are from the most under-developed village of Dhanusha district; the three Madheshi women belonging to Yadav community were the martyrs of 1990 revolution.

Madheshi organisations and scholars are organising several workshops and seminars exchanging views and ideas both in rural and urban areas. In recent months, very few organisations with Nepali people in their governing body have initiated dialogue between various stakeholders. The positive attitude and actions of some international organisations including UN Human Rights have helped Madheshi people to come closer to discussing way outs for peaceful resolution and holistic development in Madhesh. The mass media including the internet have helped a lot in terms of communication. A sense of identity deeply rooted in a common culture, a common history and the glorious past, as well as the memory and feeling of conquest and oppression by Nepali rulers have united the Madheshi people. Now the Madheshi people throughout the country both in rural and urban areas and living abroad are united and they very much feel the Madheshi nationalism. They are proud to be Madheshi and Nepalese.

Ethnopolitical Conflict

A decade long socio-political revolution led by the Communist Party of Nepal (CPN) Maoists, the agreements between the major political parties and Maoists in late 2005 in India, involvement and strong advocacy of a large number of civil society and development activists, and the mass movement of early 2006 significantly changed the political dynamics in Nepal. The king lost all the authoritarian governing power through the alliance of seven political parties (SPA) on 18 May 2006 and the SPA headed by Nepali Congress (NC) leader Mr. Girija Prasad Koirala led the multiparty secular democratic government. The people felt a great relief sensing stability and peace although the socio-political condition in the country was very much deteriorated.

Prime Minister Koirala, along with a high profile Nepalese delegation visited India in early June 2006 for a possible 'economic and political package'; the visit was considered moderately successful in terms of economic package. CPN-Maoists, who had formed local governments in rural areas and had strong hold both in Tarai and hills, were still considered a threat to the State. On 21 November, a 'Peace Accord' between the CPN-Maoist leader Prachand and the Prime Minister GP Koirala, a leader of the SPA was signed. All the Nepalese were happy about this historic event and they regained hope to leave peacefully with pride. The Maoist leaders spared no time to organise meetings with the elite groups, organisations including bi-laterals and multilaterals, and scholars in Kathmandu Valley; they listened to the participating people and tried to make them aware and convince them the 'Maoist development and governance approaches'. Many people felt them more progressive than the traditional political parties ruling the country. Very soon CPN-Maoist became urban based in Kathmandu like the other political parties, and in late March 2007 they joined the government thus forming Seven Party Alliance and CPN-Maoist (SPAM) government.

The behaviour of the State governing body led by the alliance of seven political parties towards the Madheshi people remained more or less unchanged; even the Interim Constitution of the late 2006 did not do socio-political justice to the Madheshi people, who felt their identity threatened. The Janjatis – indigenous people felt the same. The governing political parties, democrats or communists, did not think of restructuring their parties; a true representation of Madheshi, Janjati and Dalits in the decision-making body of parties was ignored. The mentality of the political leaders who are mostly from Khas community remained unchanged, disregarding the socio-political transformation that the people and the country want. Madheshi and the other disadvantaged ethnic communities felt oppressed and let down again. The Khas people are dominant groups in all the major political parties in the parliament such as Nepali Congress (NC), Nepal Congress (Democratic), United Marxist Leninist (UML), Nepal Communist Party (Maoist), Nepal Prajatantra Party, Nepal Janshakti Party and many others, and they often label Madheshi, Janjati and Dalits as 'minorities' and the dominant group consider them 'less worthy ethnic groups' in political status.

The Madheshi ethnic group or people, subjected to discriminatory treatment by the rulers who are mostly Khas people because of their cultural and ethnic traits, are now mobilized for political action to promote and defend their common group identities and interest. The disadvantaged or secluded Madheshi communal group is thus called Madheshi ethnopolitical group. This fuels the ethnopolitical protests, movement and rebellion. Usually, the ethnopolitical conflicts cause humanitarian disasters as seen in Sri Lanka , Bhutan , Myanmar and in other parts of Africa and Latin America . If prolonged, it leads to terrorism and rebellion and provokes fruitless military intervention. There are successful ethnopolitical movements such as the US civil rights movement in 1960s and Baltic nationalism in late 1980s and 1990s. A total of 32% and 22% of the country's population consist of Madheshi ethnopolitical group and Nepali Janjati ethnopolitical group respectively. About 95% of the Madheshi ethnopolitical group lives in one continuous geographical area called Tarai or Madhesh whereas people from the Nepali Janjati ethnopolitical group live scattered in high mountains, hills and Tarai regions.

Deliberate public policies, adverse socio-political practices and discriminatory treatment by the governing body of the state the ruling political parties dominated by Khas people, who secluded the Madheshi people even after the Andolan II, fuelled the ethnopolitical movement. The CPN-Maoists had promised federal state in Madhesh, rights of self-determination and many other assurances during their decade old revolution against the monarchy and the state, but in due course of time after the Andolan II in May 2006 Madheshi people found these promises to be empty. The breakaway Madheshi factions of Maoists established socio-political organisations such as the Janatantrik Tarai Mukthi Morcha (JTMM) led separately by Jay Krishna Goit and Jwala Singh.

Madheshi people had no alternative but to initiate mass movement initially through protests and mass demonstration to defend their threatened identity and to gain opportunity in governance and political power to rule their homeland, a separate Madhesh federal state extending from Mechi in the east to Mahakali in the west, and proportional representation in constituent assembly and in government organs. The Nepalgunj incidence in early December and the firing by Maoists at the unarmed demonstrators in Lahan, Siraha district on 19 December 2006 killing one person, a thoughtless action by the Maoists, resulted in mass spontaneous demonstration all over Tarai districts from Mechi in the east to Mahakali in the west. The Prime Minister on 23 January 2007 while meeting the Nepali Congress Parliamentary leaders blamed the Maoists for "escalating" violence in Tarai.

This ethnopolitical movement was based on Madheshi nationalism, which the governing political parties could not properly understand and due to their utter negligence, brutal force was used killing over 38 Madheshi people and injuring over 800 people.

The CPN-Maoists even advocated use of force to wipe out the Madheshi movement. This movement, known to the Madheshi people as Andolan III, was basically rural based unlike the earlier movements, Andolan I and II, which were mostly Kathmandu centric.

The Madheshi Janadhikar Forum, an activist organisation successfully led the movement although the Jantantrik Tarai Mukti Morcha led separately by Jay Krishna Goit and Jwala Singh were involved in this movement in a few places. In some areas, local members of the Nepal Sadbhavana Party the Madhesh based political party took part in the agitation. The movement was internationalised and there was intense pressure from UN human rights organisations, agencies and some political parties to stop police brutality; very few Civil Societies and Nepali Human Rights organisations took interest after the bloodshed in Madhesh and they were silent spectators during the brutal police action by the state. Their indifferent attitude towards Madheshi people at large became questionable, which could be a subject for research in future.

On 7 February 2007, the seven political party alliance and Maoist, the SPAM, signed an agreement guaranteeing the Tarai region representation in the Constituent Assembly in proportion to its population. The Prime Minister in his nearly midnight address to the nation broadcast live by state owned media, guaranteed the increased number of constituencies in the Tarai region in proportion to its population, increased number of seats to be elected through proportional representation systems, inclusion of Madheshi in the State organs on the basis of the principle of proportional inclusion, federal system of governance and delineation of electoral constituencies, all through immediate amendment in the Interim Constitution. He recognised the legitimate demand of Madheshi people during the movement. It has been a collective commitment of SPAM government.

This movement very much weakened the stand and influence of Maoists in Tarai region and clearly indicated emergence of democratic forces reducing the chances of spreading hard-core communism in Tarai region. The socio-cultural and linguistic southern boundary of Madheshi ethnopolitical community is Bihar and Uttar Pradesh, the politically less stable and economically less developed provinces of India. A democratic Madhesh (Tarai region) extending from Mechi in the east to Mahakali in the west would be in the interest of India as well as the Western countries which have socio-economic and political interest in India itself.

The Madheshi people believing in democratic governance system welcomed this state gesture and wished a long lasting peaceful situation in Tarai. They had already gained citizenship rights. The Madheshi Janadhikar Fourm (MJF) was elevated as a powerful political force in the country; their leaders were praised in Madhesh and the media in Kathmandu highlighted them very frequently. In Madhesh, Forum became a big name. Sensing a big share in the forthcoming Constituent Assembly election, they registered the socio-political activist group as a political party.

Most Madheshi people thought that the SPAM commitment and political and governance reforms would lead to dialogue for peaceful resolution of Madheshi ethnopolitical movement.

The base had been prepared for the future political framework for governing Madhesh region. Due to certain reasons, both the Forum and the State very much delayed the dialogue process for peaceful resolution of Madheshi unrest. Moreover, the delay in amending the Interim Constitution incorporating the SPAM commitments confused many Madheshi people. The Madheshi parliamentarians from UML , NC (Democratic), Nepal Sadbhavana Party and Nepali Congress made an alliance to press the government for legitimising the PM's declaration on Madheshi issues.

It was a difficult job to create and stabilise the alliance, which acted against the command of their political parties especially NC, UML and NC (Democratic), which are ruled by Khas people. Consequently, about 40% of the parliamentarians (MPs) from the above parties adhered to their Khas rulers in the party and some of them were reluctant to show sympathy to the alliance and their efforts. Inspite of intense party pressure, the Madheshi MPs continued their efforts and eventually the alliance efforts were fruitful. The alliance and its activities were considered pro-Madheshi by many Madheshi and Janjati people; nevertheless it made the participating MPs closer to the Madheshi community.

During the past three months the popularity of Madheshi Janadhikar Forum has declined. It could not force the government to implement the SPAM agreement such as inclusion of Madheshi in the State organs on the basis of the principle of proportional inclusion. Some of its local level cadres as well as its mid level leaders initiated actions which were not accepted by many Madheshi people. As a political party, it needs to develop codes and norms acceptable to people and gain the support of a large number of Madheshi people who strongly allied with them during the movement. At the same time, the SPAM government could not convince a large number of Madheshi people that their actions were pro-Madheshi. Their governance mentality and order remained unchanged.

Proportional representation entitles space and position of minorities at all levels and every segment of government. There has been no change in the governance system in Tarai districts; most of the administrative offices and key development offices which make socio-economic and governance decisions in Tarai have people from hill origin.

Tarai Janatantric Mukti Morcha (Jwala Singh) on the Nepalese New Year widely circulated its press release asking the government to change its discriminatory policies towards Madheshi people but these remained unnoticed by the rulers. They were active during the Madheshi movement and their actions have intensified in the past four months. In the last two months the government made a positive effort of organising dialogues with Madheshi Janadhikar Forum, but no other such efforts have been made with other agitating groups in Madhesh. Now many groups have emerged and some of them show militant characteristics similar to Maoists from about 3-4 years ago. Most of these groups are breakaway factions of CPN-Maoists. Currently, Janatantric Tarai Mukti Morcha (Goit), Janatantric Tarai Mukti Morcha (Jwala Singh), Janatantric Tarai Mukti Morcha (Bishfot Singh), Madheshi Mukti Morcha, Madheshi Tiger, Tarai Cobra Group, Madhesh Mukti Force, Tarai Tiger, AASK Group, Tharu Mukti Morcha, Chure Bhawnr Pradesh Ekta Samaj, Janajati Mahasangh are active in Tarai districts, and many other unknown groups are still emerging one after another. The law and order situation in Tarai region has very much deteriorated and the transport system has been very much affected due to strikes most of the weeks. This has adversely affected economic activities in Tarai region.

Some of the agitating groups, the breakaway fractions of CPN-Maoist, are using violent measures including kidnapping, torture and killings, similar to Maoist insurgency in the last decade which systematically employed such violent measures. They are kidnapping both Madheshi and Nepali people who are very close to the government mechanism. Most of these groups have made it clear that they are fighting for the Madheshi cause with the government ruled mostly by Nepali, and not with the average Nepali people living in Tarai unless they themselves blindly support the government system. During the movement in early 2007, property and lives of Nepali people in Madhesh were in danger which reminiscent of Maoist revolution till two years ago. All the Nepalese living either in Madhesh or hills and mountains wish for a "developed, stable and united Nepal" to be governed by Nepalese for the Nepalese but not by Nepali or for Nepali. All Nepalese, either a Nepali or Madheshi or Janjati should be given equal opportunity in nation building. This is what Madheshi people justly want and this is what a Nepalbasi wants. The world is becoming narrower with the application of science and technology. The average Nepalese questions that if China and India can develop so fast, then why is it that Nepal cannot whilst situated between these two Asian giants. Many think that the current politicians in the government do not have that vision.

Let us analyse the three questions which will positively lead to holding the CA election in November 2007.

Firstly, what do the Madheshi people want?

A current survey and workshop conducted in May 2007 involving non-political socio-economic local leaders in seven Tarai districts have identified major social, economic, cultural and political issues which they wish to be solved by the present and the future Nepalese rulers. They have pinpointed the major issues such as establishment of federal system of governance in republican setting and regional autonomy with rights of self-determination in Madhesh region, one federal Madhesh state from Mechi in the east to Mahakali in the west, proportional representation at each of the organs of the state, proportional representation of all excluded groups of Madhesh in constituent assembly, and reservation for women in CA poll. They want an end to exclusion, end of gender and caste based discrimination and co-existence with Nepali people in the country. This is what the average Madheshi people wants. Like any other Nepalese, Madheshi people want to exercise their natural birthrights.

Most Madheshi people ask the question, "Will this new constitution developed by Constituent Assembly members be pro Madheshi?"

Their eagerness is very natural. The electoral seats for CA election are 497; direct election 240, proportional election 240 and nominated 17. If the election is held fairly, under the mixed system 164 Madheshi people would be represented including 38 women. They will still be in the minority but they could democratically convince or press other CA members to address the issues of inclusion of Madheshi, Janjati and Dalit citizens. They will need to form an alliance between the other excluded communities.

Future Challenges

The national political situation is fragile. The constitution making process which is supposed to redraw the Nepali social contract and create an institutional framework of inclusive democracy is in limbo, with missed time-lines and growing inter party differences. The peace process is incomplete, with two standing armies.

And two specific issues in the Tarai unless addressed within the political framework peacefully have the potential to sow the seeds for another conflict.

The main demand of the first Madhes movement was the introduction of federalism in the interim constitution. The main achievement of the second Madhes movement was the commitment by the government to an autonomous Madhes province. The notion of self-rule in the Tarai and shared rule at the centre lies at the heart of the movement. In specific structural terms, Madhesi parties have adopted the slogan of 'one Madhes, one Pradesh' a single Madhes province across the Tarai from east to west. The logic of the parties is that this comprises a common cultural geographical zone. Communities living in the plains share a history of oppression by Kathmandu. Leaders say that such a province will be strong and will be able to counter Kathmandu. But this demand has run into rough opposition from different quarters.

The 'ultra-nationalist elite' oppose federalism in principle and feels that one Madhes is a prelude to the break-up of the country. NC and UML are reluctant converts to the cause of federalism and advocate vertical provinces that incorporates the hills and plains on the lines of old development zones77 which Madhesis saw as discriminatory. Maoists have suggested breaking up the Tarai into Tharuhat in the far west, Madhes in central and eastern Tarai with Awadh, Bhojpur, and Mithila as sub-provinces or alternately the three linguistic units as separate provinces each.

Some Tharu groups have demanded that the entire plains be constituted as Tharuhat; others demand that far west districts be a Tharu province – they feel that a single Madhes province would mean hegemony of Madhesi Hindu castes.79 Limbuwan activists agitating in the eastern hills have demanded the inclusion of far-eastern districts like Jhapa in the Limbuwan province;

Rajbanshi activists similarly claim that parts of Jhapa, Morang and Sunsari should be a part of a Kochila state. Kathmandu based planners have urged vertical provinces as economically more feasible, where both plains and hills will be able to derive mutual advantages.

And many commentators, opposed to ethnic states in principle, have raised the point that any province is bound to have people from different ethnicities and castes carving out ethnic or linguistic provinces may make the minorities within them second-class citizens, and thus defeat the purpose of federalism. The other debate is about the range of powers to be given to provinces. Regional parties have demanded an extreme form of autonomy, where states keep all powers except foreign affairs, defence, communication, and currency they would also have the right to self determination.

National parties want to retain a stronger centre, with minimal devolution of powers. The constituent assembly has ten months to take into account these contesting claims. Given that all the political actors have not shown any inclination to step down from their radical rhetoric, it is difficult to see how a consensus can be engineered in this time period.

To add to it, street politics has got legitimacy and is seen as an effective political tool. When the federal debate picks, many fear that all these groups with conflicting demands may resort to agitation, which will be difficult for the state to tackle. Political-security situation As recounted above, politics in Tarai has fragmented to unmanageable levels. Most groups have a semi-militant character. Many armed groups operate in the belt, with close ties with criminal networks. Security experts also contend that it is in such an anarchic set up, international counterfeit currency and drug networks find space.

A new security policy is essential, but it has to be accompanied with a reformed state structure which can implement it sensitively. A uni-dimensional approach, as seen during the Maoist conflict, is bound to create further resentment and generate a backlash. Any approach has to take into account the political alienation in Madhes; it must win the confidence and support of Madhesi politicians and civil society and engage in talks with groups who are political; at the same time, state mechanisms must be strengthened, police be made less susceptible to political pressure, and the border better regulated to ensure better law and order. Only then can a peaceful and just Tarai within a united Nepali framework thrive.

2

Nepal in 21st Century

Nepal is a country in South Asia bordering the Republic of India and the People's Republic of China. Mount Everest, the highest mountain in the world, is found there, as well as the Himalaya Mountains. 12 of the world's 18 highest mountain peaks are in Nepal. It is also the birthplace of Buddha. It has recently become a secular country, but it used to be the only Hindu nation the world. Nepal is a very important pilgrimage place for both Hindus and Buddhists. The population of Nepal in 2007 was almost 29 million people. Nepali is the official language, and there are many other regional languages. English and Hindi are widely understood. The capital city of Nepal is Kathmandu which has a population of over two million people. The second largest city is Pokhara. Pokhara is a major tourist attraction of Nepal. It is rich in Natural Beauty. Pokhara includes many lakes , Phewa Tal is one of them.

As we all know that Nepal country located between China and India. Besides that we have posted here in this post, more than these facts. You'll get real facts about country Nepal. We all know that the Lord Buddha was born in Nepal. The highest peak of the world, Mount Everest is located in the Himalayas of Nepal. Besides these renown's facts we have here written only the facts related to geography of Nepal. It's not only 10 facts about Nepal.

The Kathmandu Valley, the political and cultural hub of the nation, is drained by the Baghmati River, flowing southward, which washes the steps of the sacred temple of Pasupatinatha (Pashupatinath) and rushes out of the valley through the deeply cut Ċhhobar gorge. Some sandy layers of the lacustrine beds act as aquifers (water-bearing strata of permeable rock, sand, or gravel), and springs occur in the Kathmandu Valley where the sands outcrop. The spring water often gushes out of dragon shaped mouths of stone made by the Nepalese; it is then collected in tanks for drinking and washing and also for raising paddy nurseries in May, before the monsoon. Drained by the Seti River, the Pokhara Valley, 96 miles west of Kathmandu, is also a flat lacustrine basin. There are a few remnant lakes in the Pokhara basin, the largest being Phewa Lake, which is about two miles long and nearly a mile wide. North of the basin lies the Annapurna massif of the Great Himalaya Range.

The major rivers of Nepal the Kosi, Narayani (Gandak), and Karnali, running southward across the strike of the Himalayan ranges form transverse valleys with deep gorges, which are generally several thousand feet in depth from the crest of the bordering ranges. The watershed of these rivers lies not along the line of highest peaks in the Himalayas but to the north of it, usually in Tibet.

The rivers have considerable potential for development of hydroelectric power. Two irrigation hydroelectric projects have been undertaken jointly with India on the Kosi and Narayani rivers.

Discussions have been held to develop the enormous potential of the Karnali River. A 60,000-kilowatt hydroelectric project at Kulekhani, funded by the World Bank, Kuwait, and Japan, began operation in 1982. In the upper courses of all Nepalese rivers, which run through mountain regions, there are little or no flood problems. In low-lying areas of the Tarai plain, however, serious floods occur.

The rivers and small streams of the Tarai, especially those in which the dry season discharge is small, are polluted by large quantities of domestic waste thrown into them.

Towns and villages have expanded without proper provision for sewage disposal facilities, and more industries have been established at selected centres in the Tarai. The polluted surface water in the Kathmandu and Pokhara valleys, as well as in the Tarai, is unacceptable for drinking.

The people

The large-scale migrations of Asian groups from Tibet and Indo Aryan people from northern India, which accompanied the early settlement of Nepal, have produced a diverse linguistic, ethnic, and religious pattern. Nepalese of Indo Aryan ancestry comprise the people of the Tarai, the Pahari, the Newar, and the Tharus the great majority of the total population. Indo Aryan ancestry has been a source of prestige in Nepal for centuries, and the ruling families have been of Indo Aryan and Hindu background. Most of the Tibeto Nepalese groups the Tamang, Rai, Limbu, Bhutia (including the Sherpa), and Sunwar live in the north and east, while the Magar and Gurung inhabit west central Nepal. The majority of the famous Gurkha contingents in the British army have come from the Magar, Gurung, and Rai groups.

The principal and official language of Nepal is Nepâlî (Gorkhali), spoken in the Tarai and the mid-mountain region. Nepâlî, a derivative of Sanskrit, belongs to the Indo Aryan branch of the Indo European family. There are a number of regional dialects found in the Tarai and mountain areas. The languages of the north and east belong predominantly to the Tibeto Burman family. These include Magar, Gurung, Rai, Limbu, Sunwar, Tamang, Newari, and a number of Bhutia dialects, including Sherpa and Thakali.

Although Newari is commonly placed in the Tibeto-Burman family, it was influenced by both Tibeto-Burman and Indo European languages.

In Nepal a vast majority of the population is Hindu, but a small percentage follows Buddhism or other religious faiths. Hindus and Buddhists tend to be concentrated in areas where Indian and Tibetan cultural influences, respectively, have been dominant. Almost all Nepalese live in villages or in small market centres. Outside of Kâthmându, there are no major cities. Smaller urban centres (Birâtnagar, Nepâlganj, and Birganj) are located in the Tarai along the Indian border, and Pokharâ is situated in a valley in the mid-mountain region. In addition, a few townships such as Hitaura, Bûtwal, and Dharân have begun to emerge in the foothills and hill areas, where economic activity has developed.

SOCIAL DEVELOPMENT

Geographically Nepal can be divided into three zones Himalayan, Hilly and Terai realms Himalayan realm is the homeland of panoramic snowy peaks five out of eight highest peaks in the world viz Mt. Everest talk:! summit in the world, Kanchanjungha, the 3rd tales summit, Dhawalaqiri and Annapurna all over 8,000 metre. Multi dozen rivers duo perennial and non-perennial rivers do originate from them and flow down providing endless opportunities of rafting, boating, fishing, irrigating and immense hydropower potential. In fact, the mountain region is uninhabited except some scattered settlements in the mountainous valleys and plains.

Likewise, the hilly region does have divisional landscapes, insurmountable hills, fertile valleys, hilarious flora and fauna, tranquil lakes and so on. And, a low, fertile and alluvial plain the Teri realm is known as the "Food' basket", exhibits excellent wild lives in the dense forests. The mountain range has bitter cold winter where as the southern belt has a hot tropical climate. The effect of the environmental differences on crops and vegetation, results in equally striking variations in population density.

Economy

Economy of Nepal-Nepal's mineral resources are small, scattered, and barely developed. There are known deposits of coal (lignite), iron ore, magnetite, copper, cobalt, pyrite (used for making sulfuric acid), limestone, and mica. Nepal's great river systems provide immense potential for hydroelectric development. If developed and utilized within the country and exported to India (the principal market for power generated in Nepal), it could become a mainstay of the country's economy.

Nepal's gross domestic product (GDP) for 2012 was estimated at over $17.921 billion (adjusted to nominal GDP). In 2010, agriculture accounted for 36.1%, services comprised 48.5%, and industry 15.4% of Nepal's GDP. While agriculture and industry are contracting, the contribution by the service sector is increasing. Agriculture employs 76% of the workforce, services 18% and manufacturing and craft-based industry 6%.Agricultural produce mostly grown in the Terai region bordering India includes tea, rice, corn, wheat, sugarcane,root crops, milk, and water buffalo meat.

Industry mainly involves the processing of agricultural produce, includingjute, sugarcane, tobacco, and grain. Its workforce of about 10 million suffers from a severe shortage of skilled labor.

Nepal's economic growth continues to be adversely affected by the political uncertainty. Nevertheless, real GDP growth was estimated to increase to almost 5 percent for 2011 -2012. This is an improvement from the 3.5 percent GDP growth in 2010–2011 and would be the second-highest growth rate in the post-conflict era. Sources of growth include agriculture, construction, financial and other services. The contribution of growth by consumption fueled by remittances has declined since 2010/2011. While remittance growth slowed to 11 percent (in Nepali Rupee terms) in 2010/2011, it has since increased to 37 percent. Remittances are estimated to be equivalent to 25–30 percent of GDP. Inflation has been reduced to a three-year low of 7 percent.

The proportion of poor people has declined substantially since 2003. The percentage of people living below the international poverty line (people earning less than US$1.25 per day) has halved in seven years. At this measure of poverty the percentage of poor people declined from 53.1% in 2003/2004 to 24.8% in 2010/2011. With a higher poverty line of US$2 per-capita per day, poverty declined by one quarter to 57.3%. However, the income distribution remains grossly uneven.

In a recent survey, Nepal has performed extremely well in reducing poverty along with Rwanda and Bangladesh as the percentage of poor dropped to 44.2 percent of the population in 2011 from 64.7 percent in 2006—4.1 percentage points per year, which means that Nepal has made improvement in sectors like nutrition, child mortality, electricity, improved flooring and assets. If the progress of reducing poverty continues at this rate, then it is predicted that Nepal will halve the current poverty rate and eradicate it within the next 20 years.

The spectacular landscape and diverse, exotic cultures of Nepal represent considerable potential for tourism, but growth in the industry has been stifled by political instability and poor infrastructure. Despite these problems, in 2012 the number of international tourists visiting Nepal was 598,204, a 10% increase on the previous year. The tourism sector contributed nearly 3% of national GDP in 2012 and is the second-biggest foreign income earner after remittances.

The rate of unemployment and underemployment approaches half of the working-age population. Thus many Nepali citizens move to other countries in search of work. Destinations include India, Qatar, the United States, Thailand, the United Kingdom, Saudi Arabia, Japan, Brunei Darussalam, Australia, and Canada.

Nepal receives $50 million a year through the Gurkha soldiers who serve in the Indian and British armies and are highly esteemed for their skill and bravery. As of 2010, the total remittance value is around $3.5 billion. In 2009 alone, the remittance contributed to 22.9% of the nation's GDP.

A long-standing economic agreement underpins a close relationship with India. The country receives foreign aid from the UK, India, Japan, the US, and the EU, China, Switzerland, and Scandinavian countries. Poverty is acute; per-capita income is around $1,000. The distribution of wealth among the Nepali is consistent with that in many developed and developing countries: the highest 10% of households control 39.1% of the national wealth and the lowest 10% control only 2.6%.

The government's budget is about $1.153 billion, with expenditure of $1.789 billion (FY 20005/06). The Nepali rupee has been tied to the Indian rupee at an exchange rate of 1.6 for many years. Since the loosening of exchange rate controls in the early 1990s, the black market for foreign exchange has all but disappeared. The inflation rate has dropped to 2.9% after a period of higher inflation during the 1990s. Nepal's exports of mainly carpets, clothing, hemp, leather goods, jute goods and grain total

$822 million. Import commodities of mainly gold, machinery and equipment, petroleum products and fertilizer total US$2 billion. European Union (EU) (46.13%), the US (17.4%), and Germany (7.1%) are its main export partners. Recently, the European Union has become the largest buyer of Nepali ready-made garments (RMG). Exports to the EU accounted for "46.13 percent of the country's total garment exports". Nepal's import partners include India (47.5%), the United Arab Emirates (11.2%), China (10.7%), Saudi Arabia (4.9%), and Singapore (4%).

Besides having landlocked, rugged geography, few tangible natural resources and poor infrastructure, the ineffective post-1950 government and the long-running civil war are also factors in stunting the nation's economic growth and development

Industry and trade

Industrial production represents a small but growing segment of economic activity. Most industries are small, localized operations based on the processing of agricultural products. The jute industry, centred in Birâtnagar, is an important earner of foreign exchange. Sugar factories are located in Birâtnagar, Birganj, and Bhairahawâ.

There are a sawmill and a meat-processing plant in Hitaura and a number of rice and oil mills in the Tarai. Other industries include brick and tile manufacture; processing of construction materials, paper, and food grain; cigarette manufacture; cement production; and brewing of beer. In general, there are more industrial enterprises in the private than in the public sector, although most of these are cottage industries. The main areas of manufacturing concentration are Birâtnagar, the Birganj–Hitaura corridor, and the Kâthmându Valley.

Tourism represents a small but expanding industry. Foreign tourism is primarily confined to the Kâthmându Valley, which is the only area equipped with the necessary hotels, food supplies, roads, and international transport services. There are, however, many areas outside the Kâthmându Valley with potential for the development of tourism; these include Pokharâ, the Mount Everest area, and the Nârâyani area (where big game exists).

For geographic and historical reasons, nearly all of Nepal's trade is with India. Attempts have been made to diversify trade through agreements with such countries as Japan, South Korea, Pakistan, the United States, Germany, Poland, and China. The state trading agency, National Trading Limited, has expanded its activities by fostering the development of commercial entrepreneurial activity.

Large-scale commercial activity has hitherto been in the hands of foreigners, primarily Indians. Nepal's foreign trade and balance of payments have suffered setbacks, and exports have not increased enough to pay for imports of consumer goods and basic supplies. Nepal's dependence on the Indian market for most of its imports and exports and on the port of Calcutta for its access to the sea has been the source of periodic friction between the two countries.

Income

The US Central Intelligence Agency (CIA) reports that in 2005 Nepal's gross domestic product (GDP) were estimated at $42.2 billion. The CIA defines GDP as the value of all final goods and services produced within a nation in a given year and computed on the basis of purchasing power parity (PPP) rather than value as measured on the basis of the rate of exchange based on current dollars. The per capita GDP was estimated at $1,500. The annual growth rate of GDP was estimated at 2.5%. The average inflation rate in 2005 was 2.9%. It was estimated that agriculture accounted for 40% of GDP, industry 20%, and services 40%.

According to the World Bank, in 2003 remittances from citizens working abroad totaled $785 million or about $32 per capita and accounted for approximately 13.4% of GDP. Foreign aid receipts amounted to $467 million or about $19 per capita and accounted for approximately 8.0% of the gross national income (GNI).

The World Bank reports that in 2003 household consumption in Nepal totaled $4.57 billion or about $185 per capita based on a GDP of $5.9 billion, measured in current dollars rather than PPP.

Household consumption includes expenditures of individuals, households, and nongovernmental organizations on goods and services, excluding purchases of dwellings.

In 2001 it was estimated that approximately 44% of household consumption was spent on food, 7% on fuel, 5% on health care, and 14% on education. It was estimated that in 1996 about 42% of the population had incomes below the poverty line.

Labour

In the latest years for which data was available, as of 1998, Nepal's labour force was estimated to number 11 million. In 2002, the vast majority, approximately 81% of the workforce, was engaged in agriculture. Most agriculturists are peasant farmers, and there are many wage labourers, but only in the peak seasons. The service sector provides work for 16% of the labour force, and industry accounts for the remaining 3%. There is a severe lack of skilled labour. Among some tribes, women do most of the farm work, while in others, especially among strict Hindus, they do no farming at all. Many occupations are effectively restricted to certain castes, although the practice has been declared illegal. In 2001, the unemployment rate was 47%.

Unions are allowed to organize and strike. The three largest trade unions are associated with political parties, but the government does not restrict union activity. However, the right of a union to strike is limited to nonessential services. About 20% of the workforce is covered by collective bargaining agreements.

Minimum wage rates and working conditions in the small industrial sector are set by the Nepal Factories and Factory Workers' Act of 1959, as amended. In 2002, the minimum wage was $20 per month for unskilled, $21 for semiskilled, and $25 for skilled workers in the organized industrial sector. Wages can be as low as 50% of the minimum in the informal economy and the agricultural sector. The law establishes a minimum employment age of 16 years in industry and 14 years in agriculture.

Armed forces and police

Nepal's armed forces consist of the Royal Nepalese Army, predominantly an infantry force. The Army Flight Department operates all aircraft. Except for a few simple weapons, all military supplies are imported. Nepal is famous for the fighting qualities of its Gurkha soldiers; nearly 10,000 of these serve in British Gurkha units, and 50,000 in Indian Gurkha units. The British maintain a recruiting centre at Dharân. Gurkha veterans are a valuable human resource of Nepal.

For police purposes the country is divided into three zones: eastern, central, and western, with headquarters at Birâtnagar, Kâthmându, and Nepâlganj, respectively. Each zonal headquarters, under a deputy inspector general of police, is responsible for several subsections composed of four to five police districts operating under a superintendent of police. A district superintendent is in charge of police stations in his area, and each station normally is supervised by a head constable.

Cultural life

The relaxation of censorship that followed the overthrow of Rana rule in 1951 encouraged a revival of artistic and intellectual expression. In literature and poetry, Nepâlî works emphasize the cultural renaissance and national patriotism. King Mahendra, a poet whose Nepâlî lyrics have been published in English translation under the name of M.B.B. Shah (for Mahendra Bir Bikram Shah), did much to promote the revival of arts and literature. The cultural heritage of Nepal, particularly contributions made by the Newar of Kâthmându Valley to sculpture, painting, and architecture, is a source of great pride. Hindu and Buddhist religious values have provided the basic source of inspiration to Newar artisans.

The themes of most artistic works have been primarily religious; the lives of the gods, saints, and heroes and the relationship of man to society and to the universe are expounded in sculpture, architecture, and drama. In Kâthmându Valley some 2,500 temples and shrines display the skill and highly developed aesthetic sense of Newar artisans. Music and dance are favourite pastimes among the Nepalese.

Religious ceremonies require the use of drums and wind instruments preserved from ancient times. Important in most religious and family occasions are devotional songs that have elements of both classical and folk music and that have been used by some contemporary musical revivalists in their attempt to bridge the gap between the two. The government-owned Radio Nepal broadcasts programs in Nepâlî and English. The country's first television station, at Kâthmându, began broadcasting in 1986.

Newspapers and periodicals are published in Nepali and in English. Newspapers are frequently sensational in tone and are poorly staffed and financed. Gorkha Patra, published by the government, occupies a commanding position in the Nepalese press. Nepalese newspaper readers rely on the foreign press, particularly Indian newspapers, which are flown daily into Kâthmându, for more sophisticated coverage of world and national news.

After 1960 King Mahendra required newspapers to obtain official clearance for all reports of political activity. Subsequently the government increased its censorship, and in 1985 the publication of many newspapers was suspended. In 1990, reflecting the change in the country's political climate, freedom of the press was restored.

Political

Nepal's democratic transition from monarchy to a secular, federal and democratic republic has helped to establish relative peace, invent a new constitutional design, engineer broad social change and open the state to popular sovereignty, citizenship and democracy consolidation. In the midst of a historic constitution-making process by the elected Constituent Assembly (CA), Nepalese leaders now seek to establish a virtuous state ruled by law and social discipline to bring coherence to a society shattered by violent conflict and a better life to all citizens. Following the success of April the 6-24, 2006 militant mass movement against King Gyanendra's direct rule, the Nepalese government, the Seven-Party Alliance (SPA),1 took a number of initiatives—declared the country secular, suspended the monarchy, brought the Nepalese Army (NA) under civilian control, signed the Comprehensive Peace Agreement (CPA) on November 22, 2006, with the Unified Communist Party of Nepal-Maoists (UCPN-Maoist)2 to end a decade-long people's war, and the Agreement on Management of Armies and Arms. It also promulgated an Interim Constitution on January 15, 2007, which facilitated the formation of an interim legislature and interim government, with the inclusion of the UCPN (Maoist). On April 10, 2008, as an essential aspect of the peace plan, Nepal successfully held a post-conflict CA election after missing three deadlines (June 14 and 20 and November 22, 2007) and elected a 601-member CA to draft a new constitution.

In policy terms, the outcome of the election has made the UCPN (Maoist) the single dominant party in the country and offered it an opportunity to peacefully compete for power, transform its wartime class-based structures, ideology, leadership and policy into a mass-based competitive democratic party. The CA election also shifted the balance of power towards the forces of the left. Now they together control over 60 percent of CA seats. The inability of old parties, such as the Nepali Congress (NC), the Communist Party of Nepal Unified Marxist Leninist (CPN-UML) and the Rastriya Prajatantra Party (RPP), to absorb newly mobilized social groups aspiring for social transformation, as well as lack of inclusiveness, the birth of regional parties, especially the Madhesi Jana Adhikar Forum (MJAF), the Tarai-Madhesh Loktantrik Party (TMLP) and the Sadbhavana Party (SP), and weak communication and organizational capacity battered their electoral base.

Following the advent of the UCPN (Maoist) to power, the state-centric conflict became society-centric and openended as Madhesi (people of the southern flatlands), Tharus (indigenous people), Janajatis (ethnic groups), Dalits (untouchable people), and women intensified their struggle for power, resources, representation and identity, conceptualized their condition as deprived and set the motion of inversionary discourse into full play. The global pressure for conformity with and the binding power of human rights and international law presupposed that deliberative politics would lead to universal legitimacy of its constitutional discourse. But the loss of the Nepali state's legitimate monopoly on power and taxation and fragmentation of people's loyalty into ethnic, regional, linguistic and religious identification have weakened its ability to manage diversity and conflict. The yawning gaps in security and the rule of law and politicization of functional elites such as the police, bureaucracy, educational institutions and cultural industries along partisan lines show poor esprit de corps, de-motivation and erosion of the efficiency of state institutions.

The resilience of its patrimonial political culture has further sapped the political will for the creation of the rational state authority necessary to alter the policy and strategic development so vital to transforming the structural causes of the conflict. It has also refused to invest scarce resources in productive sectors and confiscated state capacity to distribute sufficient collective goods to inspire the solidarity of citizens with the state. As a result, Nepal is variously labeled by the international community as a soft, fragile and weak state3 lacking autonomy from the dominant

POLITICAL BACKGROUND OF MADHESI

The Maoist chief insists only rigging will defeat his party in the next elections. Till some years ago, before the Electronic Voting Machine era of elections, when counting of votes went on interminably, round after round, the surest sign of impending defeat was when politicians would begin yelling that the elections had been rigged. A winner would never say the election had been unfair, only a loser.

A strong flavor of that era comes through in the statements made by Pushpakamal Dahal aka Prachanda, Chairman of the Communist Party of Nepal-Maoist (CPN-M) about the elections to Parliament and a Constituent Assembly in Nepal, due on April 10. Speaking at a public meeting at Morang, around 300 km from capital Kathmandu, Prachanda said last week that his party's defeat in the elections would be "unacceptable". The Maoists have so much support, he said, that the party's defeat could only be caused by conspiracies hatched by "national and international reactionary forces". In other words, if the people didn't vote for the Maoists, they'd better watch out. And if the Maoists were defeated, India would be to blame.

This seems a bit rich coming from the chairman of a party that has 83 seats in the 303-seat Parliament just about a quarter of the total. And there are a plethora of issues the Maoists should worry about. Their lack of traction in the Terai (plains) in Nepal is the biggest. Terai is a problem for all parties, not just the Maoists. But the fact that the Madhesis have taken up arms that has so far been a Maoist prerogative suggests there are deeper problems.

Twenty two districts in Nepal are occupied by Madhesis who settled in the southern plains of Nepal, battling malaria and clearing forests to claim fertile land. Cheek by jowl with India, property and family knit the community inextricably with India.

According to the 2001 Nepal census, they comprise 57 per cent of the population. More akin to Indian culture, they speak Maithili, Bhojpuri and Avadhi. They live with Tharu tribals in the mid- and far western districts of Nepal. A majority of them are Hindu, though the Muslim population is growing. The Pahade those who live in the mountains consider the Madhesis an affront to Nepal's ethnic identity. They are seen as collaborators who forced the Nepalese to cede Sikkim, Garhwal and parts of Kumaon to the British as part of the Treaty of Segowli (1816) because Madhesi landlords helped the British effort. As Nepal prides itself on never having been anyone's colony, this defeat is a bitter fact of history for which every Nepali holds the Madhesis squarely responsible, whether it is the Maoists or the Nepali Congress.

The Madhesis consider themselves Nepalese residents but are angry that Nepal has consistently denied them their due. Hindi teaching in schools was banned by King Mahendra. Many Madhesis live in Nepal but don't have citizenship or the right to own property. India will have nothing to do with them, although they consider themselves Indian by birth. But more than 50 per cent of Nepal's GDP comes from Madhes. Nepal's biggest road, the East West Highway, runs through Madhes. An armed insurrection in this region is bad news because communication links are so good it will be impossible to control militants.

Madhesi militants are sui generis. They have banded together under Jwala Singh, as opposed to the relatively peaceful movement spearheaded by the Madhesi Janaadhikar Forum (Madhesi People's Rights Forum) or MJF or MPRF, led by former

Maoist leader Upendra Yadav. There is no love lost between them and the Maoists and they are indifferent to demands that Nepal repudiate monarchy and become a Republic. It is in Madhes that the Maoists will face their biggest challenge and they are getting ready for that defeat, which will then be visited on India's head.

The hill Nepalese are not worried about the Maoists. They can deal with them appropriately. Some sections of the population, especially women, even think the Maoist movement is the best thing that's happened to them because of the ban on drinking that

Maoists enforce on the countryside from time to time. Extortion by the Young Communists League (YCL) continues but all it needs is village-level organisation to end it. But the Nepalese have two big fears: one, the growth of Islamic movements in the countryside; and two, the ethnic powderkeg that the Madhesis represent. The April 10 elections are to decide the complexion of Parliament.

This body will convert itself into a Constituent Assembly and write the constitution of Republican Nepal. If the Madhesis are not given their due or if the Maoists are seen as obstructing/preventing the elections, it could make for an explosive situation in one of India's strategically most important neighbours. For the Maoists, it is their credibility that's at stake. For the Madhesis, it is their very existence.

MADHESI POLITICS IN KATHMANDU

The question of Terai rights was raised first by Bedananda Jha in the early 60s, but his movement ended with his co-option in the power centre. He became a Minister and Nepal's ambassador to India in the late 70s.

After the advent of democracy in 1990, leaders like Gajendra Narayan Singh demanded a fair share to Madhes. Since 2007, more regional parties, aggressive and vocal, have come into the picture. The Madhes centric leaders were discredited after failing to push their agenda during their time in power in 2008. They started to press for greater autonomy as per the March 2007 agreement only after they had fallen out with the major parties over power-sharing in late 2014.

India has being criticized in Kathmandu for having sided with the "discredited" Madhesi leaders, and shutting its eyes to the blockade that hurt the aam Nepali. Over a quarter century ago, a 15-month blockade by India led to a political change in Nepal and, subsequently, the advent of democracy. The current situation has followed India's disapproving response to the new Constitution.

The current unrest is rooted in Nepal's national identity.

However, in recent years, the increasing dominance of Maoism in Nepal's domestic politics, along with the strengthening economic and political influence of the People's Republic of China has caused the Nepalese government to gradually distance its ties with India. Prime Minister of India Narendra Modi visited Nepal in August marking the first official visit by an Indian prime minister in 17 years, provided Nepal with USD 1 billion as concessional line of credit for various development purposes to Nepal and a HIT formula, but he insisted that Indian immigrants in Nepal don't pose a threat to Nepal's sovereignty and therefore open border between Nepal and India should be a bridge and not a barrier. Nepal and India signed an important deal on 25 November 2014 as per which India will build a 900 MW hydropower plant at a cost of another USD 1 billion.

In a statement, Nepal's Home Ministry said that an "odd-even system" had been introduced Sunday, meaning "vehicles with odd number plates can only operate on odd dates and even number plates on even dates."

Ministry spokesman Laxmi Prasad Dhakal acknowledged that dozens of protesters had been injured in protests since the constitution was passed but denied there were major security concerns for the trucks to pass the checkpoints.

Dhakal told CNN demonstrations had been taking place in Nepal for months before the constitution was enshrined and trucks had been entering without major problems. "Just after the constitution was put into effect, India stops the trucks at the border citing security issues. Our stand is this is a vengeance from India as they are not happy with Nepal's new constitution.

Ministry spokesman Laxmi Prasad Dhakal acknowledged that dozens of protesters had been injured in protests since the constitution was passed but denied there were major security concerns for the trucks to pass the checkpoints.

Dhakal told CNN demonstrations had been taking place in Nepal for months before the constitution was enshrined and trucks had been entering without major problems.

"Just after the constitution was put into effect, India stops the trucks at the border citing security issues. Our stand is this is a vengeance from India as they are not happy with Nepal's new constitution. This is a trade blockade, just not officially announced," Dhakal said.

The Nepal Oil Corp. said Indian customs and the Indian Oil Corp. had not allowed the majority of trucks to enter Nepal for 10 days. Nepal now faces a "major fuel crisis situation," with only two to three weeks' supply and more than 400 fuel trucks stuck on the Indian side of the border, NOC spokesman Deepak Baral said.

MADHESIS RESENTMENT AGAINST THE CONSTITUTION

The recent turmoil in Madhes (or the Terai plains bordering India) was a stark reflection of the challenges confronting the restructuring process in Nepal. It was also a reminder to the current interim government that the problems in Nepal are not yet over and that there are serious socio-economic and political issues that need to be addressed.

The Madhesi uprising in January was marked by bans, protests, and violence in some major areas of Nepal's terai resulting in the death of over thirty people. This has in several ways changed the interim government's approach to and the management of Nepal's political restructuring and peace process. It has also raised many questions. Why was the violence so potent? Who was responsible? How will it affect the restructuring process? And so on.

These questions are palpable in the context of Nepal's fragile political restructuring process that is underway. While exploring answers to these questions, however, there is a proclivity to misinterpret the Madhesi issue. Some (mis) conceptions that have come about in the wake of the uprising are not only erroneous but also dangerous.

The Madhesi issue is not a communal issue. It is not one of Madhesis ("people of the plains") vs Pahadis ("people of the hills") as some tend to view it. This misinterpretation of the Madhesi issue commits a serious mistake by making it a community-based issue that could have grave implications for the country. To view the issue as a problem between Madhesis and Pahadis reveals a poor understanding of Nepal's complex society.

While one may have some facts supporting such an argument, it fails to explain the real issue of the Madhesis. There were also reports that certain "forces" (implicating the "Royal agents" and the "right wing" elements in India) of allegedly instigating the Terai riots to create trouble for the interim government in a bid to salvage the "monarchy" in Nepal. Hard evidence to ascertain the involvement of these forces is difficult to unearth, but many in Nepal point fingers at these forces as being responsible for the violence. Whatever the motive of those behind the terai violence, many ordinary Madhesis have lost their lives. Madhesis out on the streets at the risk of their lives were there for a different reason. For them it was a fight for a genuine object the Madhesi cause.

The Madhesi issue did not suddenly emerge in January 2007. A long history of a sense of discrimination is at the root of the Madhesi struggle. To explain the recent uprising it is necessary to understand the issue from the correct perspective. The issue relates to a movement against the state's "discriminatory" politics. It is a fight for recognition of rights political, cultural as well as economic and a struggle for equal representation and opportunity.

This forms the core ingredient of the Madhesi issue. For over five decades, the Madhesis have been waging a movement against "discriminatory" laws of citizenship and language, as well as recruitment policies to the armed forces and bureaucracy. The struggle can be traced back to 1951 when a party called the Nepal Terai Congress was formed under the leadership of Vedananda Jha to advocate "regional autonomy" for the Madhesis.

Again, in 1983, Gajendra Narayan Singh established an organization called Nepal Sadbhavana Council with the aim of combat discrimination against the Madhesis. In the post-1990 era, the organization turned into a political party called Nepal

Sadbhavana Party and in the general elections of 1991, 1994, and 1999, the party's manifesto called for a federal system of government, a liberal policy on citizenship and a separate Madhesi battalion in the army.

Despite the long struggle, however, the Madhesi issue has not been resolved partly on account of Nepal's five-decade history of being under autocratic rule 1960 to 1990 and 2002 to 2006 where political activities were restricted. Even during the short-lived democratic experiments in Nepal 1950 to 1960 and 1991 to 2002 the issue remained unresolved because of the lack of political will on the part of the successive governments.

The failure of the movement is also partly because of the internal divisions within the Madhesi leadership. The Sadbhavana Party has seen frequent infighting and splits that have further weakened the movement. It is in this context and in light of the predicaments mentioned that the Madhesi uprising of January needs to be understood.

The resolution of the Madhesi issue depends on how the interim parliament drafts a new constitution taking into account the various socio-political issues of the country. Should it fail to ensure the aspirations of the people, the recent outburst of violence in the terai will only be an indication of more chaos to follow?

China is unlikely to benefit from the tension between Nepal and India

The whole issue of new connectivity that can significantly affect our economy, I have had some interest in this area and I can tell you about the possibilities. We in Nepal have proposed that we construct a new trans-Himalayan rail link that can operate all year round between India and China via the mid region of Nepal. India's trade with China is going to be around $60 billion this year.

As a part of its development strategy India will be focusing on its north and north-eastern states because they are relatively backward. Similarly in China, the western and south western provinces including Tibet are getting increased attention. These are the provinces that will be receiving more resources in the future.

Tibet's GDP is increasing at a rate of over 10 per cent. Similarly in India, the state of Bihar which was considered a problem state has now a growth rate of around 10 per cent. This means tremendous opportunity of trade between these new growth centers of India and China via the land route in Nepal.

Lhasa, the capital of Tibet is now connected to mainland China by rail. The distance from Lhasa to Kathmandu is around 800 km and from Kathmandu to Barging, the border town adjoining India, it is another 200km. At present, trade between western China and India means over 5,000km of rail/road transport plus sea transport. The new connectivity via Nepal can create wonders for all the countries involved. India could have land connection with China via Sikkim, but I understand that the Nathula pass is not operational in the winter. In the case of Nepal, however, we have mountain passes that are less than 4,000ft above the sea level and can therefore remain open in all seasons. So we have suggested a trans-Himalayan rail link that could be owned jointly by Chinese, Indian and Nepali entrepreneurs. It could be a joint venture among the three nations. It may sound a little farfetched at the moment but the way the volume of trade is increasing between India and China, the proposal for trans-Himalayan connectivity via Nepal will be economically viable. Distances may be long, but with new investments moving towards the north and north eastern states in India and the same happening in China in the west and south western provinces there is a real possibility for this land route. In fact, when we were in the government in 2002/03 this was something that seemed to be of interest to both China and India. But somehow the relationship between the two countries has not warmed up enough to allow this kind of a venture. But I am pretty sure that the logic of economic gain is important in the decision making framework of both the nations and so the interest in such a land route will gain momentum in the future.

Government of Nepal overwhelmingly passed a new constitution last month which plans to devolve the unitary state into a federal one formed from seven new provinces . The decision was met with immediate consternation by some of the country's minority ethnic groups, most notably the Madhesi and Tharu that live in the fertile Terai region that stretches along the Indian border.

India, too, hasn't been too keen about supporting its neighbor's moves, giving indications that it's worried that friendly ethnic groups like the Madhesi might be underrepresented in the new structure. India's lack of enthusiasm about Nepal's federalization is occurring at the same time as the growing Madhesi uprising in the south (now joined by the Muslim community) that has stopped border trade between the two countries, leading Kathmandu to accuse New Delhi of implementing a de-facto blockade.

India, for its part, denies the accusations, and says that its trucks can't get through the border because of the anti-federalization unrest there. The crisis is becoming especially acute because fuel supplies are blocked at the border, and Nepal is having difficulty compensating with imports from China because of most of the border checkpoints are still impassable after the earthquake earlier this year. One of them just reopened , however, and it's already having a positive effect on ameliorating the crisis.

What had begun initially as a domestic political issue has warped into one with international dimensions, as its observable that China and India are now competing for Nepal's loyalty. China has the advantage of taking a hands off approach to its partner's internal affairs, and combined with its fuel exports to the beleaguered country, this has ingratiated it with the national government. At the same time, however, India exerts a different level of influence that's concentrated along cultural, economic, and ethnic lines. It's the Himalayan state's largest trading partner , and it has strong connections to the country's majority Hindu population and plethora of minority border region groups. There's thus a certain dichotomy when it comes to China and India's present methods of influence over Nepal Beijing's are top down, while New Delhi's are bottom up.

INDIA WANTS SEVEN AMENDMENTS TO NEPAL'S CONSTITUTION: CONFIDENTIAL DOCUMENT

The Indian government has asked the Nepali side to make seven amendments to the new constitution, according to an Indian

Government classified report published by the Indian Express. The India Ministry of External Affairs has said that the seven amendments are indispensable stating that these are the issues of concerns raised by the disgruntled Madhesi and Tharu groups. The amendments wanted by the South bloc have been forwarded to Nepali leadership via Indian ambassador Ranjit Rae. Rae, who had flown into New Delhi on Monday a day after the promulgation of the new constution, returned to Kathmandu on Wednesday and he headed straight to Prime Minister's official residence in Baluwatar to convey the message from New Delhi.

Amendment 1

India wants the electoral constituencies in Madhes to be based on population. The Article 63 (3) of the Interim Constitution states that the electoral constituencies will be based on population, geography and special characteristics," and in the case of Madhes on the basis of percentage of population." The latter phrase, however, has been omitted from Article 84 of the new constitution. India wants it re-inserted.

Amendment 2

India wants the word 'proportional' be inserted in the Article 42 of the new constitution. The article states that "the right to participate in state structures on the basis of principles of inclusion". The Article 21 of the Interim constitution, however, mentioned that various groups would have "the right to participate in state structures on the basis of principles of proportional inclusion". The word 'proportional' has been dropped from the Article 42 of the new constitution. India has asked the word to be reinstated.

Amendment 3

The amendment three is on the Article 283 regarding the special provisions relating to Citizenship of the office-bearers. The article states that the only those who have a citizenship by descent will be entitled to the position of president, vice president, PM, chief justice, speaker of the parliament, chairperson of National Assembly, head of the province, chief minister, speaker of provincial assembly and chief of security bodies.

Delhi says this should be amended to include citizenship by birth or naturalisation as a large number of Madhesis have acquired citizenship by birth or naturalisation.

Amendment 4

India wants representation in the National Assembly to be based on the population of the provinces. But the Article 86 of the new Constitution states that National Assembly will comprise 8 members from each of seven states and three nominated members.

Amendment 5

The five disputed districts Jhapa, Morang, Sunsari, Kanchanpur and Kailali be included in Madhes provinces. These districts are currently in province one (Jhapa, Morang, Sunsari) and province six (Kailali, Kanchanpur) along with hilly and mountainous districts.

Amendment 6

The article 281 (12) states that the delineation of electoral constituencies shall be put to review in every 20 years. It was to be reviewed on every 10 years in the interim constitution. India wants this time to be restored to 10 years.

Amendment 7

The Article 11 (6) states that a foreign woman married to a Nepali citizen may acquire naturalised citizenship of Nepal as provided for in a federal law.

Madhesi parties want acquisition of naturalised citizenship to be automatic on application. This also finds favour with Delhi.

BUT INDIA HOPE DFFICULT DAY

On September 20, Nepal's President Ram Baran Yadav announced that his country had a new constitution. The promulgation of the constitution is significant because it paves the way for the establishment of a democratic political system in the country. The constitution itself is the result of eight years of deliberation, including the failure of the first Constituent Assembly in 2012. It is the seventh constitution to have been adopted by Nepal in the last 67 years and the first by democratically elected representatives.

The adoption of Nepal's constitution has triggered alarm bells in India. According to reports in the Indian Express, a day after the constitution was promulgated; India expressed its displeasure about the content.

New Delhi has reportedly asked Nepal to make as many as seven amendments to address the concerns of the Madhesis and Janjatis (minority groups in Nepal). These amendments, the report suggest, have been "conveyed to Nepal's leadership through official channels."

Nepal on Sunday adopted its new fully secular and democratic Constitution, achieved after seven years of painstaking deliberations, amid violent protests by minority Madhesi groups over a seven-province federal structure.

"I call for unity and cooperation of all at this historic moment," Nepal President Ram Baran Yadav was quoted as saying by news agency PTI. Yadav was speaking at a special ceremony at the Constituent Assembly (CA) hall in Kathmandu's Naya Baneshwor to mark the Himalayan nation's transformation into a secular, federal democracy from a Hindu monarchy.

The Constitution, coming within months of the country seeing deaths of close to 9,000 people after devastating earthquakes, has 37 divisions, 304 articles and seven annexes.

But disagreement surrounding the federal structure that will divide Nepal into seven provinces has triggered violence in the country, claiming at least 40 lives including one on Sunday.

Madhesis and the Tharu ethnic communities in southern Nepal (the Terai region) and some western districts are opposed to the new Constitution as they believe it fails to address concerns raised by them. The Terai region constitutes a fifth of Nepal's landmass but accounts for over half the nation's population.

Among some of the most contentious clauses in the Constitution are those over citizenship in the country of 28 million people. The proptesting communities say that these clauses discriminate against women marrying foreigners, and deny their children equal access to citizenship. Estimates of the number of stateless people in Nepal range from 800,000 to 4 million, says a Reuters report.

Indians' worry

Quoting official sources The Indian Express reported that India was "dissatisfied" with the new Constitution of Nepal as it was "not broad-based" or "equal" and did not represent "two-thirds of the population", comprising Madhesis and Janajatis.

The report added that India's biggest concern was that Madhesis were up in arms against the secular and democratic Constitution.

A FirstPost report argued that as the Terai region shared its borders with the Indian state of Bihar, it was quite obvious that political unrest in Nepal would impact the poll-bound Indian state.

A statement released by the Ministry of External Affairs also had some apprehensions regarding the Nepali Constitution. "We are concerned that the situation in several parts of the country bordering India continues to be violent. Our ambassador to Kathmandu has spoken to the prime minister of Nepal in this regard," it said.

"We urge that issues on which there are differences should be resolved through dialogue in an atmosphere free of violence and intimidation, and institutionalized in a manner that would enable broad-based ownership and acceptance," the statement added.

Foreign Secretary S Jaishankar had on Saturday said India had always been strongly supportive of the Constitution-making process in Nepal and it would like its completion to be an occasion of joy and satisfaction, not agitation and violence.

The Terror factor

The 1950-Indo-Nepal Treaty of peace and friendship that enables the Nepalese and Indian citizens to move freely across the border without passport or visa has become a tool for terror outfits to export extremist elements to the Indian side. So, given the unrest and chaos along the Indo-Nepal border, members of several terrorist groups might enter India with sinister designs. India shares a 1,751-km border with Nepal.

According to an India Today report in April, just after the first devastating earthquake, the Intelligence Bureau (IB) had sent alerts to the Uttar Pradesh government to intensify vigil at the border in Maharajganj, Siddharthnagar, Balrampur, Shravasti, Bahraich, Lakhimpur Kheri and Pilibhit in the state.

So, it is clear that India's concerns on the unrest over promulgation of the Nepali Constitution are not unfounded, as this will impact its own internal security.

In the last few months, these communities have strongly protested against provisions of the constitution which they fear will impinge on their cultural identities. Prominent among the concerns are provisions related to the reorganization of provinces. The Madhesis largely inhabit the plain regions that border India. The protest has reportedly claimed 40 lives so far and New Delhi fears that violence may spill over to the Indian side if corrective measures are not taken.

The constitution was passed by a clear majority with 507 of the 598 constituent assembly members voting in favor. However, around 60 members from the Madhesis and Janjatis community boycotted the vote. India views the constitution as unrepresentative of a significant fraction of the population.

New Delhi's response to the constitution has come as a surprise to many. As a democratic country itself, India has arguably overstepped the limits of suggestion and rather tried to impose its views on its much smaller neighbor. In various international forums, India has repeatedly advocated for a country's right to self-determination. Unfortunately, this seems not to apply to Nepal. The concerns that India has raised may well be real. The Madhesis and Janjatis may indeed be fearful of their future at the hands of the three big political parties in Nepal. As a friendly neighbor, it is certainly not unreasonable for India to suggest concerns.

However, asking the country to made seven amendments to its constitution the day after it was promulgated goes well beyond suggestion. India must respect the will of the Nepali people and the democratic process through which the constitution was drafted and adopted.

Responding to the report in Indian Express, the Ministry of External Affairs has issued a statement stating. Government of India has not handed over any list of specific Constitutional amendments or changes to the Government of Nepal...we continue to urge that issues on which there are differences should be resolved through dialogue in an atmosphere free from violence, and institutionalized in a manner that would enable broad-based ownership and acceptance." The newspaper maintained that it "has confirmed from its sources that these amendments/changes were communicated by New Delhi to Katmandu. It stands by the report."

Indian Foreign Secretary S Jaishankar was sent on a diplomatic mission to ensure that India's concerns are amicably addressed. His visit was a failure. Immediately after Nepal adopted its constitution; India recalled its ambassador in Katmandu for a briefing. New Delhi has expressed its displeasure (and also here) without much impact.

It is likely to perceive this as its weakening grip over the Himalayan state, notwithstanding its humanitarian aid in the wake of the recent earthquake and Prime Minister Narendra Modi's visiting the country twice.

LESSONS FOR DEMOCRACY?

India may praise itself as the "world's largest democracy" but there are important lessons it can take from the new constitution of Nepal.

With the promulgation of this constitution Nepal has become the first Asian country to explicitly recognize the rights of the Lesbian, Gay, Bisexual and Transgender (LGBT) community. The provisions under Right to Equality clearly state that "no discrimination shall be made against any citizen in the application of general laws on grounds of religion, colour, caste, tribe, sex, sexual orientation, bodily condition, disability, status of health, marital status, pregnancy, financial status, origin, language or region, ideological conviction or any of these."

The constitution also states that nothing shall prevent the state from the "making of special provisions by law for the protection, empowerment or advancement of [among others] gender-based and sexually oriented minorities."

In contrast, same-sex relationship is a crime in India under Section 377 of the Penal Code, which awards punishment of "imprisonment for life or with imprisonment of either description for a term which may extend to ten years and shall also be liable to fine." The Supreme Court in 2013 upheld Section 377 but left it to the wisdom of the parliament to decide whether to retain or repeal the draconian law. The present Narendra Modi government recently informed parliament that it has no plans to repeal Section 377.

The party in the past has welcomed the apex court verdict and also termed homosexuality as "anti-India." Recognizing the rights of women, the constitution of Nepal explicitly states that "women shall have equal ancestral right without any gender-based discrimination." India has yet to introduce a similar right for women from all faiths. Moreover, ancestral property rights for women are not a fundamental right in India. Apart from this, the principles of positive discrimination and proportional inclusion have been employed in Nepal's constitution to give women the right to participate in all agencies of State mechanism and in health, education, employment and social security. Nepal also has become the second country after Bhutan in South Asia to abolish the death penalty. The Supreme Court of India in the past has accepted the fact that on various occasions innocent people have been executed. Since 1996, around 15 people have been erroneously given the death penalty. Two of them were hanged.

Under the new constitution, victims of environmental pollution or degradation in Nepal now have the fundamental right to receive compensation from the polluter. In India the "right to a clean environment" is not explicitly mentioned in the constitution, but the Supreme Court has interpreted it be included under the right to life. However, unlike Nepal, the victims of environmental pollution or degradation in India are not entitled to any compensation as a fundamental right. The state may impose a penalty on polluters but this does not necessarily mean that the affected will be compensated. The state gets richer; the victims poorer.

Similarly, while advocating for a fundamental right to education, the constitution makes special provisions for the empowerment of the differently-able citizens. It states, "Citizens with disability and economically poor conditions shall have the right to free higher education." On the other hand, in India no such provisions are available under fundamental rights for the differently able to access free higher education. Provisions for free education are limited only to the primary level.

3

Madhesis Resentment against the Constitution

It is a momentous time in the history of our nation Nepal in the process of promulgating a new constitution 2015. The constitution of Nepal finally delivered on the promises of federalism. Not to spoil the party though, however, it is clearly apparent that half of the population in southern and other parts of Nepal is still agitated despite of a new constitution that still do not address the voice of marginalized group in Nepal Nevertheless, the Madhesh-based parties did not learn any lesson from the election debacle and they could not come together to form a united front to protect their interests. By the time they formed the Unified Democratic Madheshi Front this year, it was too late to exhibit their strength, the three major political parties, including the NC, CPN-UML and UCPN-Maoist. With the promulgation of Constitution, the Madhesi people are strongly opposing the Constitution saying they are underrepresented. They have been protesting since August 15, 2015, even before constitution was drafted which took on fire after promulgation setting constitution on fire and forming human chain. During the protest more than 45 people were killed at point blank distance. They are demanding equal rights in all areas including high official positions.

Though the Madhesi people represent 51% of total population, they were able to get hardly 5% of government jobs and never in the high official positions like ministers, chief of government banks, police forces, ambassadors etc.

Another cause of protest of the Madhesi is with the demarcation of the proposed 7-states, which divide them in such a way they will never form majority in the upper house to voice for any amendments or opposition.

To bring things into perspective, I am talking about this half of population of marginalized group represented by Madhesi, JanJatis and Muslims. There is no doubt that the constitution is promulgated by the constituent assembly with a clean majority, something, that can not be denied when the three largest parties have found a common ground. This has also made easier for the ruling coalition to oversee the marginalized population's voices to incorporate in the constitution. To make it worst, the marginalized population agenda bearer political parties have diminished representation in the second constitution assembly after their failure to agree on a constitution in the first term of the constitution assembly.

Madhesi and Janajati are still protesting even so the fundamental demand of federalism is accepted, but my attempt is to find reasonings on the increasing Madhesi Resentment against the constitution building process. Madhesi definition includes Madhesi political parties (many), their activists, extreme Madhesis, moderate Madhesis and scared indifferent Madhesis. There is a clear massive resentment among the Madhesis that may be categorized in two aspects social and political.

A small disclaimer that the writing depicts a Madhesi perspective, the writer's interpretation of Madhesi resentment is with the government and leading national parties than any communal or ethnic group or any particular persons, Although, some arguments could make a no sense for a non-Madhesi.

The majority of casualties and brutality begun after the Tikapur incident where 8 policemen were killed by the angry protesters, a heinous action during a political protest cannot be justified in any circumstances. Without going to the political reasons of such a massive protest by Tharus in the Tikapur event, they would point out to the earlier clashes in Madhesh that begun from the day one when the draft constitution feedback process was initiated by the government.

In some places like Janakpur, police resorted to crowd control measures of baton charges resulting in several injuries including child, women and old people. This followed by two civilians killed in Surkhet, one killed in Rautahat, 5 civilians killed in Rupandehi, 1 killed in Karnali and 1 killed in Gaur before the Tikapur incident where the angry mob retaliated to the crown control and indiscriminate killing resulting in policemen casualties. Tikapur incident was followed by army deployment, looting and burning of Tharus houses amidst curfew and stricter measure by the security forces of Nepal police and armed police force. Further, 1 civilian bystander was killed in Rautahat, 4 killed in Birgunj, 8 killed in Jaleshwor, 3 killed in Janakpur and 4 civilians killed in Bhairahawa by the security forces with one casualty from the security force.

Nepal police on 2nd Nov opened fire killing a 19-year-old student from Darbhanga in Bihar. The police opened fire near the border to stop Madhesi protesters from reoccupying a bridge in the No-Man's Land demarcating the Raxaul-Birgunj border between India and Nepal. Ethnic minorities have taken to the streets in large-scale protests against the discriminatory provisions of the new governing order. Nepal's new constitution is highly controversial further deepening the divide.

National Human Rights and International Human rights have alluded to the fact that Nepal Security Forces have used excessive force to control the protest mentioning that often resorted to live ammunition easily with an intention to kill. This article will not go into grizzly killings of Madhesi and policemen, but, certainly uncontrolled killing of madhesi people is seen by the Madhesi as a genocide or ethnic cleansing. This is the sole reason all Madhesi from wide diaspora are protesting the bloodshed ushered by the security forces in Nepal while the rest of the country was uplifted in the mood of promulgating historical constitution. One of the major anger among madhesi is that the government spokesperson never backed up from their position on suppression, use of excessive force and killing of civilians at all. This was infuriating.

Despite the overwhelming size of population of the Madheshis and Tharus in Terai, they could get only 10 per cent seats in the

601-member Constituent Assembly (CA)-2 in the December 2013 elections. Many of the Madheshi leaders were defeated in CA-2 elections because they failed to address the people's problems. Out of lust for money and power, they did not hesitate to fragment the parties. During the CA-1 elections in 2008, only three Madhesh-based parties had contested the elections and hence they had a substantial presence in CA-1. In contrast, during the CA-2 elections in 2013, there were 13 Madhesh-based parties. Though both during CA-1 and CA-2 elections, the overall voting percentage for the Madhesh based parties remained almost the same about 12 per cent Madhesh leaders lost the elections because their votes were divided, making it easier for non-Madheshi leaders to win. Because of the insensitivity shown towards the demands of the Madheshi parties, a call was given by the Unified Democratic Madheshi Front and Tharuhat/ Tharuwan Joint Struggle Committee for an indefinite strike in Terai beginning August 8. Security Forces personnel used excessive force to suppress the agitation. Even the army was mobilized for this purpose. But the situation deteriorated fast. During the last month and half of protests, over 46 people, including 10 security personnel, have been killed. Besides, hundreds of protesters have been injured. Almost all the Terai districts have turned into war-like zones.

Immediately after the promulgation of the Constitution, the ruling political parties including Nepali Congress and CPN-UML celebrated "Diwali", while the Madheshi political parties and Tharuhat Struggle Committee observed it as a black day. Both within and outside the country, the new Constitution was welcomed by one community, while it was burnt by others. Nepal is now widely polarised between those who support and those who oppose the Constitution. China, Pakistan and a few other countries have welcomed the new Constitution, but India has indirectly shown its displeasure over the development, which is worrisome.

WHY MADHESIS RESENTMENT AGAINST THE CONSTITUTION?

The recent turmoil in Madhes (or the Terai plains bordering India) was a stark reflection of the challenges confronting the restructuring process in Nepal. It was also a reminder to the current interim government that the problems in Nepal are not yet over and that there are serious socio-economic and political issues that need to be addressed.

The Madhesi uprising in January was marked by bans, protests, and violence in some major areas of Nepal's terai resulting in the death of over thirty people. This has in several ways changed the interim government's approach to and the management of Nepal's political restructuring and peace process. It has also raised many questions. Why was the violence so potent? Who was responsible? How will it affect the restructuring process? And so on.

These questions are palpable in the context of Nepal's fragile political restructuring process that is underway. While exploring answers to these questions, however, there is a proclivity to misinterpret the Madhesi issue. Some (mis)conceptions that have come about in the wake of the uprising are not only erroneous but also dangerous.

The Madhesi issue is not a communal issue. It is not one of Madhesis ("people of the plains") vs Pahadis ("people of the hills") as some tend to view it. This misinterpretation of the Madhesi issue commits a serious mistake by making it a community-based issue that could have grave implications for the country. To view the issue as a problem between Madhesis and Pahadis reveals a poor understanding of Nepal's complex society.

While one may have some facts supporting such an argument, it fails to explain the real issue of the Madhesis. There were also reports that certain "forces" (implicating the "Royal agents" and the "right wing" elements in India) of allegedly instigating the Terai riots to create trouble for the interim government in a bid to salvage the "monarchy" in Nepal. Hard evidence to ascertain the involvement of these forces is difficult to unearth, but many in Nepal point fingers at these forces as being responsible for the violence.

Whatever the motive of those behind the terai violence, many ordinary Madhesis have lost their lives. Madhesis out on the streets at the risk of their lives were there for a different reason. For them it was a fight for a genuine object the Madhesi cause.

The Madhesi issue did not suddenly emerge in January 2007. A long history of a sense of discrimination is at the root of the Madhesi struggle. To explain the recent uprising it is necessary to understand the issue from the correct perspective. The issue relates to a movement against the state's "discriminatory" politics. It is a fight for recognition of rights political, cultural as well as economic and a struggle for equal representation and opportunity.

This forms the core ingredient of the Madhesi issue. For over five decades, the Madhesis have been waging a movement against "discriminatory" laws of citizenship and language, as well as recruitment policies to the armed forces and bureaucracy. The struggle can be traced back to 1951 when a party called the Nepal Terai Congress was formed under the leadership of Vedananda Jha to advocate "regional autonomy" for the Madhesis.

Again, in 1983, Gajendra Narayan Singh established an organization called Nepal Sadbhavana Council with the aim of combat discrimination against the Madhesis. In the post-1990 era, the organization turned into a political party called Nepal Sadbhavana Party and in the general elections of 1991, 1994, and 1999, the party's manifesto called for a federal system of government, a liberal policy on citizenship and a separate Madhesi battalion in the army.

Despite the long struggle, however, the Madhesi issue has not been resolved partly on account of Nepal's five-decade history of being under autocratic rule – 1960 to 1990 and 2002 to 2006 where political activities were restricted. Even during the short-lived democratic experiments in Nepal 1950 to 1960 and 1991 to 2002 the issue remained unresolved because of the lack of political will on the part of the successive governments.

The failure of the movement is also partly because of the internal divisions within the Madhesi leadership. The Sadbhavana Party has seen frequent infighting and splits that have further weakened the movement. It is in this context and in light of the predicaments mentioned that the Madhesi uprising of January needs to be understood.

The resolution of the Madhesi issue depends on how the interim parliament drafts a new constitution taking into account the various socio-political issues of the country. Should it fail to ensure the aspirations of the people, the recent outburst of violence in the terai will only be an indication of more chaos to follow?

THE ISSUES IN MADHES

The trigger for the first Madhesi movement in January 2007, when the interim constitution was promulgated, was the silence of the interim constitution on federalism and an inequitable electoral system. Madhesi leader Upendra Yadav burnt the interim constitution. This was followed by widespread protests in the Tarai by MJF activists, the killing of a MJF activist by the Maoists in Lahan of Siraha district, and the flare-up of the agitation across Tarai with a strong anti-Kathmandu and anti-Maoist flavour. The Maoists had contributed to militant mood in Tarai and were the first ones to characterize the exploitation of Madhes as a case of 'internal colonialism'. But they could not politically reap the benefits of this mobilization, as they were seen to have betrayed the cause after becoming a part of the Kathmandu establishment. the state was forced to relent and introduced an amendment to announce Nepal as a federal democracy. The seats from the Tarai were increased from 205 to 240 on account of its greater population. The demand for federalism reflected an aspiration for self-rule at the ground level and the creation of a political unit where the Madhesis would be able to control affairs. The demand for changes in the electoral system denoted the aspiration for shared rule at the centre with meaningful representation. But while these were the visible issues, at the root lay the Madhesi aspiration for securing respect, dignity, and equal citizenship in an erstwhile discriminatory set up.

The primary issue underlying the Madhes movement is the re definition of Nepali nationalism, which has rested on pillars like one language (Nepali) and one dress (daurasaluwar). While a hill person - irrespective of nationality in the case of Nepali speakers from Indian Himalayas - is considered Nepali, Madhesi citizens have long been treated as the fifth column because of their geographical, cultural, linguistic and kinship ties with people across the border in Bihar and Uttar Pradesh. This has manifested itself in various forms from deprivation of opportunities to insinuations about their 'patriotism' and prejudiced comments about dress, language and colour. It is in this regard that a distinction can be made between the different socio political movements that engulf the country. The quest for representation is common to all of them, but there are subtle differences as well. The Janajati movement is a fight to end the cultural oppression of the Nepali speaking,

Hindu, upper castes; the Dalit movement is against the oppressive caste structure and challenges the hierarchy inherent in it; the women's movement is a battle against patriarchy. The Madhes movement challenges the very basis of old Nepali nationalism and thus is considered politically the most dangerous and subversive.

Kathmandu has been forced to change its assumptions about Madhesis 'as Indians' and share power, but issues of who is a Nepali continues to lie at the heart of contemporary debates. Last year, the Vice President of Nepal a nominee of a Madhesi party took his oath in Hindi even as the President who was swearing him in spoke in Nepali. It led to protests by student outfits of national parties, particularly the Maoists, in Kathmandu and attacks on Madhesi party offices. Madhesi activists retaliated back in the

Tarai, burning the 'national dress' and launching protests. In July 2009, a year after the incident, the Supreme Court decided that the Vice President's oath was unconstitutional.

The Vice President and Madhesi parties have termed the decision as 'regressive' and as going against the spirit of 'inclusive federal democratic republic' other national parties and sections of the Kathmandu intelligentsia have urged the Vice President to retake his oath in Nepali.

While some language activists from the Tarai would also have preferred the VP to take his oath in one of the local languages like Maithili, the undertone of the entire debate in Kathmandu is based on the premise that Hindi is an Indian language. The incident is merely symptomatic of the contestations that mark the redefinition of Nepali identity. As journalist Prashant Jha notes, "Can a person who has darker skin, speaks Hindi or Maithili, has relatives in

Patna or Lucknow enjoy equal rights as a Nepali citizen with his cultural rights preserved? At the core, that is the essence of the

Madhes movement. Progress has been made in three years, but incidents like the Vice President's oath show that there will be continued contests on these issues. Another demand, cutting across Madhesi parties, is that of increased representation and meaningful inclusion. After the constituent assembly elections, when Madhesis were able to attain unprecedented political representation, with more than 200 members in the constituent assembly across parties, many felt that the core demand of the Madhesi movement had been addressed. The census of 2001 has put the Madhesi population at 33.2 percent; now, they constituted one-third of the house. Indeed, a fair and inclusive electoral system that made it contingent for parties to give proportional representation to marginalized communities had helped Madhesis. The identity-based voting pattern of the elections also helped, with Madhesi people deciding to give a chance to their regional parties instead of investing hopes yet again with hill origin candidates of 'mainstream' national outfits. But the quest for representation has not translated into success in the bureaucracy and security forces. Less than one percent of the total 75 Chief District Officers across the country are Madhesis.

Madhesi leaders claim that the army has only 800 Madhesis out of 93,000 plus force21, though the army contests the figures and claimed in 2007 that they have more than 7000 Madhesis in the force. Army officials also point to a separate Madhesi battalion as an example of inclusion. Police officials in Tarai districts predominantly are people of hill origin. But another perspective holds that this is merely rhetoric of Madhesi leaders; the problem is that Madhesis either do not apply or are not eligible enough for many government posts. One of the points of the eight point agreement signed between the government and Madhesi parties, after the second Madhes movement in February 2008, was 'group entry of Madhesis in the Nepal Army'but there has been little movement in this regard. An ordinance brought in by the Maoist led government proposed 45 percent reservation for marginalized communities in security forces, but this lapsed as the government fell. The new government has not taken any initiative in this regard. As commentator Tula Narayan Shah says, "Whether we like it or not, in the Nepali context, real power is exercised if you control the purse strings or decide when force can be used. That is meaningful inclusion in the state structure. Madhesis are still not present in these two areas of state authority they do not control the treasury or security forces, All the other demands – federalism, affirmative action, the allocation of services in Madhes, increased budget, autonomy stems from this basic yearning to be an equal citizen of Nepal, with a stake in its power structure. The Madhes movement except for a few armed groups with minimal support is not a secessionist movement; it is a movement to become Nepalis.

Protest

Violent protests against the proposed federal set up have shifted gradually to central Tarai. A protester succumbed to injuries from police firing at Birgunj in Parsa on Monday as the sporadic clashes between security personnel and protesters turned ugly.

More than 30 people, including a security official, were injured while demonstrators torched three police posts in Birgunj defying the curfew. Parsa, Bara and Rautahat, among other central Tarai districts, have been the flashpoints of the protracted banda enforced to protest the proposed seven state federal model lately.

The Samyukta Loktantrik Madhesi Morcha (SLMM) and Tharuhat campaigners have brought Tarai districts to a halt for the past two weeks. Various ethnic groups and political outfits also took to the streets, throwing normal life out of gear in the region. The District Administration Office (DAO), Parsa, clamped an indefinite curfew in Birgunj with effect from 4pm as the clashes between security personnel and protesters became violent. Dilip Chaurasiya, 35, of Birgunj-25 sustained bullet injuries during the curfew hour. Police had fired at him in the Radhemai area as the protesters defied the curfew. The victim succumbed to injuries in Narayani Subregional Hospital. Chaurasiya was a village committee member of the Sanghiya Samajbadi Forum Nepal. Party district Chairman Pradip Yadav claimed that about two dozen cadres were injured in police firing. The protesters staged a demonstration till the evening, defying the prohibition. Police had fired about a hundred warning shots and dozens of tear gas shells. Three police posts have been relocated citing security reasons. The enraged protesters set a government vehicle on fire and also torched the CPNUML party office at Ramgadhawa. They pulled down the statue of the late PM Girija Prasad Koirala at Chhapakaiya.

The line of trucks on either side is at least 10-km long, and the road to Nepal has become a narrow path from Ramgarhwa. "There are more than 2,000 trucks stranded here. We have no information.

No one from the Government has come to tell us anything. We don't know when the agitation in Nepal will end," said Ajay Tanti, the driver of a Bharat Petroleum tanker who arrived here 12 days ago from Kolkata Despite the uncertainty following widespread protests over Nepal's new Constitution, the situation in Raxaul is calm as officials keep watch on a large group of people gathered in the middle of the bridge that forms the border here. Madhesi activists have set up tents in the middle, in no-man's land, blocking the passage. In one tent, a young man is singing, eulogising the Madhesi struggle. The song can be heard and understood on both sides, Nepal police is at Shankaracharya gate, the entrance to Nepal.

"We are in no-man's land and that's why we are safe," said Ram Babu Kumar Yadav, president of the Sanghia Samajvadi Forum in neighbouring Bara Zila in Nepal. "Six of our children were killed in this district this is where Birganj is located. The Nepali police had come here and tried to push us out. They even fired teargas shells that fell across the border on the Indian side. But once a senior Indian officer came and demarcated the no-man's land, the Nepali police haven't come here," Yadav said. Scores of young people, who are part of the dharna, have gathered around and started shouting slogans. Yadav said the Madhesis are fighting for their rights. "We are happy that India is playing a very good role," he said, adding that the "blockade won't be lifted till Kathmandu agrees to give us the same rights that they give to the 'paharis' (hill people)". Sudhir Kumar, Superintendent, Customs, said they have no role to play in easing this blockade. "We are silent spectators sitting on this side of the bridge," Kumar told The Indian Express. "There is a dharna on since September 24 and the Madhesi protesters aren't allowing any vehicles from either side to go through," he said, adding that operations at the border were normal till August 15. "On August 16, they (madhesis) gave a two-days' protest call," said Kumar. According to the Customs official, the revenue collected on imports here was usually Rs 25 lakh on an average every day but has now dropped to Rs 5 lakh.

"After September 24, everything has stopped. No vehicle has crossed from either side ever since," Kumar said. He said that a high-level team of dignitaries are expected here on Wednesday.

"We have no idea how this will be resolved. We have been asked to file daily reports," Kumar said. The drivers stranded on the road, however, are in a difficult situation. One of them, Ram Dutt from Agra, was pleading with the Madhesis on the bridge. "There are 50 of us stranded across the bridge on the Nepal side. We were returning after unloading our goods (in Nepal) when we got stuck in this agitation. We are there for a month and eight days now. We have no money, not even to buy food, and our families are worried back home. Please tell the Government to do something for us," Dutt said. Dozens of other drivers have similar complaints. Anup Bhunia of Jhadavpur had driven a Satyam Transports tanker, carrying edible oil, across the border five days ago. "We had to go to Birgunj. It would have taken us a few hours to finish this work. Now we have no idea how long we will be stuck here," he said. "We know there is an agitation in Nepal. Please tell us whether this dharna will end anytime soon or not," said Rajinder Kumar, the driver of 18-tyre trailer carrying a load of paper from Mansa in Punjab. "I had to go to Narayangarh but I am stranded here since August 24," he added. Bijay Singh, a driver from Kolkata, said they can't abandon their vehicles and return, either. "There are tankers full of fuel stranded on the road. We hope nothing goes wrong," he said.

FROM DISARRAY TO UNITY

Despite the overwhelming size of population of the Madheshis and Tharus in Terai, they could get only 10 per cent seats in the

601-member Constituent Assembly (CA)-2 in the December 2013 elections. Many of the Madheshi leaders were defeated in CA-2 elections because they failed to address the people's problems. Out of lust for money and power, they did not hesitate to fragment the parties. During the CA-1 elections in 2008, only three Madhesh-based parties had contested the elections and hence they had a substantial presence in CA-1. In contrast, during the CA-2 elections in 2013, there were 13 Madhesh-based parties. Though both during CA-1 and CA-2 elections, the overall voting percentage for the Madhesh based parties remained almost the same about 12 per cent Madhesh leaders lost the elections because their votes were divided, making it easier for non-Madheshi leaders to win.

Nevertheless, the Madhesh-based parties did not learn any lesson from the election debacle and they could not come together to form a united front to protect their interests. By the time they formed the Unified Democratic Madheshi Front this year, it was too late to exhibit their strength. The three major political parties, including the NC, CPN-UML and UCPN-Maoist, took advantage of this split.

Because they had 90 per cent seats in the CA-2, they excluded the Madheshi parties in the constitution making process. But this was a major blunder. It was forgotten that the Madheshis and the Tharus have always been humiliated ever since the central and eastern parts of Terai were gifted away by the British East India Company to Nepal partly after the Sugauli Treaty of 1816 and partly after the Sepoy Mutiny (1857) in 1860. The hill elites always doubted the loyalty of the Madheshis towards the nation. This distrust towards the Madheshis and the Tharus provided these groups with ample reason to unite and protest against the constitution when a call was given for an indefinite strike.

Impact of Strike

The impact of the ongoing Madheshi agitation in Nepal as a whole in general and in the Terai region in particular is quite severe. For more than one and a half months now, life in the Terai region has been paralysed. All the educational institutions, hospitals, government offices, industries, banks, shops, agricultural activities and transport services have been crippled. Most of the essential items including food grains, petrol and gas are in short supply. Those who depend on daily wages for their livelihood are suffering the most. Movement of people is restricted because of continuous curfew in several places and also due to the deteriorating law and order situation. Amidst all this, unscrupulous elements hostile to India could pose a security risk by taking advantage of the open border between the two countries.

However, the government and the main political parties in Nepal are least sensitive to the needs of their own people, leave alone their concerns about security challenges such a protracted crisis could pose for Nepal and India. Instead of taking any initiative to defuse the crisis, some of them have started blaming India for the troubles in Nepal.

Rumours are rife that India has imposed a blockade as trucks loaded with goods are not coming from India to Nepal. In a deliberate manner, wrong information is being fed to the people of Nepal by the media that the sealing of the border by India at certain locations has caused food scarcity in Nepal. The truth, however, is that the private trucks plying on the Indian side of the border cannot afford to cross the border and come to Nepal because of the fragile law and order situation, which is due to the mishandling of the situation by the Nepalese government.

Madhesi including Tharus represent about 35 % of population of Nepal. With the new constitution Madhesi are looking for the equal representation in the state government and central government. There have been serious allegations made by madhesi leaders of an attempted division of madhesi and tharu clusters which would limit madhesi political representation.

As a marginalized group, Tharus in the west are combined together with hilly areas separated by geographical boundaries. A fear among them is because of parsimony and gerrymandering, their representation will be seriously flawed in future. Similarly, Madhesi in eastern districts of Sunsari, Morang and Jhapa are excluded from the central Madhesi province. Madhesi seek for one or two state encompassing their big cluster based on their settlement.

Further arguments and debates can be made on the structuring of states; however, it is a critical practice in democracy and federalism to keep the minority cluster together to increase the political representation. This was clearly not addressed in the present constitution.

Beyond that, Madhesi leaders and intellectual raised a serious issue of proportionate representation principle where the constituency for the central government are divided based on geography instead of population. Out of 165, 200 constituency are allocated among the hill territory and 65 in the Terai Madhesh, Further proportionate representation seats of 110 is added. Madhesi's are against the proportionate representation principle in a belief on the fundamental practice of democratic elections elsewhere in the world. A madhesi will ask why there is not proportionate representation of Madhesi in Army, Police and Armed Police Force. Why there is not proportionate representation in Government? Partly, answer to the lack of representation in Government service is the obvious difficulty of madhesis to get up to speed in Nepali language as a non-Nepali speakers. This applies to all other ethnicities represented as indigenous population – Janjati . There is an argument made by some people that Madhesi are not discriminated in government position sighting appointment of Madhesi President and Vice President. The answer to that is the mere Tokenism can not solve the issue of proportionate representation. A President and Vice President do not have any executive power except to protect and abide by the interim constitution. In future, however, President has significant power as commander-in-chief of army and several other functions as indicated by the draft constitution.

This is an uphill political fight for Madhesi diaspora against the government to push the agenda for equality in the new promulgating constitution.

Nepal's agitating Madhesi leaders say that government's decision to move constitution amendment bills in the Parliament would meet some of their demands but the move was not enough. This could prolong the agitation with top three parties of Nepal currently jockeying for power in the run-up to new government formation according to the agitating leaders. Worried about differences between Nepali Congress and CPN-UML on constitutional amendment the Madhesi leaders also say that the Madh ..

CONCLUSION

If the government and the main political parties are really serious about defusing the present crisis, they should accept it as a political problem and take steps to ensure that Nepalese people of all ethnicities, including the Madheshis and the Tharus, develop a sense of ownership in the new Constitution. For this, it is urgently required to initiate a dialogue with the aggrieved Madeshi and

Tharu political leaders and address some of the demands put out by them at the moment, as follows:

(1) Formation of two autonomous states in the Terai one extending from Jhapa to Parasa to be called "Mithila state" with Janakpur as its capital, and the other from Chitwan to Kanchanpur to be called "Buddha State" with Lumbini as its capital.

(2) Provision of 83 parliamentary seats for Terai Region in the new parliament

(3) Reservation of seats for the Madheshis and the Tharus in administrative, security, judiciary and diplomatic services on the basis of their population.

(4) Adequate representation of the Madheshis and the Tharus in decision-making process in all constitutional bodies, including in Public Service Commission at the central and state levels.

(5) Formation of an independent commission to investigate the excesses committed by the security forces and punish the culprits; and provision of adequate compensation for those killed during the agitation and also to those injured.

A forward looking Constitution must take adequate care to accommodate rather than leave out the genuine aspirations of a substantial cross-section of people. If such aspirations remain unmet, as the persisting movement by the people of the Terai region would indicate, the ongoing crisis may deepen causing trouble for one and all in Nepal. In such a situation, there is always a temptation to find an external scapegoat. It would require exemplary courage on the part of the Nepalese leadership to own up their mistakes and put their house in order before it is too late.

MADHES: THE CHALLENGES AND OPPORTUNITIES FOR A STABLE NEPAL

One of the least reported, but most significant changes in Nepali politics since the 2006 People's Movement is the emergence of the 'Madhes' as a political force. With the opening of the democratic space, the Madhesis, who largely but not exclusively live in the southern plains and constitute 33 percent of the population, asserted themselves. The Madhes speak languages like Maithili, Bhojpuri, Awadhi, Hindi and Urdu and have extensive cross-border ties with India. They challenged the hill centric notion of Nepali nationalism and staked claim for greater representation in the state structure. After a period of two and a half volatile years which has seen the repeated formation and fragmentation of Madhesi parties, the proliferation of militant armed groups in the Tarai, and reluctant measures by Kathmandu to share power, Madhesi politics is once again at the cross-roads.

The ouster of the Maoist government in May 2009 and the subsequent formation of the Madhav Nepal led coalition government was accompanied by striking changes in political alignments in Tarai. The biggest Madhesi party, Madhesi Janadhikar Forum (MJF) led by Upendra Yadav, split into two factions with one supporting the government and the other out in the opposition. The split was driven by personality centered as well as ideological issues. The Tarai Madhes Loktantrik Party (TMLP), which had stayed out of the Maoist government and even announced an agitation in the Tarai, has now become a participant in the ruling dispensation. The Sadbhavana Party continues to occupy one ministerial portfolio. These three Madhesi parties were critical in helping Madhav Nepal form a majority government. Even now, if two of these parties withdraw support, the coalition runs the risk of losing the confidence vote on the floor of the house. All these parties have come together on an anti-Maoist plank, sharing the belief that the Maoists must be stopped in their quest for 'total state capture'. They have termed the alliance as a broader democratic alliance. But it is riddled with internal contradictions.

The Madhesi parties are sharing power with the UML, which they have accused repeatedly of being an 'anti Madhesi' party and propping up communities in Tarai to 'divide and weaken' their movement. Among the other 22 members of the coalition are also old conservative parties which have steadfastly opposed federalism the main plank of Madhesi forces as well as forces like Chure Bhawar Ekta Samaj which claims to represent the hill population of the Tarai and tends to view most Madhesis as Indians. Even as Madhesi parties are engaged in Kathmandu centric power games, the political security situation in the Tarai continues to be worrying. The split in the MJF, and the cynical power play, has led to deep disillusionment among Madhesis in the Tarai.

Their faith in newer forces to change the political culture and win them rights as reflected in their participation in the constituent assembly elections despite threats has taken a beating. They have little trust in Kathmandu, which political actors view as the bastion of hill nationalism. The recent decision of the Supreme Court holding the Vice President's oath in Hindi as unconstitutional has further added to the trust deficit. Among Madhesis, caste based political mobilization has increased. With multiple armed groups where the line between politics and crime is blurred operating with total impunity, the fear among residents in Tarai towns has increased dramatically.

The state continues to be weak; its structures are dominated by people from hill castes; and the government has not been able to carve a response to the armed groups vacillating from engaging in talks to a solely security centric approach that has seen increased extra judicial killings in the past a few weeks. This ACHR briefing begins with a brief background of the Madhesi movement and grievances in the context of present developments. It then looks at the pre constituent assembly, political situation and agitations, and the subsequent post-election context. The paper examines in some detail the present political dynamics, the existing ground level situation in the Tarai, the multiple fault lines that characterize it, and the assertion by Tharus and other communities claiming a distinct identity. It also examines the role of the Indian establishment and cross border elements which wield enormous influence and leverage in shaping Nepali politics.

State and Madhesi groups

A deep trust deficit continues to characterize the relationship between the state either seen as the Kathmandu establishment or the CDO or SP in the district headquarters and the general Madhesi population. District administrators continue to carry the baggage of the old hill nationalism, seeing many Madhesis as Indians; the Madhesis continue to view them in an unchanging prism with suspicion. A few incidents illustrate this deficit starkly.

In January 2009, the government decided to set up integrated administrative service centres, which would perform basic government functions, on the highway in the northern parts of Tarai districts. The highway vicinity is home largely to people of hill origin.

The announcement provoked widespread opposition by Madhesi parties and residents living in the district HQs located towards the south of the district, closer to the border, which is inhabited largely by Madhesis. Madhesis saw this is a 'pahadi conspiracy' to shift administrative and welfare services to cater solely to pahadis; they claimed this was a prelude to shifting the headquarters itself.

The government, in its defence, repeatedly said that all they were doing is starting supplementary services in order to bring the government closer to residents on the highway and had no intention to shift the HQ. Protests spiraled, with Madhesis demanding that the service centres be annulled.

The government was forced to give in and postponed the decision. As they did that, people of hill origin at the highway began protests demanding that the centres be set up there. The incident is reflective of how even what may have been innocuous, and even well intentioned, government actions are viewed in the Tarai. The relationship between the state and the armed groups also reflects the difficult choices administrators have to make in a low intensity conflict, and how their choices may potentially lead to further resentment and a deterioration of the security situation. In 2007, immediately after the Madhes movement, the government made some tentative steps to invite armed group leaders like Goit and Jwala Singh for talks. But this was not followed through.

The armed groups had threatened to boycott and obstruct the elections in April 2008, but a combination of factors the desire of the Madhesi people to participate in elections, Indian pressure on groups operating from their territory meant they could not hamper the elections on any major scale.

The extortion, abductions, and killings in the Tarai however continued and even increased soon after the polls. Analysts blamed police complicity, political protection to armed activists, the proliferation of small arms, the legitimacy of the politics of violence, and an unregulated open border as primary factors leading to spiraling crime.

There are no precise figures but a Hetauda based human rights organisation, Him Rights, reported in November 2007 that in the preceding six months, there were 82 killings by armed gangs and 75 abductions in Tarai. Commentator Tula Narayan Sah, on the basis of the Human Rights Yearbooks published by INSEC between 2005 and 2008, reports that more than 1000 people have been killed between Biratnagar and Birgunj in three years and there have been more than 3000 abductions.

The Maoist led government initiated talks with many of these armed groups. By the middle of 2008, unofficial estimates suggested that the number of groups had shot up to more than 40 in the Tarai.

While the major groups – Goit's JTMM, Jwala Singh's JTMM, Manager Mahato's Madhes Rashtriya Janatantrik Morcha (Krantikari) did not participate in the talks, several others did. The government talk's team, headed by peace minister Janardhan Sharma, signed a 5 point agreement with groups that came for talks, allowing their activists to emerge over ground in return for cessation of armed activities. No reliable figures are available yet, but anecdotal evidence suggests that criminal activities had dipped partially in this period. The political uncertainty at the centre, with the fall and formation of a new government, led to a renewed spurt in these activities. The new government has decided to continue talks with some of the armed groups which had been in negotiations. On 10 August 2009, the peace minister

Rakam Chemjong held negotiations with four armed groups, the Janatantrik Tarai Mukti Morcha (Rajan faction), Madhesi Mukti Tigers, Madhesi Virus Killers, and Tarai Samyukta Janatantrik Party. But these talks were held in the backdrop of the new security policy announced by the government, and several 'encounter' killings in the Tarai.

The new security policy the full text of which has not been made public yet aims to crackdown on highway bandhs and organized crimes. It envisages an additional 16,000 security personnel in the Tarai and eastern hills. It has identified 109 armed groups operating in the Tarai alone. According to a news-paper report, a confidential Home Ministry report says that 80 percent of the 109 groups in the Tarai are based on Indian soil and are trained in India; they are supported by Indian leaders; and that 20 of these groups challenge the territorial integrity of Nepal while 60 want an autonomous Madhes province. The security policy has adopted a policy to quell those who do not come to dialogue with force. Between 20-24 July 2009 , three activists of armed groups were killed in separate incidents by the police in the Tarai. State authorities have claimed that they were shot when they confronted the police late at night or early morning with explosives and bullets But there is widespread suspicion that the police killed them while in custody.

The case of Manager Mahato has attracted attention in this regard. He is understood to have been arrested by the Jainagar police in Bihar, then handed over surreptitiously to Siraha police in Nepal, and shot in the middle of night.

Madhesi MPs have raised the issue in the legislature-parliament; Siraha based human rights organisations have condemned the incident and a senior police official was transferred out of the district. But the incident has not yet been investigated by national or international human rights organisations. Clearly, the state has found it difficult to deal with the Madhes issue. For one, there is no one Madhes issue the issues keep changing, and there are heterogeneous groups pushing different agendas.

The fact that the top echelons of the government are dominated by hill origin folk also blinds them to the sensitivity of the identity politics. The discourse of inclusion has meant that the old establishment has had to make compromises; Madhesi forces have been co-opted in the power structure. But radical forces, which are politico criminal in nature, exist and the state vacillates from engagement to coercion while dealing with them. The fact that the 'Madhes sentiment' can be whipped up by parties in the opposition, and on the look-out for an issue also means that the state authorities have to be creative and flexible in their responses a trait they lack.

4

Nepal and Constitutional Crisis

NEPAL CONSTITUTION CRISIS

Nobody knows what would be more galling for the BJP: Nepal's refusal to remain a Hindu state and instead turn secular, or Prime Minister Narendra Modi's inability to influence the Himalayan kingdom in spite of his two high-profile visits, stirring speeches, liberal economics and earthquake diplomacy.

Nepal's decision to adopt a new Constitution, in spite of objections and diplomatic pressure from India, is turning into a major embarrassment for the Modi government. The sequence of events unfolding in Nepal has put India in the unenviable position of an intrusive bully who is being continuously rebuffed by a much smaller neighbour.

The ungainly spat being played out in public has already caught the world's attention. "Modi makes a lot of overseas trips, but is he a diplomatic failure with India's neighbours?" asks Washington Post, arguing that the PM's sojourns have not yielded results.

"Just a year after Modi's high-profile visit to Nepal — where he performed an elaborate prayer ritual at a Hindu temple, gifted sandalwood worth $600,000 to the temple, offered a $1 billion line of credit and addressed the country's Constituent Assembly — comes the news that Nepal ignored many of New Delhi's inputs in writing its new Constitution," says the newspaper. Adding to India's discomfort is the Nepalese reaction to the neighbour's efforts to tweak the new constitution. For two days, the hashtag #BackoffIndia trended worldwide on twitter, with Nepali citizens asking Modi to lay off. "Tell to Modi don't mess around no more: this time strictly not," fumed Samira Sami on the popular Nepal Times website.

India's reported advice to Nepal for making seven changes in the Constitution has elicited an angrier response. Nepali people have retorted by advising India to first settle its own internal disputes with Kashmiris and Gorkhas before poking its nose in the neighbourhood.

The relations came to a boil when the Constituent Assembly of Nepal passed the new Constitution defining the Hindu-majority nation as a secular republic and divided it into seven federal provinces. The division is being opposed by people living in the Terai, especially the Madhesis and Tharus. They believe the new boundaries will lead to their marginalisation in Nepal.

The Madhesis are mostly Brahmins, Bhumihars, Rajputs and people of similar clans residing in Nepal's central Terai. They are both originally from Nepal and migrants from adjoining Indian states like UP and Bihar. They have close social and business links with people in Indian states. India sees them as a vocal support group and a buffer against any pro-Chinese tilt by the Nepal government.

Since the 1980s, there have been sporadic demands in Nepal for a separate Madhes as a single province. Since this has been ignored in the new Constitution, the Madhesis believe it is part of a conspiracy to marginalise them politically.

Apart from the Madhesis, the Tharus in the western plains and the Janjatis in eastern Nepal are also against the new Constitution. Several people have died in violent protests across Nepal against the new Constitution. India fears this may lead to large scale exodus of Madhesis and their migration to UP and Bihar.

Concerned by the development, India dispatched its foreign secretary S Jaishankar to speak to Nepal's leaders about the concerns of the Madhesis. Jaishankar also invited leaders of an alliance of Madhesis, who have been leading protests against the new Constitution to the Indian Embassy. Earlier, there were reports that Modi has advised Nepal against allowing "Five-10 people to decide the fate of the country". But nothing seems to have worked. The queer Indian response of just taking note of the

Constitution passed by a two-third majority evoked only anti-India sentiments and public derision. While the incumbent Prime Minister Sushil Koirla has refused to address India's concerns, his possible successor KP Oli has rebuffed the Modi government publicly.

"We have not done anything against Nepali people, and why should anyone bother about it when we have not done anything wrong,"

Oli said at an event on Wednesday. He went on to ominously add, "Let no friends be deluded that they can do whatever they like just because this nation is small..."

India seems to have yet again made the classical mistake of ignoring the neighbour's history, geography and psychology. Nepali people have always resented India's big brother attitude and intrusion into their affairs; they have been wary of Indian support to the Madhesi cause — seeing parallels between Sikkim's annexation and the unrest in Terai; and have taken pride in their freedom and independence.

The Modi government should have taken a cue from the Nepalese reaction to the Indian media's coverage of the recent earthquake and our boasts of providing timely relief to the victims. Perhaps the Indian reaction to the new Constitution could have been more nuanced and subtle.

This must be a major setback to Modi, who had energetically pursued a neighbour's first policy after becoming the PM in a bid to position India as a regional super power and restrict Chinese influence in the subcontinent.

After a promising beginning, India's relations with Pakistan have touched a new low. Unfortunately, Nepal too appears headed in the same direction.

Blaming India

As the agitation flares up and Indian response to the promulgation of New Constitution chills, leaders of big three are blaming India for the unrest in areas bordering India. Social media, online and print news sites are full of stories blaming India for the present problems. Even scholars regarded as soft on India are accusing the Indian establishment as a factor in the situation. Although Prime Minister Sushil Koirala is quietly describing India's role, UCPN-Maoist leader Pushpa Kamal Dahal and CPNUML leader K.P. Sharma Oli are openly chanting anti-India slogans in the public forums. UCPN-Maoist leader Prachanda threatened I ndia not to indulge in Nepal's internal politics. "Nepalese cannot bow down to anybody as they don't want to sacrifice their pride with India," said Prachanda. Out of big three, UCPN-Maoist leader Prachanda is the most vocal, followed by CPN-UML leader and prime minister aspirant K.P. Sharma Oli. The situation is such that Nepal and India are witnessing their official relations at their lowest ebb since the impasse of 1988-1989. As Nepal heavily depends on India for its economic development, the deteriorating relations with India will harm the common people. "We will talk with India on issues if there are certain misunderstandings between us," said K.P.Sharma Oli.

Political Move

As per the gentlemen's agreement, Nepali Congress, CPNUML and UCPN-Maoist have already fixed the positions of power for new Nepal, with Nepali Congress likely to get the post of president, CPN-UML leader K.P. Sharma Oli prime minister and UCPN-Maoist leader Krishna Bahadur Mahara speaker of the Legislature Parliament. Given the ongoing agitation, building pressure from agitators, the plan of the three parties is likely to change in case of early agreement. In case the leaders of the three parties agreed the proposal of the leader of Madheshi Janaadhikar Forum (Loktantrik), who proposed to incorporate the demands of disgruntled parties in bulk as political agenda, there will be new provisions in the constitution and the present power sharing model will be likely to change. Prime Minister Sushil Koirala will be in

New York for two weeks after leaving Nepal on 23 September and the parties in Kathmandu are likely to work on power sharing and accommodation of demands of Madheshis, Tharus and Janjatis through an amendment. "Since the demands of Madheshis, Tharus and Janajatis are political in nature, one cannot find these addressed looking at the legal and constitutional means," said Gachchhadar. Given the nature of the political leaders, it is unlikely that the current unity among the top brass of the three parties will remain intact forever when they will sit across the table to bargain for various constitutional and political positions.

Challenges

Nepal has promulgated seven constitutions in the past 68 years, this is the first constitution which faced the strong challenges from the hour of promulgation. Nepal has experimented with Nepal Constitutional Act, 1948, Interim Constitution of Nepal 1951, Constitution of Kingdom of Nepal 1959, Constitution of Nepal 1962, Constitution of Nepal 1990, Interim Constitution of Nepal 2007 and Constitution of Nepal 2015. However, none of the constitutions has survived for an adequate time. All the previous constitutions died because of failure of Nepalese leaders to stick to institutions and rule of law. One after another, these constitutions were burnt whenever the opposition felt betrayed. This time also, similar forces have appeared to threaten the longevity of the constitution. Instead of warm welcome or candle light, the constitution was put in fire on the same evening with blackout in half of the country. This has indicated that the new constitution is likely to face a number of challenges in its implementation.

The process of negotiations has already been initiated by prime minister Sushil Koirala, K.P.Sharma Oli and Pushpa Kamal Dahal Prachanda, who started the initiative by visiting the party offices of two leaders Mahant Thakur and Bijaya Kumar Gachchhadar.

Even as 40 days of violent agitation and clashes have already taken the lives of over 40 people, no sign of immediate solution is near the horizon. Along with Madhesis, Tharus and disgruntled Janajatis, Dalits and Hindu religious groups are opposing the constitution. And the opposition is gradually increasing expanding as the groups join hands with one another to press the rulers in Kathmandu.

NEW NEPAL, OLD POLITICS

Republican Nepal finally adopted a constitution on September 20, nearly ten years after the initiation of the peace process. It had held two elections to the Constituent Assembly to produce a constitution based on 'consensus' as agreed in the comprehensive peace agreement of 2006, which was midwifed by New Delhi. But the constitution, rather than resolving the fundamental problem of political representation and mainstreaming minority communities and women who were historically at the bottom of both the social and political structure, has marginalised them further. The issue of 'consensus' that has been at the core of writing a constitution has been eroded through majoritarianism to secure the entrenchment in power of the hill political elites. The argument that has been a driving force behind the new constitution is this: an elected Constituent Assembly (CA) representing the will of the people should write a new constitution taking into account the aspirations of the people based on transparency and consensus.

This was the reason why the Maoists had rejected the Constitution of 1990 as a compromise document dictated by the Monarchy and agreed to by the leaders of political parties who were in a hurry to acquire power when the transition was made from the Panchayat regime to multiparty democracy and constitutional monarchy. It was at that time, the Masal and Mashal radical left groups came together and formed the Communist Party of Nepal (Unity Centre), which, as part of the United National Peoples Movement (UNPM), participated in the pro-democracy movement that engulfed Nepal in 1990. One of their demands was an elected constituent assembly to write a constitution. Though the Unity Centre participated in the 1990 election, it suffered a split before the 1994 election because Prachanda's faction was not allowed to contest, which thereupon boycotted the election and declared armed struggle, a 'people's war', against a system that was a symbol of the Hindu religion, Nepali language and khas nationality. The Prachanda faction also carried forth the demand for a republic, secularism and a constitution written by the elected representatives of the people. This was reflected in the various agreements that the political parties signed after Jan Andolan II. After the formation of an elected Constituent Assembly in 2008, all the political parties jostled to frame a constitution keeping in mind their particular electoral constituency. The victory of the Maoists and the end of constitutional monarchy gave hope to the marginalised groups, especially the Janajatis, that their political aspirations would find a place in the new constitution.

Similarly,the Madhesis who have had historic grievances about the lack of proportional representation in jobs, in the army and in Parliament also aspired for accommodation. When their political concerns were not addressed in the 2007 interim constitution, the Madhesis even engaged in violent protest demanding 'ek Madhesh ek Pradesh'. The UCPN-M (United Communist Party of Nepal Maoist) was reluctant to support the cause of Madhesis because of the fear that its own support base among the Paharis would get eroded. It was only belatedly, that too after Jay Krishna Goit and Jwala Singh broke away to form a separate party, the Janatantrik Terai Mukti Morcha (JTMM), that the UCPN-M extended support for the Madhesi cause. Subsequently, the Madhesis also received assurances from Prime Minister G. P. Koirala in the form of a 22-point agreement with the Madhesi Janadhikar Forum, an umbrella group of Madhesi leaders from different political parties led by Upendra Yadav.

While Nepal managed to resolve most contentious issues, it could not resolve the issue of federalism. This remained a sticking point when Baburam Bhattarai dissolved the Constituent Assembly in 2012 and called for fresh elections. There was complete disagreement regarding the basis of creating federal units and their numbers. The problem persisted in the second Constituent Assembly. But since the Madhesis and Janajatis did not have adequate numbers of seats in the second CA, they depended on the UCPN-M's support to attain their demand. Kathmandu was rife with rumours of a post-constitution making power sharing deal between the UCPN-M and Communist Party of Nepal-United Marxist-Leninist (CPN-UML). It was therefore not surprising that

Prachanda decided to abandon the causes of Madhesis and other minorities as well as the principle of consensus that guided the peace-process. The split in the UCPNM became apparent when Baburam Bhattarai, former Prime Minister, second in command in the UCPN-M, and chairman of the CA committee on dialogue and consensus building, was not present in the ceremony where the new constitution was promulgated. His subsequent resignation from the party as well as from Parliament indicates a certain degree of disagreement within the party on the constitution.

It is true that the absence of consensus on the constitution prevented a settlement given the stance adopted by Madhesi parties and the Janajati groups. But what cannot be ignored at the same time is the fact that the Kathmandu political elites were not sincere about initiating a dialogue process to address the grievances of Madhesis and Janajatis. Ironically, the Maoists who waged a People's war demanding an elected CA to draw up a constitution by taking into account people's aspirations, now supports a constitution that is approved only by the majority and in the process marginalising the marginalised classes that at one point in time formed the backbone of their movement.

The boundaries of the new provinces have been drawn with a view to preserving the base of the political elite dominated by bahuns and chetris. It is true that the Madhesi parties have remained hopelessly fragmented. As a result, their strength declined precipitously between the first and second Constituent Assemblies; while they held 84 seats in the first CA, it declined to only 46 seats in the second CA election. This made them politically ineffective. Three issues are of major concern in the Constitution that has been promulgated. First, many of the highest constitutional positions are reserved for those who are citizens by descent only; naturalized citizens are ineligible to hold these posts. The fact that many Madhesis have marriage and familial ties across the border make them ineligible for these posts. Second, children of a Nepali mother married to a foreigner will not get citizenship by descent, thus perpetuating a gender bias in the constitution. Third is the issue of the boundaries of the newly created provinces, which affects the Tharus, Limbus and the Madhesis. In June, the four major political parties including the Madheshi Janadhikar Forum (Democratic) led by Bijay Gachchedar had agreed to the 16 point formula which promised that "The Federal Democratic Republic of Nepal will have eight provinces based on five criteria of identity and four criteria of capability."

It was also decided that since the names of the provinces and demarcation of their boundaries was a contentious issue, these would be decided by a Commission. But this agreement was struck down by the single bench of the Supreme Court as contravening Articles 82 and 138 of the interim constitution, resulting in the present crisis.

Thereafter, on August 10, top political leaders agreed to divide the country into six provinces in such a manner as to dilute the majority of the Madhesis and Tharus and reduce their political salience in terms of electoral politics. While Nepal moved to a new era of democratic politics after adopting a constitution drafted by an elected CA which made Nepal a secular, federal republic, its failure to address the grievances of Madhesis and Janajatis and women's rights make the constitution non-inclusive. Adoption of this constitution and the manner in which the provincial boundaries have been drawn only ensure that the political and electoral base of the Kathmandu based hill elites gets further entrenched.

Indian Concerns

From the outset, India had supported a consensus constitution. Prime Minister Modi while addressing Nepal's Parliament last year had emphasised upon the need to build a consensus. Nepali political leaders assured New Delhi that they will keep in mind the interests of Janajatis, Madhesis, Dalits and women in the new constitution. Yet, these were completely ignored and the constitution was passed through a majority vote. India's reaction has been curt especially since it had held a series of consultations with all Nepali leaders regarding the need to adopt an inclusive constitution. Yet, Nepal's political parties went back on the assurances that they had given to India.

Even Foreign Secretary Jaishankar's last ditch effort did not help matters with Nepal adopting the constitution by majority voting on 17 September. India has consequently not hidden its displeasure as it is concerned about the increasing polarisation in Nepali politics. The need for building a consensus is clearly reflected in the MEA statement: "India has been strongly supportive of constitution making in Nepal. We would like its completion to be an occasion for joy and satisfaction, not agitation and violence. We hope that Nepal's political leaders will display the necessary flexibility and maturity at this crucial time to ensure a durable and resilient Constitution that has broad-based acceptance."

Nepal has decided to send a Special Envoy to brief the Indian leadership about the constitution and the latest security situation. In the meanwhile, attempts are being made to initiate talks with Madhesi and Janajati leaders. Without a concrete road map and without disbanding the law and order approach to the Madhesi demand, the offer of talks is unlikely to yield result. The continuing violence by agitating parties in the Terai has created a situation where Indian trucks carrying goods and oil are reluctant to venture into Nepal.2 Economic hardship due to shortage of fuel and goods would have a long term impact on India-Nepal relations.

Given the fact that India shares an open border with Nepal, the consequences of violence and instability in the Terai would have consequences for India's security and may threaten the security of Indian businessmen and traders who are engaged in business in Nepal. Moreover, cross border ethnic linkages and familial ties makes India an interested party. While Nepali political leaders blame India and Indian 'interference' and try to arouse anti-Indianism, the same political leaders use New Delhi to further their political ambitions and do not hesitate to take New Delhi's help to entrench themselves in power. If Nepal does not want India's involvement, it needs to not only ensure that developments in the Terai do not have a spill over effect but also stop courting the Indian establishment to gain political power.

5

Nepal's Constitution Controvercial, Why ?

NEPAL'S NEW CONSTITUTION IS HIGHLY CONTROVERSIAL

The protests began in the final weeks of Nepal's protracted constitution drafting process. Drafting a constitution through an elected Constituent Assembly was a central plank of the peace agreement signed in 2006 to end a decade long Maoist insurgency and civil war. The first Constituent Assembly was elected in 2008, but it failed to complete the new charter, in large part due to differences over the delineation of federal provinces. A second Constituent Assembly elected in 2013 was also deadlocked for over a year. However, in the aftermath of the devastating earthquake which struck Nepal in April 2015, four major political parties reached an agreement to complete the charter by a "fast track" process.

However, marginalized groups in the Terai the lowland region that stretches across southern Nepal between the Indian border and the foothills of the Himalayas objected to this "fast track" process and the constitution which emerged from it. Once again, the delineation of federal provinces was the most contentious issue. In particular, protests against the new constitution involved two relatively large ethnic or social groups: Madhesi's concentrated in the eastern and central Terai; and Tharus, concentrated in the far western Terai. They objected to the new federal boundaries and to other aspects of the new constitution which they claim abrogate previous commitments made to their communities and create "second-class" citizens.

Objections include the unequal distribution of parliamentary constituencies and restrictions on the right of women to pass citizenship to their children.

Underlying these grievances is a long standing history of discrimination by successive governments, which remains dominated by traditional social elites from Nepal's hilly regions, against marginalized groups including Madhesis and Tharus. Members of these groups are underrepresented in government, public employment, and other influential institutions such as the media, and also on average have lower economic, health, and education indicators. While the government insists that the constitution guarantees "inclusion," protesters believe that it fails to address their marginalization and may even deepen it.

As the protests spread in August and deadly violence repeatedly occurred, the major political parties backing the process argued that it was essential to urgently pass the charter. They urged dissatisfied groups to come to Kathmandu for talks, but declined to pause the drafting process in order to discuss their demands. Those leading the process argued that the constitution was endorsed by the overwhelming majority of elected Constituent Assembly members and could be amended later to address the demands of protesting groups. Some also argued that the protests were instigated by neighboring India. According to the government, the extent of violence by protesters left police with no option but to resort to lethal force, although available evidence indicates this was not the case. Deadly violence has continued since the promulgation of the constitution on September 20 Much of the Terai, which is home to half of Nepal's population, remains at a near standstill due to ongoing strikes and protests. The town of Tikapur, in Kailali district, has been under curfew since August 24.

Community leaders on both sides have used crude populist language which risks inflaming tensions. In Kailali district, communally-motivated attacks on property took place, most notably after protesters killed the eight police officers on August 24.

However, it is important to note that aside from events in Kailali where the property of the members of the Tharu community was attacked, there are, according to the authorities, no known instances of protesters attacking people or property with an evident ethnic, caste, or other discriminatory motive in the areas covered by this report. This is despite the fact that the political differences underlying these protests are largely polarized along communal lines, and despite the contrary impression too often given in national media coverage of the events. At the same time, many people we spoke to in the affected areas said that police used insulting and derogatory language toward them. There has also been a worrying eruption in crude, prejudiced commentary on social media. There is a widespread fear among commentators in Nepal that the situation in some regions of the country could deteriorate into communal violence.

Local authorities have declared curfews and "restricted" or "prohibited" zones declared with the stated aim to contain public unrest and protests, some of which have been in effect for considerable periods. Some of these restrictions have severely constrained freedom of movement and economic activity.

In many parts of the Terai, bandhs (closures or strikes, also affecting road transport) organized by Madhesi and Tharu groups dissatisfied with the new constitution began in early August, and have at the time of writing been in effect for almost two months.

Some of the bandhs, seemingly supported by a significant portion of the Terai population, have resulted in serious economic disruption.

Many of the incidents described in this report are well known in the regions where the violence has occurred, but have not been reported in the rest of the country. While the media has consistently characterized the protesters as violent, it has also avoided reporting on the details of police violence, despite some illegal killings by the police having been witnessed and even filmed by numerous journalists. Newspaper editors explain these decisions as being made to "protect social harmony."

The government needs to immediately ensure that security forces cease the use of disproportionate force against protesters, and in particular that they abide by the United Nations Basic Principles on the Use of Force and Firearms by Law Enforcement Officials. The security forces need to immediately stop using unlawful violence. Intimidation and abusive language toward members of the public should end. The government should immediately establish independent bodies to investigate the unlawful killing of protesters and prosecute perpetrators, while ensuring the due process and fair trial rights of all accused of crimes, including those accused of killing police officers.

Human Rights Watch urges protesters and protest leaders to take all feasible steps to ensure that all protests are peaceful, and fully cooperates with the authorities in ensuring those responsible for serious crimes are brought to justice. It is especially important that those on all sides of this political dispute, including protesters and the government, avoid any action which could incite communal tensions.

The international community should urgently press the Nepali government to uphold basic international human rights and allow a credible and timely independent investigation of the events described in this report and in credible reports of local media, nongovernmental organizations, and the National Human Rights Commission (NHRC), among others.

Protest

Violent protests against the proposed federal set-up have shifted gradually to central Tarai. A protester succumbed to injuries from police firing at Birgunj in Parsa on Monday as the sporadic clashes between security personnel and protesters turned ugly.

More than 30 people, including a security official, were injured while demonstrators torched three police posts in Birgunj defying the curfew. Parsa, Bara and Rautahat, among other central Tarai districts, have been the flashpoints of the protracted banda enforced to protest the proposed seven-state federal model lately.

The Samyukta Loktantrik Madhesi Morcha (SLMM) and Tharuhat campaigners have brought Tarai districts to a halt for the past two weeks. Various ethnic groups and political outfits also took to the streets, throwing normal life out of gear in the region. The District Administration Office (DAO), Parsa, clamped an indefinite curfew in Birgunj with effect from 4pm as the clashes between security personnel and protesters became violent. Dilip Chaurasiya, 35, of Birgunj-25 sustained bullet injuries during the curfew hour. Police had fired at him in the Radhemai area as the protesters defied the curfew. The victim succumbed to injuries in Narayani Subregional Hospital. Chaurasiya was a village committee member of the Sanghiya Samajbadi Forum Nepal. Party district Chairman Pradip Yadav claimed that about two dozen cadres were injured in police firing. The protesters staged a demonstration till the evening, defying the prohibition. Police had fired about a hundred warning shots and dozens of tear gas shells. Three police posts have been relocated citing security reasons. The enraged protesters set a government vehicle on fire and also torched the CPNUML party office at Ramgadhawa. They pulled down the statue of the late PM Girija Prasad Koirala at Chhapakaiya.

The line of trucks on either side is at least 10-km long, and the road to Nepal has become a narrow path from Ramgarhwa. "There are more than 2,000 trucks stranded here. We have no information.

No one from the Government has come to tell us anything. We don't know when the agitation in Nepal will end," said Ajay Tanti, the driver of a Bharat Petroleum tanker who arrived here 12 days ago from Kolkata Despite the uncertainty following widespread protests over Nepal's new Constitution, the situation in Raxaul is calm as officials keep watch on a large group of people gathered in the middle of the bridge that forms the border here. Madhesi activists have set up tents in the middle, in no man's land, blocking the passage. In one tent, a young man is singing, eulogising the Madhesi struggle. The song can be heard and understood on both sides. Nepal police is at Shankaracharya gate, the entrance to Nepal.

"We are in no man's land and that's why we are safe," said Ram Babu Kumar Yadav, president of the Sanghia Samajvadi Forum in neighbouring Bara Zila in Nepal. "Six of our children were killed in this district this is where Birganj is located. The Nepali police had come here and tried to push us out.

They even fired teargas shells that fell across the border on the Indian side. But once a senior Indian officer came and demarcated the no-man's land, the Nepali police haven't come here," Yadav said. Scores of young people, who are part of the dharna, have gathered around and started shouting slogans. Yadav said the Madhesis are fighting for their rights. "We are happy that India is playing a very good role," he said, adding that the "blockade won't be lifted till Kathmandu agrees to give us the same rights that they give to the 'paharis' (hill people)". Sudhir Kumar, Superintendent, Customs, said they have no role to play in easing this blockade. "

We are silent spectators sitting on this side of the bridge," Kumar told The Indian Express. "There is a dharna on since September 24 and the Madhesi protesters aren't allowing any vehicles from either side to go through," he said, adding that operations at the border were normal till August 15. "On August 16, they (madhesis) gave a two-day' protest call," said Kumar. According to the Customs official, the revenue collected on imports here was usually Rs 25 lakh on an average every day but has now dropped to Rs 5 lakh.

"After September 24, everything has stopped. No vehicle has crossed from either side ever since," Kumar said. He said that a high-level team of dignitaries are expected here on Wednesday.

"We have no idea how this will be resolved. We have been asked to file daily reports," Kumar said. The drivers stranded on the road, however, are in a difficult situation. One of them, Ram Dutt from

Agra, was pleading with the Madhesis on the bridge. "There are 50 of us stranded across the bridge on the Nepal side. We were returning after unloading our goods (in Nepal) when we got stuck in this agitation. We are there for a month and eight days now. We have no money, not even to buy food, and our families are worried back home. Please tell the Government to do something for us,"

Dutt said. Dozens of other drivers have similar complaints. Anup Bhunia of Jhadavpur had driven a Satyam Transports tanker, carrying edible oil, across the border five days ago. "We had to go to Birgunj. It would have taken us a few hours to finish this work. Now we have no idea how long we will be stuck here," he said. "We know there is an agitation in Nepal.

Please tell us whether this dharna will end anytime soon or not," said Rajinder Kumar, the driver of 18-tyre trailer carrying a load of paper from Mansa in Punjab. "I had to go to Narayangarh but I am stranded here since August 24," he added. Bijay Singh, a driver from Kolkata, said they can't abandon their vehicles and return, either. "There are tankers full of fuel stranded on the road. We hope nothing goes wrong," he said. India denies imposing a blockade, saying its truck drivers are concerned for their safety after protests inside the Himalayan nation.

Nepal tell we, the people of Nepal, in exercise of the sovereign powers inherent in us, Internalizing the sovereign right of the people and the right to autonomy and self-rule, by maintaining Nepal's independence, sovereignty, geographical integrity, national unity, freedom and dignity, Remembering the glorious history of historical peoples' movements and armed struggles time and again and the sacrifice made by people for national interest, democracy, progressive change, and recognizing the martyrs, the disappeared citizens and the victims, Ending all forms of discriminations and oppression created by the feudal, autocratic, centralized and unitary system, Internalizing multi-caste, multi-lingual, multi-cultural and diverse geographical specificities, by ending discriminations relating to class, caste, region, language, religion and gender including all forms of racial untouchability, in order to protect and promote unity in diversity, social and cultural solidarity, tolerance and harmonious attitudes, we also express our determination to create an egalitarian society on the basis of the principles of proportional inclusion and participation, to ensure equitable economy, prosperity and social justice,

Expressing commitment to create the bases of socialism by adopting democratic norms and values, including peoples' competitive multi-party democratic governance system, civil liberty, fundamental rights, human rights, adult franchise, periodic elections, press freedom, an independent, impartial and competent judiciary, and the concept of rule of law,

NOW THEREFORE, in order to fulfill the aspirations for sustainable peace, good governance, development and prosperity through the medium of federal democratic republican governance system, hereby promulgate this constitution through the Constituent Assembly.

We know that, No constitution is perfect. Yet, This constitution is far more progressive than any other in the past or even compared to that of India. In the world, There are very few instances where the new constitution has been made with 90% suppport from its representative of the country. But, Nepal successfully drafted new constitution supported by 90% of the member of the constitution assembly, who represented the people of different geography and ethnicity. Nepal thus, has a constitution of the people, for the people and by the people.

There are some disagreements in some parts of the country but that will be solved within the country. The people disagreeing are our own people and we will come to some agreements.

The first seeds of discontent were from sections of Nepalis themselves- from restoring the world's only Hindu kingdom to bringing back the king- murmurs were starting around 2007-08 itself.

In 2007, Madesh erupted centuries of neglect, second class citizenry as well as being politically, socially, culturally

- economically dominated by Khas Arya finally had run its course. Madesh bandh was called & the call for federalism and delimitation of constituencies was first made. It must be noted that the issues on which Madesh bandh was first called were the same issues that Maoists themselves championed throughout their armed revolution (1996-2006). However, Maoists cadres opened fire on demonstrators turning the protest violent. Subsequent violence saw Madeshis attacking (destroying/pillaging) anything

- everything Pahadis and large scale ethnic conflict looked inevitable. However, it is important to note that during the entire Madesh uprising of 2007, violence was one way only- pahadis were the victim and no retaliation was witnessed in the hill areas and/or by pahadis.

It was then federalism was added into the interim constitution. The interim constitution promised to look into the historic grievances of various communities and suddenly you had Newer asking for a Newa Rajya, Limbus for Limbuwans, Tamangs for Tamsaling,

Tharus for Tharuhat etc. The new demands for states based on ethnicity became the new currency in the political discourse. All political parties were championing this rajya or that rajya.

When the first Constituent Assembly elections were held in 2008, Maoist emerged surprisingly victorious and both, the Nepali Congress (NC) & United Marxists and Leninists (UML) were decimated. Madesh was swept by Madeshi Janadhikar Forum (MJF). Obviously then the NC & UML also hopped into the federalism bandwagon and thus started a period of political musical chairs where governments were formed & governments dismissed with no actual agenda, no intention to write the constitution and political parties raising issues of one ethnicity or other to remain relevant, to show political strength and/or to come to power.

All in all, every party was at fault here but the biggest culprit was the Madesh based parties themselves. Such was the ferocity of the Madesh uprising that it put Madeshi issues right on the forefront.

Kathmandu could no longer ignore Madesh. Political parties were forced to concede space and Madeshis were elected as President & Vice President. However, Madesh based parties revelled in their new found power and all vexing issues were treated as a tool to be exploited for political gains. Genuine demands were relegated to the back burner.

The period of 2008-2013 were the ones in which the Maoist party had an upper hand and were dictating terms to other political parties. As federalism is/was a pet Maoist agenda, all major political parties also supported/pretended to support this agenda to cut Maoist to size. Hence, political winds of those times demanded that federalism was a forward looking agenda and any party that opposed it was destined be consigned into the dustbins of history. But that was then...

The second Constitution Assembly elections were held in late 2013. The results were also surprising-2008 elections turned on its head. NC & UML decimated the Maoists & Madesh based parties. Another surprise package was the emergence of a pro monarchy party the RPP (N). Once, the Maoists and the Madesh based parties were decimated, the big 2 (NC & UML), backtracked on federalism issue. The political saga went on & life went ahead as usual- with the constitution no where in sight.

Then the earthquake (April 2015) happened. Along with it came widespread anger and political parties wisely & hastily announced that constitution will be promulgated soon. In the ensuing 5 months, negotiation, renegotiation, give & take, this agenda, that agenda-all were discussed & finally the constitution was promulgated on the 20th of September 2015.

In between May 2015 to September 20 2015, the government first asked for suggestions. Then many demands were made on the streets and in Madesh, things took to the worse. The agitating Madeshis (and Tharus) lynched policemen and policemen shot demonstrators. Curfew were imposed the decimated politcal parties of Terai (Madesh) saw an opportunity to cash in the violence and propel itself back into power.

The violence of Madesh was attributed to India by arm chair Kathmandu intelligentsia. India is an easy scapegoat for everything wrong in Nepal. From 14 states promised to 6 declared (later increased to 7), no one thought to question the dillydallying hill based political parties, who first sowed the seeds of discontent & then claimed one up man ship the fault was squarely laid on India's feet- since Madeshis and Biharis look the same, this is a problem initiated by India- no discussion- chapter closed.

So what's the issue with the new constitution and why is it affected our (India-Nepal) relationship?

1) A large part of Madesh-Terai shares an open border with Indian states of Bihar & UP
2) Hill Nepalis have historically looked upon Madeshis as non Nepalis & are suspicious of anything Madeshis do
3) Madeshis are considered Indians and are 2nd class citizenry
4) A Madeshi has to prove allegiance time & again

India, especially after Narendra Modi became Prime Minister, has worked overtime to repair its relationship with Nepal, the anti-India stance of the pahad/hills notwithstanding. India has always stressed on the constitution being broad to encompass every aspiration of all Nepalis. As a neighbor, from the government standpoint, it has played everything correctly.

However, the relationship between Nepal & India is not just government to government. A large section of Indians support Nepal because of religion, cultural and historically affinity. What happens in Nepal has political ramifications in India too & vice versa. The religious & cultural homogeneity of the Madesh and

Indian states of Bihar & UP is closer than what Madeshis share with the hill people. They speak the same language, follow similar customs, have similar societies, religious customs and also marry across the border. Hence, Madesh issue finds some resonance in UP & Bihar- a spill over is highly likely.

When the constitution was about to be promulgated, with Madesh on fire, India suggested encompassing its aspiration so that the issue doesn't overflow into UP & Bihar. Who's in the wrong here?

1) Indian government showed insensitivity by calling its ambassador & sending a special envoy
2) Nepal government showed insensitivity by being indifferent to India's concern India's biggest concern of the flareup in Madesh is the state elections to be held in October-November 2015 in Bihar and in 2016 in UP. A misstep by its Central government will see public support nosedive, with a potential to lose an elections everyone already sees it winning.

On Nepal's part, any further delay could potentially mean derailing of an almost ready constitution & moving onto its next phase of nation building. Who's right here?

1) Nepal is right because the constitution took a long time in the making and it was necessary to immediately secure it
2) India is right because with Madesh burning, a low/high scale intensity would be a terrible security headache for both, India & Nepal down the line

With passions flying high due to impeding elections in Bihar, Indian government is in a tight spot vis a vis Nepal. It is common knowledge that when the Indian Prime Minister visited Nepal twice last year, both the time, he avoided meeting the Madesh based leaders and the leaders of pro monarchy RPP(N), instead telling them from a public platform to coordinate & compromise with the main parties. When the Indian envoy recently visited Nepal, he made it clear to the leaders of the Madesh based party to align itself with the aspiration of all Nepalis and not to make 10-12 demands, rather settle all issues with 1-2 critical demands. Similarly, the leaders of NC, UML and Maoists were also requested to try and encompass everyone in the new constitution so spillovers can be avoided.

The first mistake political leaders did here was to speak to the media. I mean that alone created a huge hue & cry regarding Indian interference. What should have been a closed door meeting & understanding became headlines of newspapers.

Today there was a rumor of an economic blockade, which again had Kathmandu & hill people high on anti-India dosage.

All this could have been avoided by both, India & Nepal.

China's handling of Nepal and its interference is totally overlooked by Kathmandu based media & general populace. That Tibetans are hounded in Buddha by Chinese plain clothes police is an open secret- just nobody speaks about it. The northern mountainous areas of Nepal are culturally close to Tibet & Chinese activities there is a separate essay in itself. There's nothing- absolutely nothing-Nepal does in the northern areas without explicit permission from Beijing. However, China speaks slowly and carries a big stick.

That's something India needs to learn. Nepalese monarchy also finds a lot of support in India- it's a potential vote catcher for Indian politicians, as is the restoration of erstwhile Hindu state. While blaming India for Madesh burning is easy, it's important to note that the restoration of monarchy, Nepal as a Hindu state aren't demands Madesh and/or its leaders are espousing. Federalism benefits missionary supporting countries like EU/ Scandinavian countries the most. The more divided a country is, the easier it becomes for missionary to propagate Christianity. Sometimes, it's necessary to look beyond raw emotions & chest thumping nationalism based on being anti-India. The number of mushrooming I/NGOs in Nepal should give a thinking man a clue where the federalism agenda is being funded from.

On Nepal's part, blaming everything on India and taking the easy way out venting & ranting without rhyme & reason needs to stop. On India's part, it needs to shore up its diplomatic nuances & relook into its bureaucracy handling sensitive nations like Nepal.

A relationship can only be built if two parties willingly try in the last one year, Narendra Modi has tried his best- but as the saying goes it takes two to tango.

6

Constitution Bill of Nepal 2015 (1972)

PREAMBLE

The people of Nepal, in exercise of the sovereign powers inherent in us, Embracing the sovereign right of the people and the right to autonomy and selfrule, by maintaining Nepal independence, sovereignty, geographical integrity, national unity, freedom and dignity, Remembering the glorious history of historical peoples movements and armed struggles time and again and the sacrifice made by people for national interest, democracy, progressive change, and recognizing the martyrs, the disappeared citizens and the victims, Ending all forms of discriminations and oppression created by the feudal, autocratic, centralized and unitary system, Embracing multi-caste, multi-lingual, multi-cultural and diverse geographical specificities, by ending discriminations relating to class, caste, region, language, religion and gender discrimination including all forms of racial untouchability, in order to protect and promote unity in diversity, social and cultural solidarity, tolerance and harmonious attitudes, we also express our determination to create an egalitarian society on the basis of the principles of proportional inclusion and participation, to ensure equitable economy, prosperity and social justice, Expressing commitment to create the bases of socialism by adopting democratic norms and values, including peoples' competitive multi-party democratic governance system, civil liberty, fundamental rights, human rights, adult franchise, periodic elections, complete press freedom and an independent, impartial and competent judiciary, and the concept of rule of law, NOW THEREFORE, in order to fulfill the aspirations for perpetual peace, good governance, development and prosperity through the medium of federal democratic republican system of governance, hereby promulgate this Constitution through the Constituent Assembly.

Preliminary PART 1 -

1. Constitution as the fundamental law:

(1) This constitution is the fundamental law of Nepal. All laws inconsistent with this constitution shall, to the extent of such inconsistency, be void.

(2) It shall be the duty of every person to uphold this constitution.

2. Sovereignty and state authority: The sovereignty and state authority of Nepal are vested in Nepali people. The use of which shall be as provided for in this constitution.

3. Nation: Having multi-ethnic, multi-lingual, multi-religious, multi-cultural characteristics with common aspirations of people living in diverse geographical regions, and being committed to and united by a bond of allegiance to national independence, integrity, national interest and prosperity of Nepal, all the Nepali people collectively constitute the nation.

4. State of Nepal:-

(1) Nepal is an independent, indivisible, sovereign, secular, inclusive democratic, socialism-oriented federal democratic republican state.

(2) the territory of Nepal shall comprise:

(a) the territory existing at the commencement of this constitution,

(b) such other territory as may be acquired after the commencement of this constitution.

5. National interest:-

(A) Independence, sovereignty, territorial integrity, nationality, autonomy, protection of self-respect, rights of Nepali people, protection of boundaries, and economic progress and prosperity, shall be the fundamental subjects of Nepal s national interest.

(B) Act and character against national interest shall be punishable by law.

6. Language of the nation: All the mother tongues spoken in Nepal shall be the national language.

7. Language of official transaction:

(a) The Nepali language written in Devnagiri script shall be the language of official business in Nepal.

(b) In addition to Nepali language, a province shall select one or more national language that is spoken by majority of people in that province as the language of official business, as provided for by the provincial law.

(c) Other matters concerning language shall be as decided by the Government of Nepal on the recommendation of the Language Commission.

8. National flag:

(a) The national flag of Nepal, consists of two juxtaposed triangular figures with a crimson colored base and deep blue borders, there being a white emblem of the crescent moon with eight rays visible out of sixteen in the upper part and a white emblem of a twelve rayed sun in the lower part.

(b) The method of drawing the flag and other particulars relating thereto shall be as set out in Schedule 1. 9. National anthem, Fundamental Rights and Duties

16. Right to live with dignity:

(a) Each person shall have the right to live with dignity.

(b) No law shall be made for capital punishment.

17. Right to Freedom:

(1) Except as provided for by law no person shall be deprived of her/his personal liberty.

(2) Every citizen shall have the following freedoms:

(a) freedom of opinion and expression,

(b) freedom to assemble peacefully and without arms,

(c) freedom to form political party,

(d) freedom to form unions and associations,

(e) freedom to move and reside in any part of Nepal,

(f) freedom to engage in any occupation or be engaged in employment, establish and operate industry, trade and business in any part of Nepal.

Provided that,

(1) Nothing in sub-clause (a) shall be deemed to prevent the making of an Act to impose reasonable restrictions on any act which may undermine the nationality, sovereignty, independence and indivisibility of Nepal, or federal units, or jeopardizes the harmonious relations subsisting among the people of various caste, ethnicity, religion, or communities, or incites racial discrimination, or untouchability, or disrespects labour, or any act of defamation, or contempt of court, or an incitement of offence, or is contrary to decent public behavior or morality.

(2) Nothing in sub-clause (b) shall be deemed to prevent the making of an Act to impose reasonable restrictions on any act which may undermine the nationality, sovereignty, independence and indivisibility of Nepal, or jeopardize the harmonious relations between federal units, or public law and order situation.

(3) Nothing in sub-clause (c) shall be deemed to prevent the making of an Act to impose reasonable restrictions on any act which may undermine the nationality, sovereignty, indivisibility or Nepal, or an act of espionage against the nation, or disclosing national secrets, or helping foreign state or organization that may jeopardize Nepal security, or an act of treason, or an act that undermines the harmonious relations subsisting between federal units, or instigates communal animosity, or jeopardizes the harmonious relations subsisting among

different caste, ethnicity, religious groups and communities, or an act of acquiring or depriving the membership of a political party only on the grounds of caste, language, religion, community or gender, or the formation of a political party that creates discrimination against citizens, or an act that incites violence, or is contrary to decent public behavior .

(4) Nothing in sub-clause (d) shall be deemed to prevent the making of an Act to impose reasonable restrictions on any act which may undermine the nationality, sovereignty, indivisibility or Nepal, or an act of espionage against the nation, or disclosing national secrets, or helping foreign state or organization that may jeopardize Nepal security, or an act of treason, or an act that undermines the harmonious relations subsisting between federal units, or instigates communal animosity, or jeopardizes the harmonious relations subsisting among different caste groups, ethnicity, religious groups and communities, or an incitement of violence, or an act which is contrary to public morality.

(5) Nothing in sub-clause (e) shall be deemed to prevent the making of an Act to impose reasonable restrictions on any act which may undermine the interest of the general public, or the good relations between federal units, or the harmonious relations subsisting among various caste groups, ethnicity, religious groups or communities, or an act of committing crime or violence, or inciting such acts.

(6) Nothing in sub-clause (f) shall be deemed to prevent the making of an Act to impose reasonable restrictions on any act which may undermine the good relations between federal units, or restricting an act which may have negative impact on public health, decent behavior and morality, or the particular industries, trade, business or services which only the state may engage in, or setting conditions or eligibility to engage in industries, trade, business, livelihoods or occupation.

18. Right to equality:

(1) All citizens shall be equal before law. No person shall be denied the equal protection of law.

(2) There shall be no discrimination in the application of general laws on the grounds of origin, religion, race, caste, tribe, sex, physical conditions, disability, health condition, matrimonial status, pregnancy, economic condition, language or geographical region, or ideology or any other such grounds.

(3) The state shall not discriminate among citizens on grounds of origin, religion, race, caste, tribe, sex, physical condition, disability, health conditions, matrimonial status, pregnancy, economic condition, language or geographical region, ideology and such other matters. Provided that nothing shall be deemed to prevent the making of special provisions by law for the protection, empowerment or advancement of the women lagging behind socially and culturally, Dalits, Adibasi (indigenous groups), Madhesi, Tharus, Muslims, oppressed class, backward communities, minorities, marginalized groups, peasants, labourers, youths, children, senior citizens, sexual minorities, persons with disability, incapacitated and the helpless persons, and of the citizens who belong to backward regions and financially deprived citizens including the khas arya.

Explanation: With reference to this Part and Part 4, "financially deprived" means the person having the income less than prescribed in a federal law.

(4) There shall not be any gender discriminations regarding remuneration for the same work and social security.

(5) There shall be no gender discrimination regarding the right to parental property with regard to all family members.

19. Rights to communication:

(1) There shall be no prior censorship of publications and broadcasting, or information dissemination, or printing of any news item, editorial, article, feature, or other reading

material, or the use of audio-visual material by any medium, including electronic publication, broadcasting and printing. Provided that nothing shall be deemed to prevent the making of laws to impose reasonable restriction on any act which may undermine the nationality, sovereignty, and indivisibility of Nepal, or the good relations between federal units, or jeopardizes the harmonious relations subsisting among different caste groups and tribes, or communities, or an act of treason, or defamation of social dignity of individuals through the publication and dissemination of false material, or contempt of court, or material that incites criminal offence, or an act that is contrary to decent public behavior and morality, or disrespects labour, or incites untouchability or gender discriminations.

(2) If there is any broadcasting, publishing or printing, or dissemination of news, article, editorial, feature, or other material through the medium of electronic equipment or the use of visuals or audio-visuals, no radio, television, online publication or any kind of digital or electronic equipment, or press, or other kind of media outlet, shall be closed, seized, or their registration cancelled for publishing, or transmitting, or broadcasting such material. Provided that nothing in this sub-clause shall be deemed to prevent the making of Acts to regulate radio, television, online or the use of any other kind of digital or electronic equipment, printing press or other medium of communication.

(3) No means of communication including the press, electronic broadcasting and telephone shall be obstructed except in accordance with law.

20. Rights to Justice:

(1) No person shall be detained without being informed of the ground for such an arrest.

(2) The person who is arrested shall have the right to consult a legal practitioner of her/his choice and be defended from the time of arrest. The consultations held with the legal

practitioner and the advice given thereon shall remain confidential.

Provided that this clause shall not apply to a citizen of an enemy state.

Explanation: For the use of this clause "legal practitioner" shall mean a person who has the legal right to represent any person in any court or office.

(3) Every person who is arrested shall be produced before a judicial authority within a period of twenty-four hours after such arrest, excluding the time necessary for the journey from the time and place of arrest to such authority, and the arrested person shall not be detained in custody beyond the said period except on the order of such authority.

Provided that, this sub-clause shall not apply to a person in preventive detention or to a citizen of an enemy state.

(4) No person shall be punished for an act which was not punishable by law when the act was committed, and no person shall be subjected to a punishment greater than that prescribed by law at the time of the offence.

(5) No person accused of any offence shall be assumed to be an offender until proven guilty.

(6) No person shall be prosecuted or punished for the same offence in a court of law more than once.

(7) No person accused of any offence shall be compelled to be a witness against herself/himself.

(8) Every person undergoing trial shall have the right to be informed about the proceedings of the trial.

(9) Every person shall be entitled to a fair hearing from an impartial, independent and competent court or judicial authority.

(10) An indigent person shall have the right to free legal aid as provided for by law.

21. Right of victim of crime:

(a) The victim of crime shall have the right to be informed

about the investigation and proceedings of the case regarding his/her victimization.

(b) The victim of crime shall have the right to social rehabilitation and justice with compensation as provided for by law.

22. Right against torture:

(1) No person in detention shall be subjected to physical or mental torture, or be treated in a cruel, inhuman or degrading manner.

(2) Any such act pursuant to clause (1) shall be punishable by law and a victim of such an act shall have the right to compensation as provided for by law.

23. Right against preventive detention:

(1) No person shall be held under preventive detention unless there is sufficient ground to believe that there exits an immediate threat to the sovereignty and territorial integrity of Nepal or public peace and order.

(2) Family member or close relative of the person in preventive detention pursuant to clause (1) shall have to be immediately informed about his/her condition as provided for by law.

Provided that this clause shall not be applicable to a citizen of an enemy state.

(3) If an official is found to have held any person under preventive detention against the law and with malicious intention, such person shall be entitled for compensation as per the law.

24. Rights against untouchability and discrimination:

(1) No person shall be treated with any kind of untouchability or discrimination in any private or public place on grounds of caste, ethnicity, origin, community, occupation, or physical condition.

(2) No person belonging to a particular caste or ethnicity shall be prevented from buying an object or getting services or facilities in the process of production of such objects or in the distribution or delivery of services, or no such objects

shall be sold to, or facilities or services distributed or delivered to persons belonging to a particular caste or ethnicity only.

(3) Racial discriminations shall not be encouraged in any way, or there shall not be any behavioral attitude to exhibit high or low status on grounds of a particular caste, ethnicity or community, or physical condition of a person, or there shall not be any behavioral attitude that justifies social discrimination based on caste, ethnicity, or untouchability, or encouragement for the propagation of attitudes based on caste superiority and untouchability, or hatred.

(4) There shall not be any racial discrimination in the workplace by indulging or not indulging in untouchability.

(5) All forms of untouchability or discrimination contrary to this provision shall be punishable by law as a serious social crime, and the victim of such an act shall have the right to compensation as provided for by law.

25. Right to property:

(1) Every citizen shall, subject to laws, have the right to acquire, enjoy own, sell, have professional gains, and otherwise utilize, or dispose of property.

Explanation: For the purpose of this Article, "property" means all type of movable and immovable property and the word also includes intellectual property.

Provided that the state may impose tax on property and income of a person according to the norms of progressive tax.

(2) The State shall not, except in the public interest, acquire, requisition, or create any encumbrance on the property of any person.

Provided that this sub-clause shall not be applicable to property acquired through illegal means.

(3) In the case when the land of a person is acquisitioned by the State according to sub-clause (2), the basis of compensation and the relevant procedure shall be as prescribed by Act.

(4) The provisions of clauses (2) and (3) shall not obstruct the state in carrying out land reforms, management and regulation by law in order to increase the production and productivity of land, modernize the agriculture and make it professional, environment protection and managed housing and urban development.

(5) In case the state has acquired property of any person for public interest pursuant to clause (3), there shall be no hindrance to use such property for any other public interest, other than the public interest for which it has been acquired.

26. Right to religious freedom:

(1) Each person shall be free to profess, practice, and preserve his/her religion according to his/her faith.

(2) Every religious denomination shall, maintaining its independent existence, have the right to manage and protect its religious places and religious trusts in accordance with law. Provided that it shall not be deemed to have hindered to make law to operate and protect a religious place or religious trust and to manage the trust property and land.

(3) While exercising the right as provided for by this Article, no person shall act or make others act in a manner which is contrary to public health, decency and morality, or behave or act or make others act to disturb public law and order situation, or convert a person of one religion to another religion, or disturb the religion of other people. Such an act shall be punishable by law.

27. Right to information: Every citizen shall have the right to seek information on any matters of concern to her/him or the public. Provided that nothing shall be deemed to compel any person to provide information about which confidentiality is to be maintained according to law.

28. Right to privacy: Except in circumstances provided by law, privacy in relation to the person, and their residence, property, documents, records, statistics and correspondence, and their reputation are inviolable.

29. Rights against exploitation:

(1) Every person shall have the right against exploitation.

(2) No person shall be subjected to any kind of exploitation on the basis of religion, custom, tradition, culture, practices or any other bases.

(3) No person shall be subjected to human trafficking or bonded labour, and such an act shall be punishable by law.

(4) No person shall be subjected to forced labour. Provided that nothing in this sub-clause shall prevent the enactment of a law requiring citizens to be engaged in compulsory service for public purposes.

(5) Any act contrary to clause (3) and (4) shall be punishable by law and the victim of such an act shall have the right to compensation from the perpetrator.

30. Rights regarding clean environment:

(1) Each person shall have the right to live in a healthy and clean environment.

(2) The victim of environmental pollution and degradation shall have the right to be compensated by the pollutant as provided for by law.

(3) Provided that this Article shall not be deemed to obstruct the making of required legal provisions to strike a balance between environment and development for the use of national development works.

31. Rights to education:

(1) Every citizen shall have the right to access to basic education.

(2) Every citizen shall have the right to compulsory and free basic education, and free education up to the secondary level.

(3) The physically impaired and citizens who are financially poor shall have the right to free higher education as provided for in law.

(4) The visually impaired person shall have the right to free education with the medium of brail script.

(5) Every Nepali community living in Nepal shall have the right to acquire education in its mother tongue up to the secondary level, and the right to open and run schools and educational institutions as provided for by law.

32. Rights to language and culture:

(1) Each person and community shall have the right to use their language.

(2) Every person and community shall have the right to participate in the cultural life of its community.

(3) Each community living in Nepal shall have the right to preserve and promote its language, script, culture, cultural civilization and heritage.

33. Rights to employment:

(1) Every citizen shall have the right to employment. Terms and conditions of employment and unemployment benefits shall be as determined by federal law.

(2) Every citizen shall have the right to select employment.

34. Right regarding labour:

(1) Every labourer shall have the right to proper work practices. Explanation: For the purpose of this Article, "labourer" means a worker or labourer who offers physical or mental work for an employer for remuneration.

(2) Every labourer shall have the right to appropriate remuneration, facilities and contribution-based social security.

(3) Every labourer shall have the right to form trade union, participate in it, and organize collective bargaining.

35. Right to healthcare:

(1) Every citizen shall have the right to seek basic health care services from the state and no citizen shall be deprived of emergency health care.

(2) Each person shall have the right to be informed about his/her health condition with regard to health care services.

(3) Each person shall have equal access to health care.

(4) Each citizen shall have the right to access to clean water and hygiene.

36. Right to food:

(1) Each citizen shall have the right to food.

(2) Every citizen shall have the right to be protected from a state of starvation, resulting from lack of food stuffs.

(3) Every citizen shall have the right to food sovereignty as provided for in law.

37. Right to housing:

(1) Each citizen shall have the right to appropriate housing.

(2) No citizen shall be evicted from the housing owned by him/ her, or encroached on the housing, except in accordance with law.

38. Right of women:

(1) Every woman shall have equal right to lineage without any gender discriminations.

(2) Every woman shall have the right relating to safe motherhood and reproductive health.

(3) There shall not be any physical, mental, sexual or psychological or any other kind of violence against women, or any kind of oppression based on religious, social and cultural tradition, and other practices. Such an act shall be punishable by law and the victim shall have the right to be compensation as provided for in law.

(4) Women shall have the right to access participate in all state structures and bodies on the basis of the principle of proportional inclusion.

(5) Women shall have the right to special opportunity in the spheres of education, health, employment and social security on the basis of positive discrimination.

(6) Both the spouses shall have equal rights in property and family affairs

39. Rights of children:

(1) Each child shall have the right to his/her identity with the family name, and birth registration.

(2) Every child shall have the right to education, health care nurturing, appropriate upbringing, sports, recreation and overall personality development from family and the State.

(3) Every child shall have the right to formative child development, and child participation.

(4) No child shall be employed in factories, mines, or in any other hazardous works.

(5) No child shall be subjected to child marriage, illegal trafficking, kidnapping, or being held hostage.

40. Rights of Dalits:

(1) Dalit shall have the right to participate in all agencies of the state based on the principle of proportional inclusion. There shall be special legal provision of empowerment, representation, and participation of Dalit community for employment in other area also including the public service.

(2) Provisions of free education with scholarships shall be made for Dalit students from the primary to higher level of education as provided for in law.

Special provision shall be made in law for Dalits to pursue higher education in technical and professional subjects.

(3) In order to provide health care and social security to Dalit community, special arrangements shall be made in accordance with law.

(4) Dalit community shall have the right to use, preserve and develop their traditional occupation, knowledge, skill and technology. The State shall give priority to modern profession of Dalits in relation to their traditional occupation, by providing them with necessary skill and resources.

(5) The State shall have to make legal provision to provide land to landless Dalits for one time.

(6) The State shall enact law to make housing arrangements for Dalits who do not have housing of their own.

(7) The facilities provided to the Dalit community according to this Article, shall have to be justly distributed to Dalit

women and men and all the Dalit communities living in different parts of the country, ensuring that all Dalits receive the facilities proportionally.

41. Rights of senior citizens: Senior citizens shall have the right to special protection and social security from the State.

42. Right to social justice:

(1) Socially backward women, Dalits, Adibasi, Janjati, Khas Arya, Madhesi, Tharu, minority groups, persons with disability, marginalized groups, Muslim, backward classes, gender and sexually minority groups, youths, peasants, labourers, the oppressed and the citizens of backward regions, shall have the right to employment in state structures and public service on the basis of the principle of inclusion.

(2) Citizens who are economically very poor and communities on the verge of extinction, shall have the right to special opportunity and facilities in the areas of education, health, housing, employment, food and social security, for their protection, progress, empowerment and development.

(3) People with physical impairment shall have the right to a dignified way of life and equal access to social services and facilities, along with their diversity identity.

(4) Each peasant shall have the right to access to land as provided for in law for agricultural purposes, along with the right to choose and preserve traditionally adopted and used endemic seeds and agricultural species.

(5) The families of martyrs who sacrificed their lives in the people s movements, armed conflicts and revolutions for a democratic progressive change in Nepal, the families of those who were disappeared, persons who fought for democracy, victims of conflict and the displaced, persons who were physically maimed, the wounded and the victims, shall have the right with priority, as provided for by law, to education, health, employment, housing and social security, with justice and appropriate respect.

43. Right to social security: Economically poor, physically

incapacitated and helpless person, helpless single women, persons with physical impairment, children, persons who cannot look after themselves and the citizens who belong to communities that are on the verge of extinction, shall have the right to social security as provided for by law.

44. Rights of consumers:

(1) Each consumer shall have the right to quality foodstuffs and services.

(2) A person who has suffered from sub-standard object or service shall have the right to be compensated as provided for by law.

45. Right against exile

46. Rights to constitutional remedy: There shall be right to constitutional remedy as per the Articles 133 or 144 in course of implementation of rights granted in this part.

47. Implementation of fundamental rights: For the enforcement of the rights conferred in this Part, the State shall make legal provisions, as required, within three years of the commencement of this constitution.

48. Duties of citizens: Each person shall the following duties:

(a) Protect nationality, sovereignty and integrity of Nepal by pledging allegiance to the nation,

(b) Abide by the constitution and law,

(c) Compulsorily enlist when the nation needs the service.

(d) To protect and conserve public property.

PART 6 President and vice-President

61. President:

(1) There shall be a President in Nepal.

(2) The President shall be the head of the State. He/she shall perform his/ her duties according to this Constitution and federal laws.

(3) The President shall promote national unity of Nepal.

(4) Compliance and protection of the constitution shall be the main duties of the President.

62. Election of the President:

(1) An electoral college, consisting of voting members of the federal parliament and the members of provincial assembly, shall elect the President. It shall be done as provided for in law with the difference of weightage in voting of the members of the federal parliament and the members of provincial assembly.

(2) Notwithstanding anything contained in clause (1), it shall not be deemed to prevent the formation of an electoral college for the use of the election of the President simply because of the reason that an election of provincial assembly has not been held in any province.

(3) The person who receives majority votes of the total number of existing members of the Electoral College as provided for in clause (1), shall be elected as President.

(4) If any candidate fails to receive majority votes according to clause (3), there shall be a second round of voting between the two candidates who receive the highest votes, and a person getting more than fifty percent of vote in this voting shall be elected as president.

(5) If none of the two candidates obtain more than fifty percent of the votes in the voting held under clause (4), then a re-voting will be conducted. Any person getting the majority of votes cast in this re-voting shall be elected as president.

(6) If a person who is elected to the position of the President already holds a political position through election, nomination, or appointment, the position held by such a person shall automatically become vacant.

(7) The election of the President and other related arrangements shall be as provided for by law.

63. Term of Office of President:

(1) The term of the President shall be for five years.

(2) The President whose term has expired pursuant to clause (1), shall continue to work according to this Constitution until the newly elected President joins the office.

64. Qualifications of the President:

(1) A person shall be eligible to be President if he/she fulfils the following qualifications:

(a) He/she is eligible to be a member of the federal parliament.

(b) He/she has attained at least 45 years of age,

(c) Is not ineligible by any law.

(2) Notwithstanding anything contained in clause (1), a person who has already been elected President for two terms, shall not be eligible to be a presidential candidate for the presidential election thereafter.

65. The circumstances in which the President ceases to hold office The President shall cease to hold office under the following circumstances:

(a) If a written resignation is tendered to the Vice-President.

(b) If an impeachment motion against the president is passed pursuant to Article 101.

(c) If the term of office expires. (d) If he/she dies

66. Functions, duties and powers of the President:

(1) President shall exercise his/her rights and duties as provided for by this constitution and federal laws

(2) While exercising rights under clause (1), the President shall perform all the works with the consent and recommendation of the Council of Ministers, except in case where the works have to be performed expressly under the recommendation of some agency or official. Such consent and recommendation shall be made to the President through the Prime Minister.

(3) The decision or order made in the name of the President as provided for by clause (2) and the certification of credentials in that regard, shall be done as specified by federal law.

67. Vice-President:

(1) There shall be a Vice-President in Nepal.

(2) The vice-President shall perform the duties of the President until a new President is elected in the case when the President ceases to hold Office due to reasons other than when the President is absent or the term of office has expired.

(3) If a person is elected to the position of Vice-President already holds a political position through election, nomination or appointment, the position held by such a person shall automatically become vacant.

68. The circumstances in which the Vice-President ceases to hold office: The Vice-President shall cease to hold office under the following circumstances:

(a) If he/she tenders a written resignation to the President,

(b) If an impeachment motion against the vice-president is passed pursuant to Article 101,

(c) If the term of office expires,

(d) If he/she dies.

69. Other provisions regarding the Vice-President: The qualification of the VicePresident, election process, and other provisions regarding the term of office, shall be simi-lar to that of the President.

70. President and Vice-President to belong to different gender or community: While conducting election of the President and vice-president under this constitution, the election shall be held so as to represent different gender or communities.

71. Oath of office of the President and Vice-President: The President shall take the oath of office and secrecy before the Chief Justice, and, the VicePresident before the President, as provided for by law, before assuming the responsibilities of the office.

72. Remuneration and other benefits to the President and Vice-President: The remuneration and other benefits to the President and Vice-President shall be as determined by an Act, and until such Act is made, it shall be as specified by the Government of Nepal.

73. Office of the President and the Vice-President:

(1) Separate offices shall be set up to assist the works of the President and the Vice-President.

(2) The Government of Nepal shall provide necessary personnel and make other arrangements for the management of the works of the offices pursuant to clause (1).

PART 8 Federal PARLIAMENT

83. Federal Parliament: There shall be a Legislature, called Federal Parliament, consisting of two Houses, namely the House of Representatives and the National Assembly.

84. Constitution of House of Representatives:

(1) The House of Representatives shall consist of two hundred and seventy five members as follows:-

(a) One hundred and sixty five members elected through the first-pastthe-post electoral system consisting of one member from each of the one hundred and sixty five electoral constituencies, formed by dividing Nepal into 165 constituencies based on geography, and population.

(b) One hundred and ten members elected from proportional representation electoral system where voters vote for parties, while treating the whole country as a single electoral constituency.

(2) Provision shall be made according to federal law for the representation of political parties to file candidacy for the election of the House of Representatives for proportional representation system through closed list, of women, Dalit, Adibasi, Janajati, Khas Arya, Madhesi, Tharu, Muslim, and backward regions. Such candidacy shall also consider balance in geography and province.

Explanation: For the purpose of this provision, Khas Arya means Chhetri, Brahmin, Thakuri and Sannyasi (Dasnami) community.

(3) While filing candidacy by political parties pursuant to clause (2), provision of representation of persons with disability shall also be made.

(4) Every Nepali citizen who has attained the age of eighteen years, as provided in law, shall be entitled to vote in any constituency.

(5) Subject to law, any Nepali citizen, who is entitled to vote in election for House of Representatives, and who meets the requirements under Article 91, shall be allowed to file candidacy from any constituency.

85. Term of House of Representatives

(1) Except when dissolved earlier, the term of House of Representatives shall be five years

(2) Provided that, in situation when the order for the state of emergency is made and when such state of emergency exists, term of House of Representatives may be extended, not exceeding one year, in accordance with federal law.

(3) The term extended under clause (1) shall, ipso facto, end within six months of the end of state of emergency.

86. Constitution of National Assembly and terms of members:

(1) National Assembly shall be a permanent house.

(2) There shall be fifty-nine members in the National Assembly as follows:-

   (a) Fifty six members elected from an Electoral College comprising members of Provincial Assembly and chairpersons and vicechairpersons of Village councils and Mayors and Deputy Mayors of Municipal councils, with different weights of votes for each, with eight members from each province, including at least three women, one dalit, one person with disability or minority;

   (b) Three members, including at least one woman, to be nominated by the President on the recommendation of Government of Nepal.

(3) The tenure of members of National Assembly shall be six years.

Provided that after the commencement of this Constitution, arrangements shall be made by drawing lottery to retire one-third of the members on the expiry of two years, another one-third on the expiry of four years, and the final one-third on the expiry of six years.

(4) The tenure shall be considered to have commenced from the day of first meeting of the National Assembly.

(5) In case of vacancy of a seat in National Assembly, it shall be filled in the manner through which the said member had been elected or nominated.

87. Qualifications for Members:

(1) Persons who meet the following requirement shall be considered eligible to be the member of Federal Parliament:-

(a) citizen of Nepal,

(b) who has attained twenty five years of age for the House of Representatives and thirty five years of age for the National Assembly;

(c) who has not been punished for any criminal offence involving moral turpitude

(d) not ineligible under any law,

(e) not holding an office of profit.

Explanation: "Office of profit" in this section means any position, other than a political position which is to be filled by election or nomination, for which a remuneration or economic benefit is paid out of a government fund.

(2) No person shall be a member of both Houses at the same time. (2) No one person can be a member of both the houses at the same time

(3) If a person who is elected or nominated to the position of the member of federal parliament already holds a political position through election, nomination, or appointment, the position held by such a person shall automatically become vacant from the day of his/her taking oath of office.

88. Oath: Every member of the Federal Parliament shall, before taking part for the first time in the meeting of the parliament at its committees, have to take an oath as provided in law.

89. Vacation of seat: The seat of a Member of Parliament shall be vacant in the following circumstances:-

(a) if he or she resigns in writing to the Speaker or Chairperson,

(b) if he or she does not meet the requirements under Article 91,

(c) if his or her term of office expires or if the term of the House of Representatives and National Assembly expires,

(d) if he or she remains absent from ten consecutive meetings without notification to the House,

(e) if the party of which he or she was a member when elected provides notification in the manner set forth by law that he or she has abandoned the party.

(f) if he or she dies

90. Decision as to Disqualification of Members: If a question arises as to whether a Member of Parliament is dis-qualified or has ceased to possess any of the qualifications set forth in Article 91 the final decision shall be made by the Consti- tutional Court.

91. Speaker and Deputy-Speaker of the House of Representatives:

(1) The House of Representatives shall, within fifteen days of commencement of first meeting, elect a Speaker and a Deputy Speaker from among its members.

(2) While electing speaker and deputy speaker as per clause (1), either Speaker or Deputy Speaker shall be a woman and belong to different parties. Provided that, no more than one party is elected to the House of Representatives or does not seek to file its candidacy even when elected, nothing in this article shall bar from having Speaker and Deputy Speaker of the same party.

(3) If the office of the Speaker or the Deputy Speaker falls vacant, the House of Representatives shall fill the vacancy through election from among its members.

(4) The Deputy Speaker shall, in the absence of the Speaker of the House of Representatives, chair the meeting of House of Representatives.

(5) In case the election of the Speaker and Deputy Speaker has not taken place, or both positions remain vacant, the senior-most member of the House of Representatives shall preside the meeting of the House of Representatives.

92. Chairperson and Vice-Chairperson of National Assembly:

(1) After the commencement of its first session, the National Assembly shall, within fifteen days of commencement of first meeting, elect a Chairperson and Vice chairperson from among its members.

(2) While electing chairperson or vice chairperson as per clause (1), either Chairperson or Vice chairperson Chairman shall be a woman and belong to different parties. Provided that no more than one party is elected to the National Assembly or does not seek to file its candidacy even when elected, nothing in this article shall bar from having Chairperson and Vice chairperson from the same party.

(3) If the office of the Chairperson or Vice chairperson falls vacant, the National Assembly shall fill the vacancy through election from among its members.

(4) The Vice-Chairperson shall, in the absence of the Chairperson of the National Assembly, chair the National Assembly.

(5) If the election of the Chairperson and Vice chairperson has not taken place, or if both the positions have become vacant, the senior-most member of the National Assembly shall preside over the meeting of the National Assembly.

93. Summoning and Prorogation of Sessions:

(1) President shall summon a session of parliament within one month after the elections to the House of Representatives are held. Thereafter, President shall summon other sessions from time to time in accordance with this Constitution: Provided that the interval between two consecutive sessions shall not be more than six months.

(2) President may prorogue the session of both or either of the Houses of Parliament.

(3) If, during the prorogation or recess of the House of Representatives, one-fourth of its members submit a request stating that it is desirable that a session or meeting of House of Representatives be called, the President shall call the session or meeting of the Parliament by setting date and time for this within a fortnight, and House of Representatives shall convene or commence its session on the specified date and the time thus fixed.

94. Quorum: Except as otherwise provided in this Constitution, no resolution shall be presented for decision in either House of Parliament unless one-fourth of the total number of members of the concerned House are present.

95. Address by President:

(1) President may address either House or a joint sitting of both the Houses of Parliament, and s/he may summon the members for that purpose.

(2) President shall address the first session after an election to the House of Representatives and a joint sitting of both the Houses of Parliament after the commencement of the first session of each year.

96. Deputy Prime-minister, State Minister and Assistant Minister Entitled to Take Part in Both Houses: A Minister shall be entitled to attend and take part in the proceedings and deliberations of any of the House of Parliament or its committees. Provided that s/he shall not be entitled to vote in a House or committee of which s/he is not a member.

97. Formation of Committees:

(1) House of Representatives and National Assembly shall have the right to form committees according to the law.

(2) If a resolution is passed by either House demanding that a Joint Committee of both the Houses be constituted for the purpose of managing the working procedure between the two Houses, resolving disagreements on any Bill, or for any other specified function, a Joint Committee thereon shall be constituted.

The Joint Committee shall consist of up to a maximum of twenty-five members in the ratio of five members from the House of Representatives to one member from the National Assembly.

98. Transaction of Business in case of vacancy of Members: Both House of Federal Parliament shall have the power to transact its business notwithstanding any vacancies in the seats of its members, and no proceedings shall become invalid even if it is subsequently discovered that a person not entitled to take part in the proceedings of either House had participated therein.

99. Voting: Except as otherwise provided in this Constitution, all questions submitted for decision in either House of Parliament shall be decided by a majority vote of the members present and voting. Normally, the member presiding shall not have the right to vote.

But he may exercise the right to cast decisive vote in case of a tie.

100. Provision related to Vote of Confidence and Motion of no-confidence:

(1) The Prime Minister, while he holds office, may, whenever he is of the opinion that it is necessary or appropriate to obtain a vote of confidence from the members of the House of Representatives, shall table a resolution to that effect in the House of Representatives.

(2) The Prime Minister may, if his or her party is fragmented or the coalition partner withdraws its support, to obtain a vote of confidence from the members of the House of Representatives, table a resolution to that effect in the House of Representatives within thirty days.

(3) A decision on a resolution tabled pursuant to clauses (1) and

(2) shall be made by a majority of the total number of members of the House of Representatives.

(4) One-fourth of the total number of members of the House of

Representatives may table in writing a no-confidence motion against the Prime Minister: Provided that a no-confidence motion shall not be presented up to first two years of appointment of the Prime Minister and if a no-confidence motion fails, another motion cannot be tabled within a year of its failure.

(5) The name of the member proposed for Prime Minister should be mentioned when tabling the no-confidence motion under clause (4).

101. Impeachment:

(1) At least one-fourth majority of the total number of the then members of House of Representatives may table a motion of impeachment against the President or Vice-President on the charge of serious violation of the Constitution by him/her. If at least two-thirds majority of the total number of the then members of joint session of both Houses of Federal Parliament passes the motion, the President or Vice President shall ipso facto be relieved of his or her office.

(2) A motion of impeachment against the Chief Justice or any other Judge of Supreme Court, Judge of Constitutional Court, member of Judicial Council and Head or official of Constitutional Bodies may be moved by at least one-fourth majority of the total number of the then members of House of Representatives on the grounds of his or her incompetence, misbehavior or failure to discharge the duties of his or her office in good faith or his or her inability to discharge his or her duties because of physical or mental reason; and if the motion is passed by a two-thirds majority of the total number of the then members of joint session of both Houses of Federal Parliament, he or she shall ipso facto be relieved of his or her office.

(3) A motion of impeachment recommendation committee shall be formed in House of Representatives to recommend charges of impeachment under clause (1) and (2).

(4) The committee formed under clause (3) shall comprise of eleven members.

(5) The committee under clause (3) shall recommend the motion of impeachment to the House of Representatives when the charges of serious violation of constitution, other grounds of his or her incompetence, misbehavior or failure to discharge the duties of his or her office in good faith or his or her inability to discharge his or her duties because of physical or mental reason, are proven with evidence by at least three members.

102. Penalty for Unauthorized Presence or Voting: If a person sits or votes in a meeting of either House of Parliament as a member without taking an oath pursuant to Article 88, or knowing that s/he is not qualified for membership in the House, s/he shall, on order of the person chairing the House, be liable to a fine of five thousand rupees for each day of such presence or voting. The fine shall be recovered as government dues.

103. Privileges:

(1) Subject to the provisions of this Constitution there shall be full freedom of speech in both Houses of Parliament and no member shall be arrested, detained or prosecuted in any court for anything said or any vote cast in the House.

(2) Subject to the provisions of this Constitution, each- House of Parliament shall have full power to regulate its internal business, and it shall be, the exclusive right of the House concerned to decide whether or not any proceeding of the House is regular. No question shall be raised in any court in this behalf.

(3) No comment shall be made about the good faith concerning any proceeding of either House of Parliament and no publication of any kind shall be made about anything said by any member which intentionally distorts or misinterprets the meaning of the speech.

(4) The provisions laid in clause (1) and (3) shall also apply to any person, other than a member, who is entitled to take part in a meeting of the House.

(5) No proceedings shall be initiated in any court against any

person for publication of any document, report, vote or proceeding which is made under authority given by a House of Parliament.

Explanation: For the purpose of this clause and clauses (1), (2), (3) and (4), the word "House" shall mean and include the House of Representatives and National Assembly and shall also mean a joint sitting of Parliament or a meeting of the Joint Committee.

104. Procedures relating to the Conduct of Business:

(1) Each House of Federal Parliament shall, subject to the provisions of this Constitution, frame rules for conducting its business, maintaining order during its meetings and regulating the constitution, functions and procedures of the committees or any other matter of the Federal Parliament or committees. The Federal Parliament shall determine its own conduct of business until such rules are framed.

(2) Matters relating to the conduct of business of a joint sitting of Federal Parliament and the constitution of its Joint Committee and the functions and procedures thereof shall be in accordance with rules approved by the joint session of the both Houses.

105. Restriction on discussion: No discussion shall be held in either House of Federal Parliament on a matter which is under consideration in any court of Nepal, and about anything done by a Judge in course of performance of his duties. Provided that nothing in this Article shall be deemed to bar the expression of opinion about the conduct of a Judge during deliberations on a motion of impeachment.

106. Secretary General and Secretary of Federal Parliament:

(1) Secretary of the House of Representatives shall be appointed on the recommendation of its Speaker, the Secretary of the National Assembly shall be appointed on the recommendation of its Chairperson, the secretary-general appointed in consultation with both the Speaker and the Chairperson.

(2) The qualifications, duties, functions, rights and other services of Secretary General the Secretary of the National Assembly, and the Secretary of Federal House of Representatives shall be as determined by law.

107. Secretariat of Federal Parliament: A Secretariat shall be established for the purpose of conducting the business of Parliament. Other matters related thereto shall be as determined by law.

108. Remuneration: The remuneration and benefits of the Speaker and Deputy Speaker of the House of Representatives, the Chairperson and ViceChairperson of the National Assembly and Chairperson of committees and members of Federal Parliament shall be as determined by the law. Until so determined it shall be as specified by the Federal Government.

PART-19 Local Financial Procedure

228. No tax to be levied or loan to be raised:

(1) No tax shall be levied and collected except in accordance with law.

(2) The local level shall impose tax in areas within its jurisdiction, without causing any adverse impact on the national economic policy, transportation of goods, services, capital and labour, and on neighboring Province or local levels.

229. Local Consolidated Fund:

(1) There shall be a Local Consolidated Fund in every Village Council and Municipality under the local level. All revenues received by the local Village Council or Municipality, grants and loans received from the Government of Nepal and the Provincial Government and any amount received from other sources shall be deposited in such Fund.

(2) Provision relating to expenditures from the Local Consolidated Fund, pursuant to Clause (1), shall be as provided for in the local law.

230. Estimate of Revenue and Expenditure of Village Council and Municipality:

(1) The Village Executive and Municipal Executive shall, with respect to every fiscal year, present before the Village Assembly or Municipal Assembly annual estimates of revenues and expenditure, and have it passed.

(2) If the Village Executive and Municipal Executive have to develop a deficit budget while presenting a budget under clause (1), they shall, pursuant to Federal law and Provincial law, also propose sources to fulfill the deficit.

PART-24 Election Commission

245. Election Commission:

(1) There shall be an Election Commission in Nepal consisting of a Chief Election Commissioner and four other Election Commissioners. The Chief Election Commissioner shall act as the Chairperson of the Election Commission.

(2) The President shall, on the recommendation of the Constitutional Council, appoint the Chief Election Commissioner and the Election Commissioners.

(3) The term of office of the Chief Election Commissioner and the Election Commissioners shall be six years from the date of appointment.

(4) Notwithstanding anything mentioned in Clause (3), the office of the Chief Election Commissioner and Election Commissioner shall be deemed vacant in the following circumstances:

(a) if she/he submits a written resignation to the President,

(b) if she/he attains the age of sixty-five,

(c) if a resolution of impeachment is passed against her/him as per Article 101,

(d) if she/he dies.

(5) The Chief Commissioner and commissioners appointed pursuant to clause (2) shall not be eligible for reappointment. Provided that nothing in this Clause shall be deemed to be a bar to the appointment of a commissioner of the Election Commission as chief commissioner thereof, and when a member is so appointed as the Chief

Commissioner, her/his term of office shall be computed so as to include her/his tenure as commissioner as well.

(6) Any person who possesses the following qualifications is eligible to be appointed as the Chief Election Commissioner or an Election Commissioner:-

(a) holds a Bachelor's Degree from a recognized university,

(b) is not a member of any political party immediately before the appointment;

(c) has attained the age of forty five,

(d) possesses high moral character.

(7) The remuneration and other conditions of service of the Chief Election Commissioner and the Election Commissioners shall be as determined by law. The remuneration and other conditions of service of the Chief Election Commissioner and the Election Commissioners shall not, so long as they hold office, be altered to their disadvantage. Provided that this provision shall not apply in the case of declaration of a State of Emergency due to extreme economic disarray.

(8) A person who has been the Chief Election Commissioner or the Election Commissioner shall not be eligible for appointment in other Government Services. Provided that, nothing in this Clause shall be deemed to be a bar to the appointment to any political position or to any position which has the responsibility of making investigations, inquiries or findings on any subject, or to any position which has the responsibility of submitting advice, opinion or recommendation after carrying out a study or research on any subject.

246. Functions duties and, powers of Election Commission:

(1) The Election Commission shall, subject to this Constitution and other laws, conduct, supervise, direct and control the election of the President, the VicePresident, Federal Parliament, Provincial assemblies, local bodies. The Election Commission shall be responsible for preparing the voters list for the purpose of election.

(2) The Election Commission shall hold referendum on subject of national importance as per this Constitution and federal laws

(3) If candidacy nominations have been registered for the election of the President, the Vice-President, the member of Federal Parliament and Provincial Assembly but a question arises before the completion of the election about the illegitimacy of a candidate, a final decision thereon shall be made by the Election Commission.

(4) The Election Commission may delegate any of its functions, duties and powers to the Chief Election Commissioner, Election Commissioner or any employee of the Government of Nepal to be exercised and followed in compliance with the conditions specified.

(5) Other functions, duties and powers and working procedures of the Election Commission shall be as regulated by law.

247. Necessary Cooperation to be Extended:

The Government of Nepal, provincial government and local government shall provide necessary employees and extend other cooperation as may be required to perform the functions of the Election Commission in accordance with this Constitution.

PART-25 National Human Rights Commission

248. National Human Rights Commission:

(1) There shall be a National Human Rights Commission in Nepal consisting of the following Chairperson and four other members:

(2) The President shall, on the recommendation of the Constitutional Council, appoint the Chairperson and the Members of the National Human Rights Commission.

(3) The term of office of the Chairperson and Members of the National Human Rights Commission shall be six years from the date of appointment.

(4) The Chairperson and members appointed pursuant to clause

(2) shall not be eligible for reappointment. Provided that nothing in this Clause shall be deemed to be a bar to the appointment of a member of the Commission as chairperson thereof, and when a member is so appointed as the Chairperson, her/his term of office shall be computed so as to include her/his tenure as member as well.

(5) Notwithstanding anything contained in Clause (3), the office of the Chairperson or the Members of the National Human Rights Commission shall be deemed vacant in the following circumstances:

(a) if she/he submits a written resignation to the President,

(b) if a resolution of impeachment is passed against her/him as per Article 101,

(c) if he or she dies.

(6) Any person who possesses the following qualifications is eligible to be appointed as the Chairperson or a member of the National Human Rights Commission :-

(a) for the position of Chairperson, a person from among the retired Chief Justices or Judges of the Supreme Court who has made an outstanding contribution to the protection and promotion of human rights, or a person who holds a high reputation and has rendered an outstanding contribution in the field of protection and promotion of human rights or various sections of national life for at least twenty years,

(b) for the position of members, persons from among the persons who hold high reputation and have been actively involved in the field of, and rendered an outstanding contribution to, the protection and promotion of human rights or children rights, or various sections of national life for at least twenty years,

(c) holds a Bachelor's Degree from a recognized university,

(d) has attained the age of forty five,

(e) is not a member of any political party immediately before the appointment,

(f) possesses high moral character.

(7) The remuneration and other conditions of service of the Chairperson and the Members of the National Human Rights Commission shall be as determined by law. The remuneration and other conditions of service of the Chairperson and the Members of the National Human Rights Commission shall not, so long as they hold office, be altered to their disadvantage. Provided that this provision shall not apply in the case of declaration of a State of Emergency due to extreme economic disarray.

(8) A person who has been the Chairperson or a Member of the National Human Rights Commission shall not be eligible for appointment in any other government service. Provided that nothing in this Clause shall be deemed to be a bar to the appointment to any political position or to any position which has the responsibility of making investigations, inquiries or findings on any subject, or to any position which has the responsibility of submitting advice, opinion or recommendation after carrying out a study or research on any subject.

249. Functions, duties and powers of National Human Rights Commission:

(1) It shall be the duty of the National Human Rights Commission to ensure the respect, protection and promotion of human rights and their effective implementation.

(2) In order to perform the duty pursuant to Clause (1), the National Human Rights Commission may carry out the following functions:-

(a) conduct inquiries into, and investigations of, and recommen-dation for action against the perpetrator of, instances of violation or abetment of violation the human rights of any person or a group of persons, upon a petition or complaint presented to the

Commission by the victim herself/himself or any person on her/ his behalf or upon information received from any sources, or on its own initiative,

(b) forward a recommendation to the authority concerned to take departmental action against any authority that has the duty of responsibility to prevent violations of human rights, if it failed to perform such duty or responsibility or showed recklessness or lack of interest in performing that duty,

(c) make recommendations if necessary, to lodge a petition in the court, in accordance with the law, against a person or institu-tion that has violated human rights,

(d) work jointly and in a coordinated manner with civil society to enhance awareness of human rights,

(e) forward a recommendation to the relevant authority for taking departmental action against or imposing punishment on the vio-lators of human rights, giving clear reasons and basis therefor,

(f) review existing laws relating to human rights on a periodic basis and to recommend to the Government of Nepal necessary reforms and amendment thereto,

(g) recommend with reasons to the Government of Nepal that it become a party to any international treaties and agreements on human rights, if it is desirable to do so, and to monitor the imple-mentation of the international treaties and agreements on human rights to which Nepal is a party and if found not to be implement , forward recommendations to the Government of Nepal for effective implementation of such agreements,

(h) Publicize the names of any official, person or bodies not following or implementing the recommendations and directions of the National Human Rights Commission regarding the violations of human rights in accordance with law, and to record them as human rights violators.

(3) The National Human Rights Commission in performing

its functions and duties, may exercise the following powers:-

(a) exercise same powers as the court in requiring any person to appear before the Commission for recording their statement and information or examining them, receiving and examining evidence, and ordering the production of any physical proof,

(b) in case the Commission has received the information from any source that a serious incident of violation of human rights has occurred or is likely to occur, it may enter a person s residence or office, conduct a search and seize any documents and evidence relating to human rights violations therein,

(c) enter any government premises or other places, without prior notice, in case the Commission has received information that violation of human rights of a person is occurring thereon and immediate action is required, to provide rescue,

(d) order compensation for the victims of human rights violations in accordance with law,

(4) The National Human Rights Commission may delegate any of its functions, duties and powers to the Chairperson, any member or any employee of the Government of Nepal to be exercised and followed in compliance with the conditions specified

(5) Other functions, duties and powers and procedural of the National Human Rights Commission shall be as specified by federal law.

PART 30 Provision regarding National Security

261. National Defense Council:

(1) There shall be a National Defense Council to formulate policies for Nepal s overall national interests, security and defense, and in order to make recommendations to the Council of Ministers, Government of Nepal on mobilization, operation and management of Nepal Army comprising following Chairperson and members:-

(a) Prime Minister	-Chairperso
(b) Defense Minister, Government of Nepal	-Member
(c) Home Minister, Government of Nepal	-Member
(d) Minister for Foreign Affairs, GoN	-Member
(e) Finance Minister,Government of Nepal	-Member
(f) Chef Secretary of Government of Nepal –	Member
(g) Chief of the Army Staff	-Member

(2) The Secretary of Ministry of Defense shall work as the Secretary of National Defense Council.

(3) The National Defense Council shall submit its annual report to the President; the President shall make it present to the federal legislature through the Council of Ministers, Government of Nepal.

(4) Other provisions of National Defense Council shall be in accordance with federal law. 262. Provision relating to Nepal Army:

(1) There shall be an organization of Nepal Army, committed to democratic principles, inclusive in character and national in form, for the protection of Nepal s independence, sovereignty, territorial integrity, autonomy and national unity.

(2) The president shall be the supreme commander-in-chief of the Nepal Army.

(3) The entry of women, Dalit, indigenous community, Khash Arya, Madhesi, Tharu, Muslim, people of backward class and backward region shall be ensured in Nepal Army, based on the principle of equality and proportionate representation as provided for in the law.

(4) The Government of Nepal may, in accordance with law, mobilize Nepal Army for works relating to development, disaster management and others.

(5) The President shall appoint or remove the Commander-in-Chief of Nepal Army on the recommendation of the Council of Ministers.

(6) Except for mobilization of Nepal Army for disaster management, the decision by Council of Ministers, Government of Nepal on recommendation of National Defense Council, shall have to be presented to the federal legislature within a month, such decision shall have to be approved by the Federal Legislature.

(7) Other provisions relating to Nepal Army shall be as provided by law.

263. Provision relating to Nepal Police, Armed Police Force, Nepal and National Investigation Organization:

(1) There shall be Nepal Police, Armed Police Force, Nepal and National Investigation Department at the federal level.

(2) There shall be a provincial police organization in each province.

(3) Operation, supervision and coordination of Nepal Police and provincial police shall be as provided for by federal law

(4) Other provisions relating to Nepal Police, Armed Police Force and National Investigation Department shall be as provided by federal law.

PART 31 Provision relating to Political Parties

264. Constitution, registration and operation of Political Parties:

(1) Persons who are committed to a common political ideology, philosophy and program shall, subject to the laws under section (b), clause (2) of the Article (22), be entitled to form and operate the political parties and to generate or cause to be generated publicity in order to secure public support and cooperation from the general public for their ideology, philosophy and program, and to carry out any other activities for that purpose.

(2) The political parties formed under clause (1) shall be required to register their names under the Election Commission in accordance with the procedure determined by law.

(3) While submitting application for registration pursuant to clause

(2) above, the political parties shall be required to submit the documents relating to constitution of the party, annual auditing report and other documents as required by law. (4) While applying for the registration of the parties pursuant to clause (2) above, the political parties shall have to meet the following conditions:-

(a) The constitution and rules of the political party should be democratic,

(b) There should be the provision, in the constitution of the political party, of the election of the office bearers in the federal and provincial levels, at least once in five years. Provided that in case election of the office bearers could not be held within five years due to situation arising out of special circumstance, there shall be no hindrance to make provision in the statute of a political party to hold such election within a period of six months.

(c) There should be the provision of proportional participation so as to reflect the diversity of Nepal, in the executive committees at various levels of the party. (5) No political party shall be registered if its name, objective, symbol and flag is of a character that may disturb the country s religious or communal unity or is divisive in character.

265. Prohibition on the imposition of restrictions on political parties:

(1) Any provision, law or the decision that prohibits formation, registration and operation of political parties under Article 264, and generate or cause to be generated publicity in order to secure public support and cooperation from the general public for ideology, philosophy and program of the parties, shall be deemed against this constitution and shall ipso facto be void.

(2) Any law, arrangement or decision which allows for participation or involvement of only a single political party or persons having a singlepolitical ideology, philosophy

or programs in the election, political system of the country or conduct of sates affairs shall be considered against this constitution and shall ipso facto be void.

266. Registration required for securing recognition for the purpose of contesting elections as a Political Party:

(1) Any political party, formed under Article 264, wishing to secure recognition from the Election Commission for the purpose of elections, shall be required to register its name with the Election Commission in accordance with the procedures determined by the law.

(2) While applying for registration pursuant to clause (1), a politi-cal party shall have to clarify the details under clause (3) of Article 264, submit annual audit report, and also meet the conditions set in clause (4) of the same article.

267. Other provisions relating to Political Party: Other provisions relating to formation, registration, operation and facilities of the political parties shall be as provided in law.

PART 32 Emergency Powers

268. Emergency Powers:

(1)In case a grave emergency arises in relation to the sovereignty or integrity of Nepal or the security of any part thereof, whether by war, external attack, armed revolt, extreme economic disarray, natural calamity or epidemic outbreak, the President may, by Proclamation or Order, declare a state of emergency to be enforced in Nepal or any specified part thereof.

(2) Notwithstanding anything contained in clause (1), in case a grave situation arises, whether by natural calamity or epidemic outbreak, in any province, the concerned province may request the Government of Nepal to declare, by Proclamation or Order, a state of emergency to be enforced in the province or any specified area of the province.

(3) The Proclamation or the Order issued pursuant to clause (1) shall be presented before the meetings of both houses of federal legislature for approval within a month from the date of its issuance.

(4) If the Proclamation or the Order presented for the approval pursuant to clause (3) is approved by a two-third majorities of the total members present at the meetings of both the houses of federal legislature, such Proclamation or Order shall continue in force for a period of three months from the date of Order or Proclamation.

(5) If the Proclamation or Order presented before both houses of federal legislature pursuant to clause (4) is not approved, such Proclamation or Order shall, ipso facto, be invalid.

(6) Notwithstanding other provisions in this article, the proposal to extend the period of the Proclamation or Order of state of emergency for another period, not exceeding for three months, may be forwarded in the federal legislature, stating that the cir-cumstances under clause (4) still exist.

(7) Pursuant to Clause (6), if the resolution for Proclamation or Order of state of emergency for another period is passed by a majority of the two third members present of both the houses of the federal legislature, the state of emergency for the said period shall continue to exist.

(8) In case of dissolution of House of Representatives, the power of federal parliament as per clause (3), (4), (6) and (7) shall be exercised by National Assembly.

(9) After the state of emergency has been declared pursuant to clause (1), the President may issue necessary orders to meet the exigencies. Orders so issued shall be operative with the same force and effect as law so long as the state of emergency is in operation.

(10) While issuing the Proclamation or Order of state of emergency pursuant to clause (1), the President may suspend the fundamental rights provided in Part 3 so long as the Proclamation or Order is in operation. Provided that, Article 16, 17(2) section (c) and (d), Article 18, 19 (2), 20, 21, 22, 24, 26 (1), 29, 30, 31, 32, 35, 36 (1) and (2), 38, 39, 40 (2) and (3), 41, 42, 43, 45 and the right to constitutional remedy and right to habeas corpus related to article 46 shall not be suspended.

(11) In circumstances where any Article of this constitution is suspended pursuant to clause (10), no petition may be made in any court of law, nor any question be raised for the enforcement of the fundamental rights conferred by such Article.

(12) If, during the continuation of a Proclamation or Order pursuant to this article, any damage is inflicted upon any person by an act of any official done in contravention of law or in bad faith, the affected person may, within three months from the date of termination of the Proclamation or Order, file a petition for compensation for said damage. In case the petition is filed, the court may arrange for the appropriate compensation according to the law, or punish the guilty.

(13) The President may, at any time during its continuance, revoke the proclamation or order relating to state of emergency

PART 36 DEFINITIONS AND INTERPRETATIONS

300. Definitions and Interpretations:

(1) Unless the subject or context otherwise requires, in this Constitution:-

(a) "Minority" means those caste, language, and religious communities, whose population is less than that determined by the law, and who has their own specialties, and who aim to protect them; it also signifies those groups who have faced discrimination and harassed.

(b) "Law" means a federal law, provincial law, and local law.

(c) "Article: means an Article of this Constitution.

(d) "Municipality" means metropolitan and sub metropolitan city as well.

(e) „Citizen" means citizen of Nepal.

(f) "Province" means the area and structure of the federal unit carved in accordance with this Constitution.

(g) „Remuneration" means and includes salary, allowances, pension and any other forms of emoluments.

(h) "State power" means powers of the Executive, the Legislative and the Judiciary.

(i) "Bill" means a draft of a Constitution or an Act which has been introduced in the federal legislature or a provincial assembly.

(j) "Federation" means the federal structure that is the apex body of the federal system.

(k) "Federal Unit" means federation, provincial or local level.

(l) "Constitutional body" means Commission for Investigation of Abuse of Authority, Auditor General, Public Service Commission, Election Commission, National Human Rights Commission, National Natural Recourses and Finance Commission, National Women Commission, National Dalit Commission and National Inclusion Commission, established in accordance with this Constitution.

(m) "Marginalized" means those who have been forced to fall backward politically, economically and socially, those who have been unable to avail services because of discrimination and harassment, and because of geographical disconnection, and those communities whose standard of living has been below the legal standard as specified in the Human Development indicators. It also signifies the ultra-marginalized and communities on verge of extinction.

(n) "Local level" means village council, municipal council and district assembly to be formed in accordance with this Constitution.

(2) Unless the subject or context otherwise requires, the prevailing law of Nepal relating to interpretations shall, subject to the provisions of this Constitution, apply to the interpretation of this Constitution in the same manner that law applies to the interpretation of the laws of Nepal.

7

Current Political Situation in Nepal

The mass movement of April 2006 in Nepal sought to restore parliament for the democratic process to continue and to initiate a peace process for the end of a ten-year long armed conflict. This required the Communist Party of Nepal (Maoist) to join democratic competition which in turn necessitated the devising of a constitution to manage root causes of conflicts afflicting the nation. Hence, a Constituent Assembly (CA) election, that would pave the way for an inclusive state responsive of social diversity and sustainable peace, was seen as the compromise solution among all the political forces.

A train of processes and events was thus set off resulting in the advent of current Nepalese politics. A Comprehensive Peace Agreement (CPA) was signed between an alliance of the seven political parties (six after the merger of Nepali Congress and Nepali Congress-Democratic) and the CPN (Maoist) on November 21, 2006. An Interim Constitution drafted and the restored parliament dissolved to pave the way for an interim legislature and interim government that included the CPN (Maoist) in 2007. The ruling seven-party alliance (SPA) announced substantive structural reforms, such as declaration of the country secular, federal and republican. Civilian control of Nepal Army (NA), nationalization of royal property, empowerment of the Premier as head of state, abolition of the national unification day and substitution of the national anthem were announced as time went by. There were also reform measures such as greater inclusiveness regarding marginalized people in the CA, the bureaucracy and police. However, all these measures have allowed a neo-patrimonial regime to incubate, sapping the political will necessary to alter the policy and strategic development vital to transform the "structural causes of conflicts". This has hindered efforts for cultural, social, economic and political transformation needed to establish a well-organized virtuous state capable of instituting sound democratic governance. The political transition has remained highly turbulent due to the open-ended nature of the conflict system. It is, therefore, hard to say whether Nepal has actually entered a post-conflict phase.

The continuation of high political dynamics in the country now indicates a steady erosion of the writ of state and the low level of constitutional and government's stability. This has resulted in a new bargaining environment for armed non-state actors and movement-oriented ethno-regional forces thus further limiting the scope for complex reforms, both involving long-term institutional restructuring and short-term policy interventions. The weakness of state institutions has further spoiled efforts to promote relief to vulnerable sections of the population and address conflict residues. Social movements of marginalized groups—women, Dalits (untouchable underclass), Janajatis (ethnic groups), Aadibasis (indigenous groups) and Madhesis (people living in the southern plains) — for identity, proportional representation, federalism and self-determination and insurrectionary activities of two-dozen non-state armed actors have upset the coherence of state-society relations in an unprecedented manner. While the mainstream parties have interest in restructuring the state, the social forces favour restructuring political parties to expand the social base of politics.

As a result, the SPA has missed three deadlines (June 14 and 20 and November 22) for the CA elections to draft a new constitution. It was forced to amend the Interim Constitution three times in eight months-(May 9, June 14 and December 18) to give in to rising demands that the political process was exacting and to give in to the voice of various agitating groups. Among the provisions included in the amendments the more significant ones empower the parliament to abolish the monarchy, if found plotting against the CA elections, and declare the country a federal democratic republic, subject to ratification by the elected CA, or even before that by a two-thirds legislators if the King poses a threat to the elections. Despite voices emerging for a space for monarchy and efforts of CPN (Maoist), NC and CPN-UML to woo its supporters, King Gynendra remains aloof from the power struggle. All this has not changed the political dynamics for the better. The Madhesi People's Rights Forum (MPRF), a group which organized violent protests in the Tarai where scores of people were killed last year, is demanding a fourth revision of the constitution to address the grievances of the Madhesis.

HISTORICAL CIRCUMSTANCE TO THE PRESENT POLITICAL POSITION

Nepal has been an independent kingdom since 1768. Never colonized, the country was almost totally isolated from outside influence until the early 1950s. A transition from strict rule by the king to constitutional monarchy began in 1959, when then-King Mahendra issued a new constitution and held the country's first democratic elections. In 1960, however, the king declared the parliamentary system a failure, dismissed the fledgling government, suspended the constitution, and established a partyless system of rule under the monarchy. Although officially banned, political parties continued to exist and to agitate for a return to constitutional democracy. In February 1990, student groups and the major political parties launched the Movement for the Restoration of Democracy.

The centrist Nepali Congress (NC) party joined with the leftist parties to hold peaceful demonstrations in Nepal's urban centres. In April 1990, after more than 50 people were killed when police fired on a crowd of demonstrators, then-King Birendra turned power over to an interim government. This government drafted a constitution in November 1990 establishing Nepal as a parliamentary democracy with a constitutional monarch as head of state. The king at that time retained limited powers, including the right to declare a state of emergency with the approval of a two-thirds majority of parliament. In February 1996, the leaders of the underground CPN-M launched a "People's War" in the mid-western region of Nepal, with the aim of replacing the constitutional monarchy with a one-party Communist regime. The uprising appears to have been fuelled by widespread perceptions of government corruption and failure to improve the quality of life of citizens, including providing access to cultivable land. The Maoists ran a parallel government, established their own tax system, burned land records, and redistributed seized property and food to the poor, in 45 districts. The insurgency was waged, in part, through torture, killings, and bombings targeting police, the military, and public officials. A number of bank robberies, combined with "revolutionary tax" revenue, made the Nepali Maoists one of the wealthiest rebel groups in Asia. The Kathmandu government faced additional turmoil in June 2001, when Crown Prince Dipendra shot and killed his parents, King Birendra and Queen Aishwarya, seven other members of the royal family, and himself reportedly after a disagreement over whom he should marry.

This incident did much to undermine the legitimacy of the monarchy. King Gyanendra, the former king's brother, was crowned on June 4, 2001, and he appointed a commission to investigate the assassinations. By mid-June, the country began returning to normal following rioting and widespread refusal to believe official accounts of the massacre. In July 2001, Prime Minister Girija Prasad Koirala stepped down amid fears of continuing instability and his government's failure to deal with the growing Maoist insurgency. He was replaced by NC leader Sher Bahadur Deuba, who then became the head of Nepal's eleventh government in as many years.

Constitutional Crisis

During the summer of 2002, the government of Nepal was thrown into a constitutional crisis that interfered with its ability to effectively combat the Maoist insurgency. The crisis began in late May, when King Gyanendra, at the request of the prime minister, dissolved parliament and unilaterally declared a three-month extension of emergency rule, which had expired on May 24, 2002. The prime minister, who also scheduled early elections for November 2002, reportedly took such action after his centrist Nepali Congress party refused to support his plan to extend emergency rule. Following the prime minister's actions, 56 former members of parliament filed a lawsuit against him, claiming there was no constitutional precedent for the dissolution of parliament during emergency rule. In August 2002, the Supreme Court rejected this lawsuit. Although opponents of the prime minister agreed to accept the verdict, they emphasized the difficulty of holding free and fair elections two years ahead of schedule when much of the country was under either rebel or army control. Although the prime minister pledged that there would be no emergency rule during the scheduled November 2002 elections, Maoist attacks and threatened strikes prompted the government to consider various measures to prevent a Maoist disruption of the polls.

The government discussed imposing a partial state of emergency in areas most affected by the insurgency. However, opposition parties, which urged the government to open a dialogue with the Maoists, argued that by curbing civil liberties, emergency rule would inhibit free and fair elections. As an alternative, the government announced in September 2002 that it would hold the elections in six stages over two months, starting in mid-November, so that government troops could be transferred around the country to protect voters and candidates. After further deliberation, however, Nepal's cabinet concluded that the security situation was too risky to hold elections. On October 3, 2002, the cabinet asked King Gyanendra to postpone the national elections for one year. The next day, the king dismissed the prime minister, disbanded his cabinet, and assumed executive powers.

The King's Takeover

The security situation in Nepal deteriorated after the collapse of the ceasefire between the Maoists and the government on August 27, 2003. The Maoists favoured drafting a new constitution that would abolish the monarchy. The king opposed such a move and wanted the Maoists to relinquish their weapons. Accommodation between the king and opposition democratic elements had been thought to be key to creating the unified front necessary to defeat the Maoists. With his direct assumption of powers, and arrest of opposition democratic elements, the king decided to try to defeat the Maoists on his own. This move proved to be the beginning of the end of the power of the monarchy in Nepal. After seizing direct power in February 2005, King Gyanendra exerted control over democratic elements, but made little progress in the struggle against the Maoists. The king reportedly thought he could take advantage of a split in the Maoist leadership and disarray amongst democrats to seize control and use the Royal Nepal Army (RNA) to defeat the Maoists. The seizure of power by the king appears to have been aimed as much, if not more so, at asserting the king's control over democratic forces.

Many observers felt that a military solution to the conflict with the Maoists was not achievable and that a concerted effort by the king and the democrats was needed to establish a unified front to defeat the Maoists. When the king assumed power he stated that he would take steps to reinstate a constitutional democracy within 100 days, which he then failed to do. Although some political prisoners were released by the king, hundreds of others remained under arrest and restrictions on civil liberties, such as public assembly and freedom of the press, remained in place. A U.N. Office of the High Commissioner of Human Rights team was established in Nepal in April 2005 to monitor the observance of human rights and international humanitarian law.

By moving against the democrats, who under different circumstances could have worked with the king against the Maoists, the king strengthened the position of the Maoists. By some estimates almost half of the RNA was occupied with palace security, civil administration, and efforts to restrict communications and civil rights. The king's legitimacy with the people was weakened due to the circumstances under which he assumed the throne, the way he seized direct rule, and due to poor popular perceptions of his son, Prince Paras Shah. The former Crown prince was unpopular with Nepalis "for his drunken antics and playboy lifestyle." Maoist Reaction. From February 13 to 27, 2005, the Maoists reacted to the king's actions by blockading major highways linking the country's

75 districts, as well as international road links to India and China. This led to clashes between Maoists and the RNA and brought trade by road to a standstill. The army organized armed convoys which allowed limited trade to continue. The Maoists had earlier cut off land routes to Kathmandu in August 2004. During the week-long blockade in 2004, prices of some basic foods more than doubled and fuel was rationed. This increase in food prices reportedly recurred in the 2005 blockade. By blockading Kathmandu, the Maoists successfully increased pressure on the king's government and demonstrated their power.

Democratic Rebellion

On April 24, 2006, mounting popular resistance in support of the political parties led King Gyanendra to hand over power to the Seven Party Alliance. This followed weeks of violent protests and demonstrations against direct royal rule in Nepal. The Seven Party Alliance that opposed the king in April included the parties. The Maoists were not part of the Seven Party Alliance, though they worked with the alliance to oppose the monarchy. This was made possible by the king's political crackdown on the democrats.

- The Nepali Congress (NC)
- Communist Party of Nepal Unified Marxist Leninist CPN (UML)
- Nepali Congress (Democratic) or NC (D)
- Nepal Sadbhavana Party (Anandi Devi) or NSP (A)
- Jana Morcha Nepal
- Samyukta Baam Morcha (United Left Front) or ULF
- Nepal Workers and Peasants Party (NWPP).

The seven parties worked together through their alliance to promote a more democratic Nepal in the face of direct rule by the king. In May 2006, six of the seven political parties formed a coalition government. On November 8, 2006, the Seven Party Alliance and the Maoists reached a peace agreement ending a decade-old insurgency that claimed over 13,000 lives. In it, the Maoists agreed to put down their arms and postpone a decision on the future disposition of the monarchy until after the election of a Constituent Assembly. Under the peace agreement, Constituent Assembly elections were to be held by the end of June 2007. The June election date slipped but Constituent Assembly elections were eventually held in April 2008.

PRESENT SITUATION

After the royal massacre of June 1, 2001, the Maoists have intensified their military campaign. While dealing with the Maoists, King Birendra was not in favour of using the Nepalese Army. As commented by commentator Li Onesto 'One of the biggest disputes within the government over the last year has been whether or not to send the army against the Maoists. Some troops have been deployed to areas hardest hit.

Birendra has been reluctant to unleash the army against the guerrillas.' The Maoists, even though they regarded King Birendra as part of the feudal system, yet they considered him 'a nationalist.' The reasons for that according to Senior Maoist leader Dr. Baburam Bhattara were, 'he introduced democracy and took a keen interest in the well being of our country, for which extremist reactionaries assassinated his whole family.' Regarding the royal massacre as a conspiracy, the Chairman of the CPN (Maoist), Prachanda said, 'terming it a family conflict, planned propaganda of both national and international reactionaries, and the drama seen while performing the last rites clearly prove that the massacre is a result of conspiracy. To think that King Birendra's patriotic stand and liberal political ideology were not the reasons for the royal deaths would be very misleading politics.

The late King was not in favour of PM Koirala's plan to mobilise the army against the people's war.' Prachanda also said, 'this pre-planned massacre designed in this political background will have a long-term effect on the future of Nepal and Nepali history. This massacre portrays the end of the present political system.' He threatened that Maoists will step up their activities. As a reaction to the royal massacre the Maoists gathered in Kathmandu for planning their strategy for a revolution and stepped up their military activities in June 2001. However, in July 2001 Nepalese Prime Minister and the Maoists agreed on a cease-fire and held their first round of peace talks. During the second round of talks, held in September 2001, the Maoists put before the government their thirty-one demands.

These demands were based on the previous forty demands given in 1996. The government rejected the three main demands by the Maoists. These were, (a) calling for a republic, (b) an interim government and (c) a constitutional assembly. The government agreed to consider the other demands. The Government's argument was that the Constitution does not allow the government to act on the three demands. 'There is no clause in the Constitution for an interim government or Constitutional assembly. The clause providing for a Constitutional monarchy is also unchangeable.' The third round of talks concluded in November 2001, without any progress. Two human rights activists, Padma Ratna Tuladhar and Daman Nath Dhungana, were involved in the peace talks as facilitators.

On November 21, 2001, the Maoist leader, Chairman Prachandra, withdrew from the peace talks, saying: 'ceasefire had lost its justification because of the governments insincerity in finding a peaceful solution.' The Maoists then formed the 'central people's government' called the Central Revolutionary People's Council Committee, headed by a top Maoist ideologue Dr. Baburam Bhattarai.

On November 24, 2001, the People's Council subsequently formed the People's Liberation Army (PLA). On the same night, the PLA launched an attack at the district headquarters of Dang and Syanjya and a military base camp and killed dozens of policemen and Royal Nepal Army (RNA) personnel, and injuring many more. Similarly, the Maoists launched a daring attack in Solukhumbu district and killed the police personnel including the Chief District Officer, on November 25, 2001. King Gyanendra, on the recommendation of the Council of Ministers, announced a State of Emergency on November 26, 2001, and formally deployed the Royal Nepal Army and imposed the Terrorist and Disruptive Activities (Prevention and Control) Ordinance 2001 (TADO 2001). The Emergency was extended in March 2002. However, on April 4, 2002, the government relaxed the State of Emergency.

During the Emergency period, the Maoists stepped up their activities of target attacks on police posts and also their calls for strike. As this study goes to print, the Maoists are demanding that Prime Minister Deuba should hold talks on the question of redrafting of the Constitution. The Government has refused to hold talks until the Maoists lay down their arms. However, there is division within the ruling party and the opponents are supporting a political settlement of the Maoist uprising. The opponents in the party have already given proposals for Constitutional amendments to Prime Minister Deuba. Also there is pressure on the government from other political parties for a political solution. For example, the Nepal Communist Party (UML) the main opposition party in Nepal, has said that the government should resume talks with the Maoists immediately without pre-conditions.

THE RESPONSE OF POLITICAL

The political response has been dogged by the lack of continuity in Government. There have been 10 prime ministers in 10 years and " the peoples representatives (seem to remain) preoccupied with the game of forming and bringing down governments" In addition the Maoist threat is not the only challenge to stability, which is also challenged by wide spread student strikes aimed against the use of English in the curriculum, the agitation of Bhutanese refugees in the eastern part of the country. The question of 'reform first' or 'insurgent surrender first' has dogged the negotiations that have occurred, particularly during the ceasefire of 2001. Maoists insisted that the Government should hold elections to an assembly to draft a new constitution.

PM Sherbahadur Deuba riposted that the Maoists should surrender their weapons, hostages and ammunition first. There has been no common ground identified which will allow useful negotiation to begin, and no attempt seems to have been made to exploit fault lines in the Maoist ranks. For example in 1998 a group of Maoists broke away in response to what they described as Comrade Prachandra's "imposing dictatorship and suppressing any criticism" but the government has been too fragmented itself to take the initiative in this area.

Security Forces

The Police and the Army have different approaches to the Insurgency. Until November of 2001 the response was very much a Police operation; the Army sought to remain outside the conflict. The Police and the national polity may have cooperated in this: the Police have been keen to attract the funding that the increased tempo of operations would bring to them and politicians have been suspicious of the Army, concerned that constitutionally it is not under democratic control.

Police and Paramilitaries

The police are under resourced, poorly paid and armed, and ineffective. Recruits, after 6 weeks training, are deployed into the field with little specialist counter-insurgency training. Their main effort during their 6 month deployments is survival. They are scruffy, truculent and unimpressive: they are not a force that projects pride in their role. In recognition of the shortcomings of the police the Government has tried to create a 'third force'. Variously described as the Armed Police Force (APF) or the Special Police Force (SPF) it was to have consisted of 10,000 men organized into 9 battalions spread over 5 security regions. Tasked with ambushing and night operations the intent was to focus sufficient force at the point of effort to make certain a resounding defeat for the rebels. The SPF has claimed some success, announcing the capture of a number of weapons and "a large number of arrests" which has provided a "morale boost-up (sic) of security personnel" and " secured feelings by the local people" but one must doubt the strategic effect of these local successes, even if they could be verified. Though issued with the Israeli Galil rifle the SPF are in all other respects equipped little better than the insurgents that they are seeking to defeat. Their operations have been hampered by the lack of helicopters, radios and good intelligence.

The police have not until now subscribed to the classical CI doctrine used by the RNA. They see the insurgency as a criminal issue, and have made no attempt to address the root causes of discontent. Indeed they are now substantially part of the problem. If they are to be an effective force their morale and equipment must be improved, and they must be brought inside the full inter-agency process.

RNA

" The Army is a creation of the Monarchy". It is more loyal to the King than the elected government. Its constitutional position is perhaps anomalous in a democratic constitutional monarchy and is a legacy of the times of an absolute King.

The Army is 46,000 strong. It consists of 14 infantry battalions, one artillery battalion, one engineer battalion and an armored recce squadron. It is organized in five brigades. The 'Royal' Brigade is based in Kathmandu, 1 Bde is also based in Kathmandu to cover the Central Region, 2 Bde in Daran to cover the Eastern Region, 3 Bde at Biratnagar to cover the Eastern Region and 4 Bde to cover the Western Region from Nepal Ganj.

It has considerable peace keeping experience in Bosnia, Croatia, Haiti, The Lebanon and a battalion is now deployed in Sierra Leone. It has some CI experience from operations against the Khampas in Mustang from 1974. A peace-keeping College has been established near Kathmandu.

The Nepalese Officer corps is trained at home, in India and in the United Kingdom. In as much as a coherent CI doctrine exists it is modeled on that of the Indian Army, which in itself is derived from British teaching, further developed from experience in Assam and Sri Lanka. The Doctrine stresses the primacy of a political solution to all insurgencies: a 'peace' rather than a 'victory'. The aim is to win-over the people, not suppress them, thus denying the insurgents their support. The area of insurgency should be dominated by Security Force patrols which are aimed at gradual attrition and isolating the guerillas from their sympathizers.

The use of the RNA has been delayed by conflict between the Palace and the Government and by confusion within the government itself. The RNA has always maintained that prior to their deployment there must be all-party agreement and Royal assent, and neither of these preconditions existed until recently.

Even the Prime Minister constantly changed his mind. PM Koroila once said: "I am not in favour of mobilizing the Army...

it is the ultimate weapon. If it fails, do we then call in the Chinese or Indian Armies?" but he clearly came round to the idea by 10 April 2001 : "Why can't we use the Army here when it can serve in different countries as peacekeepers?" Some commentators claim that the King may have deliberately held back the Army in order to enable the insurgents to embarrass the government. This is highly unlikely but indicative of the Nepali delight in conspiracy theories; given fresh impetus by the mass murder of the Royal family on 01 June 01.

Prior to its full deployment in November 2001 The King had allowed the use of military resources in 5 districts for a hearts and minds campaign called the Integrated Social Development Plan (ISDP). This effort has been discontinued since the declaration of a State of Emergency. It is impossible therefore to assess the effectiveness of RNA doctrine so far.

The RNA does not have a substantial technological advantage over the insurgents. It has good rifles, Ferret scout cars and a number of ex-East German BTR 70s. There are a few howitzers of varying calibers. In support of the Army is an air wing using Skyvan, Puma and Super Puma. It has the capability to lift two companies at any one time. In spite of this morale is high, and the Army, at least so far, does not feel tainted by the failure of the Police or the corruption of the administration. Much, however, still remains to be done. The structure for inter-agency liaison must be improved and the RNA must come under clear political control. Improvements in communications, intelligence gathering and dissemination, particularly the collection of HUMINT must be made to give the RNA an edge over the insurgents.

PARTYLESS POLITICAL SYSTEM

Democracy and Conflict Era (1990 – 2007). Since the restoration of democracy in 1990, various attempts have been made to advance learning programmes and make them comprehensive in a planned way, in line with democratic norms and values, based on the demands of time and the aspiration of the people. However, the "education sector faces various problems. Basic education is still not available to all the people. More than half of the population is illiterate" (NPC 1998: 607).The national goal of universalisation of primary education requires a significant increase in girls' enrolment. The lack of progress in this direction remains a serious problem.

Similarly, in view of the fact that as many as 44.5% people are illiterate, the present efforts to raise the literacy rate are most inadequate. For example, in the case of non-formal learning and the literacy rate of 15 years and above was 39% in 1992 (NPC1992: 463), the government target to achieve "63% by the year 2002" (NPC 2002: 399) in fact only achieved "49.2%" (ibid: 29). The literacy rate for the population of six years and above only reached 55.5% (ibid: 399), when it was planned to reach 70% by the end of the Ninth Plan i.e. 2002.

Hence, the rate of progress is approximately 1% per year; which is no difference from that of the Panchayat era (pre 1990). The present efforts made to raise the literacy rate are very inadequate. Male and female literacy rate is "65.8% and 35.4%" (NPC 2002: 31) respectively. The literacy rate in urban area is 63.50% and rural area is 34.50%" (ibid). It thus is apparent that there is a higher percentage of male literacy than the female and a higher literacy rate in urban areas as opposed to rural districts. The literacy rate in the Eastern region is "41.90%, Central 35.10% and Western 34.60 %" (ibid: 92).

In order to address some of these issues, the Tenth Plan intends to set up 205 CLCs "to make 1,866,000 adults particularly women literate" (NPC 2002: 385). In addition, the Plan has set a target providing basic primary education to "200,000 boys and girls of school age" (ibid: 385) via non-formal primary education. The government's long-term plan is to hand over the responsibility of the running CLCs to the local bodies. The government has started implementing one CLC in each constituency, which does not seem practicable considering the size of the constituencies. The majority of the constituencies are so huge that it takes two to three days to walk from one end to the other as walking is the only means of travel. Therefore, when and how the sparsely distributed CLCs will maintain the process of literacy education and lifelong learning remains unclear in the policy document.

LIFELONG LEARNING PRACTICE IN RURAL NEPAL

Ward 4 Kunjari, Sikaicha Village Development Committee (VDC). Kunjari is the rural research site where I conducted my research. It is one of the most remote villages of Nepal, mainly occupied by Limbus. Even though Kunjari is a Limbu village and their religion is Kirat, they are not completely free from the influence of the Hindu religion, which is not as much or as strong as in Ward 18 KMC. However, the Limbu communities' informal teaching and learning processes are based on both Kirat and Hindu philosophies. Informal learning mainly takes place in extended family system and communities. In order to explore this issue, I carried out interviews and discussions with local people and an interview with Ward Chairman as follows:

Researcher: There was not even a school when you reached school age. Hence, can you please tell me how you gained all this knowledge without attending any formal education? Chairman: It is not necessary to attend formal education to gain knowledge. You can learn by work, experience, mistakes, difficulties, pain, sorrow, parents, senior citizens, juniors, friends, wife, and children, religions, etc. There are many more ways to gain knowledge. You only need to go to school to earn certificates. People from this village survived many hundred years without any schooling. Even now older generations like me are illiterate. Some people can hardly write their name even but we know how to cultivate, cure diseases using local herbal medicines and live, bring up children and manage the whole village.

Kunjari is one of the villages that has been totally marginalised and excluded from the centre because the majority of people from this village are Limbus, an indigenous nationality with no voice at the centre where the power lies. This village is virtually neglected by the Government including in the field of non-formal learning. The village was only allocated a short term literacy course in 2002 because there were no takers from other villages.

In this regards, the local teacher who has spent twenty years in the village said *"I was surprised to see the literacy programme in the village. I personally applied* many times for the funding for adult education and a literacy programme but results were always negative because this village had no voice at the headquarters. There is no voice since almost all youths join the British and Indian Armies. The government bureaucrats have a tendency to neglect the *voiceless villages*."

Formal learning was introduced in Kunjari in 1967 in a bamboo makeshift hut by an ex-British Gurkha soldier. Initially, he was the only teacher to more than 150 students. On the first day the villagers constructed a bamboo makeshift hut as a school while the teacher was registering the students' names in an attendance record book in the far corner of the field. My grandfather took me to this teacher and registered my name.

There was neither curriculum nor books. We had to take a wooden plank and chalk stones with us to read and write. In this manner, the practice of formal learning started in Kunjari. Since that time, 40 years ago, the school has been upgraded to secondary level. Until recently the local people, despite their meagre income, funded it.

HISTORICAL POLITICAL SYSTEM OF NEPAL

Though the 1959 Constitution provided a bi-cameral parliament, political parties were banned and the King had strong executive, legislative and judicial powers. As the demand for democracy and constitutional reforms gained strength in Nepal, the 1962 constitutional amendment established a partyless Panchayat system, which continued for thirty years. Dr. Ananta Raj Poudyal, a Nepali Professor of Political Science, wrote in one of his articles 'Politically, the 30 years were characterised by inconsistencies and contradictions. Not only politics but also the economy of the country deteriorated under the Panchayat system. Its objectives like 'exploitation-less society' became a fantasy, and the rhetoric 'politics for development' had little impact on the life styles of the general public.' Therefore, in view of the pressures from the pro-democracy movement and wide-spread unrest in the country, in 1990, King Birendra had to abolish the partyless Panchayat system. He established a constitutional monarchy and an elected parliament based on a multi-party system. According to Bertil Lintner, a journalist, in an article he published in 1997, more than 500 demonstrators were killed in violent clashes with the police in Kathmandu before the King eventually gave in to popular demands for an end to the old system.

As a result of the constitutional changes there emerged several political parties, such as, the Nepal Communist Party-United Marxist Leninist (NCP-UML], Nepali Congress (NC), Rastriya Prajatantra Party (RPP), Nepal Sadbhavana Party (NSP), Rastriya Jana Morcha, Nepal Workers & Peasants Party (NWPP), and Samyukta Janmorcha Nepal. As a result, the first general elections in three decades on a party basis were held in 1991. The Nepali Congress Party emerged as the major party. However, in about ten years of parliamentary democracy in Nepal, there have been eight different prime ministers as one government after another was not able to perform successfully. As observed by Dr. Karl H. Kramer, a German scholar, 'in practice, the politicians have not been able to implement many aspects of the constitution. Even fundamental rights guaranteed by the constitution, like that of equality of all citizens, have not even legally been realized after ten years. Corruption and selfishness of the politicians and traditional ways of thinking must be regarded as the main reasons for such shortcomings. The poor state of affairs is reflected by the instability of governments. It opens room for the development of radical forces like that of the Maoists who reject the current constitution and fight a violent so-called 'people's war' that has cost the life of more than 1.500 people since February 1996.' Dr. Ananta Raj Poudyal, in one of this articles written in 1997 concludes, 'A lot needs to be done to consolidate the democratic process of Nepal. The most urgent seem to be bringing about democratic behaviour among the political parties and raising of civic consciousness among the people.'

As a result of the unconstitutional practices of political parties, the movement for constitutional reforms gained momentum in Nepal and three schools of thought emerged by the end of the year 2000. One school of thought supported a complete replacement of the political system; the second school advocated substantial amendments; and the third supported continuity with suitable reforms. As pointed out by the Nepali scholar, Lok Raj Baral, 'The Maoist and the die-hard supporters of the dismantled partyless regime represented the replacement school. Demands for substantial constitutional amendments came from the left opposition parties. The view for continuity with minor changes came from the rest of the parties.'

CPN (MAOIST)'S PEOPLE'S WAR

The Communist Party of Nepal (Maoist) launched the 'People's War' on February 13, 1996, with the aim 'to smash the existing semi-feudal and semi-colonial state and build a people's New Democratic State.' According to Dr. Baburam Bhattarai, Chairman United People's Front, 'An armed People's War has been initiated in Nepal from February 13, 1996 under the leadership of the Communist Party of Nepal (Maoist) with the proclaimed aim of establishing a New Democratic socio-economic system and state by overthrowing the present socio-economic structure and state. This should be understood under the background that Nepal has slided to the status of the second poorest country in the world in terms of physical and cultural developments.'

Explaining the rationale behind the 'People's War', Dr. Baburam Bhattarai emphasised that 'the Nepalese Maoists' attempt to create a new democratic system through People's War began only after all attempts to carry out reforms within the old semi-feudal and semi-colonial system had failed. The ruling classes want to continuously exploit the people through the present socio-economic system, and international forces also exploit the people through internal means.

From this point of view the People's War in Nepal is part of the world anti-imperialist national liberation movement.' Ms. Li Onesto, a commentator for the Pacific News Service, in 1999 visited the Maoist-controlled areas in western, central and eastern Nepal. In her reports, she stated that the rural areas were underdeveloped, without electricity, running water and basic sanitation. The statistics of deprivation according to Shom Prasad Luitel, that make Nepal the second poorest country in the world are: '71% of the population is below absolute poverty level; 46.5% of national income is in the hands of 10% of the richest people; more than 60% of its total population are illiterate, more than 90% of its total population live in rural areas and 81% of the labour force is engaged in backward agricultural occupations; 10% are totally unemployed and 60% are under-employed or in disguised employment.'

As commented by Ms. Onesto, the rural population, including farmers and women, supported the Maoists as they were advocating land ownership rights, development and equality for women. According to other reports, the Maoists in these regions, 'burned property-ownership records and redistributed land among farmers. Women, in these areas, were also given various rights.' Thus, the Maoists gained support at the grass roots level by appealing to their sense of deprivation and grievances.

The CPN (Maoist) has two organisational structures, the political front, and the military front. The political front's responsibility is to organize, create awareness and spread Maoist ideas. The military front organises attacks on police and other targets. It has around 5000-armed personnel; including the militia. Various other organisations affiliated with the Maoist party are the All-Nepal National Free Students Union (Revolutionary), All Nepal Women's Association (Revolutionary), All Nepal Trade Union Federation and National People's Movement Coordination Committee.

When in 1994 the Samyukta Jana Morcha, led by Baburam Bhattarai disassociated itself from the Communist party (UML) and continued its armed rebellion in the rural areas, the State authorities intensified their campaign to crush the movement. The Nepali government launched 'Operation Romeo' in November 1995 against the extreme communists.

It was in this backdrop that Samyukta Jana Morcha united with the Communist Party (Maoist) and launched the People's War. According to Bertil Lintner this campaign is based on the Peru's Shining Path model. 'It has established strongholds in remote mountain regions, where police outposts are few and far between, enabling the guerrillas to move about freely.' Their arms are primitive and generally collected in the villages from farmers or snatched from the police in encounters. However, some small arms, as pointed by Lintner, were bought in the black arms market in the Indian State of Bihar. During this period there was anti-India feeling among the Nepalese because of the water and hydroelectric power issue (the Mahakali Treaty). The Maoists also exploited these nationalist feelings and won support in the rural community. Dr. Bhattarai in his article 'Politico-economic Rationale of People's War' states: 'the biggest direct manifestation of world imperialist oppression and exploitation in Nepal is Indian expansionist exploitation and oppression.'

The CPN (Maoist)'s political front, as part of it People's War in 1996, put forward forty demands to the government headed by Nepali Congress Party. These were within the following categories:

Demands Related to Nationalism

1) Regarding the 1950 Treaty between India and Nepal, all unequal stipulations and agreements should be removed.
2) The Government (HMG) should admit that the anti-nationalist Tanakpur agreement was wrong, and the Mahakali Treaty, incorporating the same, should be nullified.
3) The entire Nepal-Indian border should be controlled and systematized. Cars with Indian number plates, which are plying the roads of Nepal, should not be allowed.
4) Gorkha recruiting centres should be closed and decent jobs should be arranged for the recruits.
5) In several areas of Nepal, where foreign technicians are given precedence over Nepali technicians for certain local jobs, a system of work permits should be instituted for the foreigners.
6) The monopoly of foreign capital in Nepal's industry, trade and economic sector should be stopped.
7) Sufficient income should be generated from customs duties for the country's economic development.
8) The cultural pollution of imperialists and expansionists should be stopped. Hindi video, cinema, and all kinds of such newspapers and magazines should be completely

stopped. Inside Nepal, import and distribution of vulgar Hindi films, video cassettes and magazines should be stopped.

9) Regarding NGOs and INGOs: bribing by imperialists and expansionists in the name of NGOs and INGOs should be stopped.

Demands Related to the Public and its Well-being

10) A new Constitution has to be drafted by the people's elected representatives.

11) All the special rights and privileges of the King and his family should be ended.

12) Army, police and administration should be under the peoples' control.

13) The Security Act and all other repressive acts should be abolished.

14) All the false charges against the people of Rukum, Rolpa, Jajarkot, Gorkha, Kavre, Sindhuphalchowk, Sindhuli, Dhanusha and Ramechap should be withdrawn and all the people falsely charged should be released.

15) Armed police operations in the different districts should immediately be stopped.

16) Regarding Dilip Chaudhary, Bhuvan Thapa Magar, Prabhakar Subedi and other people who disappeared from police custody at different times, the government should constitute a special investigating committee to look into these crimes and the culprits should be punished and appropriate compensation given to their families.

17) People who died during the movement should be declared as martyrs and their families, and those who have been wounded and disabled should be given proper compensation. Strong action should be taken against the killers.

18) Nepal should be declared a secular state.

19) Girls should be given equal property rights to those of their brothers.

20) All kinds of exploitation and prejudice based on caste should be ended. In areas having a majority of one ethnic group, that group should have autonomy over that area.
21) The status of dalits as untouchables should be ended and the system of untouchability should be ended once and for all.
22) All languages should be given equal status. Up to the middle-high school level (uccha-madyamic) arrangements should be made for education to be given in the children's mother tongue.
23) There should be guarantee of free speech and free press. The communications media should be completely autonomous.
24) Intellectuals, historians, artists and academicians engaged in other cultural activities should be guaranteed intellectual freedom.
25) In both the terai and hilly regions there is prejudice and misunderstanding in backward areas. This should be ended and the backward areas should be assisted. Good relations should be established between the villages and the city.
26) Decentralization in real terms should be applied to local areas, which should have local rights, autonomy and control over their own resources.

Demands Related to the People's Living

27) Those who cultivate the land should own it. (The tiller should have right to the soil he/she tills.) The land of rich landlords should be confiscated and distributed to the homeless and others who have no land.
28) Brokers and commission agents should have their property confiscated and that money should be invested in industry.
29) All should be guaranteed work and should be given a stipend until jobs are found for them.
30) The government (HMG) should pass strong laws ensuring that people involved in industry and agriculture should receive minimum wages.

31) The homeless should be given suitable accommodation. Until the government (HMG) can provide such accommodation they should not be removed from where they are squatting.
32) Poor farmers should be completely freed from debt. Loans from the Agricultural Development Bank by poor farmers should be completely written off. Small industries should be given loans.
33) Fertilizer and seeds should be easily and cheaply available, and the farmers should be given a proper market price for their production.
34) Flood and drought victims should be given all necessary help.
35) All should be given free and scientific medical service and education and education for profit should be completely stopped.
36) Inflation should be controlled and salaries of labourers should be raised in direct ratio with the rise in prices. Daily essential goods should be made cheap and easily available.
37) Arrangements should be made for drinking water, good roads, and electricity in the villages.
38) Cottage and other small industries should be granted special facilities and protection.
39) Corruption, black marketing, smuggling, bribing, the taking of commissions, etc. should all be stopped.
40) Orphans, the disabled, the elderly and children should be given help and protection.

The government of Nepali Congress Party rejected these demands and adopted repressive measures to suppress the Maoist activities. In reaction, the Maoists increased their guerrilla activity. According to official reports, since 1996 about 1800 people have died, whereas unofficial reports claim about 4,000 deaths, mostly of Maoists, police and villagers. The Maoists have influence in sixty-eight of Nepal's seventy-five districts. According to Government sources thirty-two are regarded as 'hardest hit' areas.

In five western districts the Maoists have organised a parallel government. Theses are Rolpa, Rukum, Jararkot, Salyam and Kalikot.

In the Maoist related issues, human rights groups in Nepal have been active in two respects. First, they have supported an end to human rights violations. Second, they have stressed upon and mediated peace talks between the Maoists and the government. The Maoists have also shown a more accommodating attitude towards the human rights institutions and activists.

International organisations have called for respect of human rights by the Government of Nepal and by the Maoists. For example, Amnesty International in one of its reports says: 'Amnesty International joins human rights defenders in Nepal in demanding accountability from the authorities in upholding the fundamental human rights guaranteed in Nepal's Constitution. We also urge the leadership of the CPN (Maoist) to put an end to abuses and issue strict orders to its cadres not to attack civilians, take hostages, kill or torture prisoners or recruit children into their ranks.'

COMMUNIST PARTY OF NEPAL

The Communist Party of Nepal (Maoist) adheres to the ideals, aspirations and course of action based on Mao's style of dictatorship of the proletariat. As one of the extreme left organisation, its main objective is to 'establish a 'people's government' through a 'people's war.' The executive head of the CPN (Maoist) is its general secretary Pushpa Kamal Dahal (Prachanda). Baburam Bhattarai, considered a moderate, is the political face of the Maoists. The political party structure consists of a politburo central committee, regional bureaus, sub-regional bureaus, district committees and cell committees. The party has emphasised its course of action on political and military strategies. For administrative convenience it has divided the country into three zones and twenty-seven districts. On the military front it has a central military commission, regional military commissions and the district military commissions. The Maoists have maintained fraternal and ideological linkages with the People's War Group and Maoist Communist Centre in India who also provide them with arms and ammunition.' The Communist Party of Nepal (Maoist) is a member of the Revolutionary Internationalist Movement (RIM). It has links especially with the Maoists in Peru, India, Turkey, Philippines, Bangladesh, Sri Lanka, Iran, Italy, New Zealand and the United States. The CPN (Maoist) has support groups and solidarity forums outside the country in India, Hong Kong, Germany and in Belgium.

In 1990, the two major communist factions united into the United Marxist-Leninist party 'UML'. The Communist Party (UML) emerged as the second main party in the parliament during the first general elections, held in 1991.

The Nepali Congress, led by G. P. Koirala, emerged as the major party and formed the government. However, G. P. Koirala resigned in 1994, and during the ensuing mid-term elections the Communist Party (UML) won and formed the government under the leadership of Manmohan Adhikari. However, the communist government was not able to perform well and fell after nine months. According to Bertil Lintner, 'the CPN (UML) was not radical enough; it resembled a European social democrat party rather than a militant organisation that was going to introduce any radical political or economic changes.' It was because of these reasons that differences arose within the party and the main factions, Samyukta Jana Morcha (United People's Front), under the leadership of Dr. Baburam Bhattarai, left the Communist Party (UML). This faction had won nine seats during the 1991 elections. Dr. Baburam Bhattarai was dissatisfied with the working of the left parties who according to him, had digressed from the Marxist goal of creating a classless society. The Samyukta Jana Morcha united with the Communist Party (Maoist) and launched the 'People's War' in 1996.

CONSTITUENT ASSEMBLY ELECTIONS

The Election Commission (EC) has already published the CA election schedule and enforced the election code of conduct from January 16. The parties contesting it will have to submit their closed list of candidates for proportional representation system by February 22, registration of candidature for direct voting will be opened from February 22 to 25 and the candidates will be given election symbols on March 2. The Interim Constitution recognizes the SPA but says that anyone else willing to register a new political party must submit 10,000 signatures to EC. Many opposition parties-MPRF (Yadav), MPRF (Bishwas), Rastriy Prajatantra Party (RPP)-Nepal, Rastriya Janashakti Party (RJP), RPP, Nepal Sadbhava Party and Tarai-Madhesh Loktantrik Party (TMLP) have depicted the SPA as undemocratic in spirit and attitude and argued that setting the date for elections without creating a proper security and political environment is meaningless. The MPRF and TMLP blaming the deployment of Special Task Force "for creating terror in Tarai and helping the Maoist-affiliated Young Communist League (YCL), have threatened to stage a decisive agitation if their demands are not addressed by January 18. Nepal Federation of Indigenous Nationalities (NEFIN), a coalition of 54 ethnic groups, has put its dilemma this way: if it wages its movement, the SPA will be demolished; if not, the SPA refuses to implement the 20-pint accord it signed with the government.

The meeting of the high level seven-party coordinating committee, a SPA coordination mechanism, is currently discussing the possibility of conducting elections in two phases, keeping in mind the security situation in the Tarai. It decided to request the EC to postpone the implementation of the code of conduct for 15 days so that local bodies can be constituted. Finance Minister R. S. Mahat has requested Nepal's international development partners to extend an additional assistance of $4.76 million to implement the 23-point accord among the SPA and to hold the elections.

At the same time, an influential section of NC has warned of "Tarai disintegration" if election takes place in two phases. The decision of the government to distribute $15,870 to each legislator for the development of their constituency also stoked the fire of protest in the civil society. The pre-election perk out of the government coffer does not make the election competitive process. It is such controversies that overturned the election apple-cart in the past. A badly designed election can easily foment social divisions, fragment the political sphere, institutionalize sub-national conflicts and embroil the nation into the centrifugal pressure of regional geopolitics.

Tarai's Geopolitics

Twenty-two districts in Nepal's southern plains bordering India constitute the Terai or Madhesh. It is fertile area and is linked to Nepal's major supply routes to hills. After the declaration of secular state and talk about redistributive land reforms, the glue that bind hill and Tarai communities got lost. The Madhesi movement spearheaded by the MPRF wants the declaration of the Madhesh as an autonomous region, talks with armed Madhesi groups, balanced distribution of state revenue and income to Madhesh, proportional representation in all the governance institutions including the NA, appointment of chief administrators in Madhesh from the Madhesi communities, return weapons captured by Maoists to the concerned people and declaration of those killed during the Madhesh movement as martyrs including compensation for their families. The TMLP has expressed its desire to have its own state organs for the plains. The two radical components of Janatantrik Tarai Mukti Morcha (JTMM) demand international mediators like the UN to resolve their issues and a separate independent state. India's assertion that "Tarai's demands should be addressed," has provoked a prickly reaction from various political forces. Premier Koirala who had earlier assertion that the "Tarai problem can be resolved within a minute with India's cooperation" has led to suspicions about an 'Indian hand' in the unrest. India's main opposition, Bharatiya Janata Party (BJP), however, criticizes the Indian government for remaining silent on the collusion of Indian and Nepali communists for creating turmoil in both countries and quashing of the symbols of Nepal's stability and unity-Hindu state and monarchy. An open border with India, existence of co-ethnics across the border and affiliation of each group and political party with like-minded ones in India create a context in which resolution of conflict requires confidence-building measures from both sides.

The violent conflict in the Tarai has forced the hill people to migrate to safe places and create their own mechanisms in the area, like the Chure Bhavar Unity Society (CBUS) that positions itself in the foothills bordering the Terai and the mountains, for autonomy and self-defense. The autonomy movement in the

Madhesh has snowballed into ethnic Tharus, Rais, Limbus, Tamangs, Gurungs, Magars, Dalits and Newars also demanding autonomous federal states based on the right to self-determination. But, there is no unity among Madhesi groups due to their multiple caste, language, religious and ethnic identities. For example, TMLP leadership is dominated by high caste groups, MPRF by intermediary caste groups and JTMM by lower caste groups. The government's Special Task Force (STF), deployed in Kathmandu and eight Terai districts, has failed to penetrate, divide and destroy criminal networks and create public security for local governance to operate. Nepal's problems cannot be tackled without taking this regionalism into account and identifying ways to address it. No matter how one looks at this problem, it seems obvious that there is no military solution. The political package must create a situation favorable to all groups where they see they have more to gain through peace than violence. An election in a security and authority vacuum will neither have legitimacy nor ability to institutionalize democratic polity.

Law and Order

The Nepalese army has expressed its commitment to democracy and a nationally-owned security sector reforms. But, Chief of Army Staff, Gen. R. Katawal clearly said "No" to integrate the CPN (Maoist) combatants. The UN has verified 19,602 politically indoctrinated People's Liberation Army (PLA) out of its total force of over 32,000. Premier G. P Koirala agrees with the army's viewpoint and has given options to Maoists-to integrate the PLA into industrial security groups or give them priority in foreign employment. Nepal's total strength of security forces stands at 165,000– NA (92,000), the civilian police (48,000) and Armed Police Force (25,000). The NA is holed up inside barracks as per the peace accord. The existence of these two adversarial structures does not provide any incentive for confidence building and to pursue a viable peace process for the future. Similarly, without disarming all autonomous armed groups and improving civil-military relations, the chances of free and fair elections remain fragile.

Erosion of state monopoly on power, taxation and loyalty of citizens, growth of competitive violence and failure of statehood in governance have confiscated the state's capacity to provide security in the country. As a result the ability of the political system to maintain balance of power between different governance organs is severely undermined which is telling on its capacity to enforce rule of law, provide service delivery and resolve the multi-layered conflict. SPA's control over the legislature, the executive control over the judiciary and a lack of legitimate opposition have established monopoly rule. There is an absence of institutions protecting property rights and promotion of collective goods.

Nepal has a very weak middle class and poor mediating agencies to protect the rights and welfare of the poor. Tax contributes 12 percent to GDP and the contribution of public sector output to GDP is only about 7 percent. Foreign aid constitutes 70 percent of development outlays. Domestic revenue raising capacity is very poor. Easy borrowing from international institutions has established the government's autonomy from their tax paying citizens. As a result, the government is less concerned with institutional capacity of the state to deliver governance goals. The substantial contribution of remittance to GDP (17 percent) too has detrimental effect on the accountability of government. GDP growth rate of 2.3 percent hardly balances out the population growth of 2.2 percent. The daily per capita income of $ 1 puts Nepal's human security condition at the bottom of world development statistics. Feudalism, caste hierarchy and patriarchy have suppressed social mobility of the underclass. This lack of social and economic security has made Nepal's politics highly inflammable amidst radical appeals and growing frustration.

Nepal's bureaucracy, police and public institutions are highly politicized along partisan lines, de-motivated, show poor esprit de corps and weak to enforce rule of law and deliver essential public services. "The rulers have no trust in the constitution, leading to its failure," Chairman of the Constitution Drafting Committee, Laxman Aryal said on January 15. To him, the constitution emerged as a compromise among SPA constituents for the transition politics until the CA election is conducted. It, therefore, does not hold the principles of constitutionalism. He added, "We saw nothing during its first year, but chaos and deterioration of law and order." This condition has made national integrity system ineffective in controlling crime, corruption and impunity. Public institutions and enterprises are still monopolized by ruling parties. Sense of public trust in the authority, assuming that the government is trustworthy and acting in the public interest, is sharply declining. Lack of a boundary between leaders' personal and institutional interests has given birth to a political culture of clientalism although new social movements of women, youth, Dalits, indigenous people and ethnic groups are increasingly challenging the position of authority fixed at birth, lineage and patronage. They are seeking to remold the pre-modern political culture of mutual distrust, betrayal and revenge and into post-conflict modern culture of a shared future based on social justice, democracy and peace.

VOICE AND PARTICIPATION OF MARGINALIZED

The struggle for human rights in Nepal for liberation, entitlements and social opportunities still remains unfinished. Chairman of the National Human Rights Commission of Nepal (NHRC) K. N. Upadhaya stresses the need for joint efforts among the human rights organizations and individuals to mitigate human rights violations in an effective manner. The government's presence is felt to some extent only in Kathmandu and some urban nodes. Killing, kidnapping, extortion, strikes, food shortages, rocketing prices, shrinking job opportunities and growing fear have deteriorated human rights conditions in the periphery. Last year, 130 civilians got killed by various forces.

Seventy-two political parties have applied in the EC for registration. This number represents asymmetry and diversity in Nepalese social life. A number of social groups are struggling for social, gender and inter-generational justice in the party structure of mainstream parties. Internal party democracy is essential to make political power proportional to its representativeness and end the fissiparous tendencies that have sapped their social integration potential.

The country has 102 ethnic groups and more than 82 languages. No single group claims more than 18 percent of the population. This means it is a country of minorities and there is no institutional mechanism to prevent the minority from becoming a majority. Civil society groups are columnized along partisan lines. This condition has marred the possibilities for cooperative action for public service. Despite the legislation of the Right to Information Act, the media is unevenly distributed just like the per capita income and, therefore, people of backward and remote areas have no access to the public sphere in shaping the agenda.

In contrast, the apex body of media persons, Nepal Federation of Journalists, revealed the condition of media freedom this way: Between April 24, 2006 to December 1, 2007 one journalist was killed, one disappeared, 74 detained and 128 threatened. There were 203 attacks on media houses, 129 journalists lost their jobs and 55 media houses were shut down.

Expectation of People at the Grassroots Level

The media and the political leaders have generated unrealistic expectations among the population that the CA is the panacea that will fulfil all their needs and desires. It was important to cast the message that CA is meant to frame a draft of the constitution and the necessary laws for governance. People at the grassroots level are expecting informed and reason-based knowledge about the constitution-making process, the suitability of the election system, improvement in security and are concerned about political stability, cooperation from outside, avoidance of unnecessary foreign intervention, knowledge about the modern state, functions of political systems, government, political parties and leadership, enfranchisement of citizens and their stake-holding in public institutions, social cohesion, support in education, health and economic activities and social justice. Minorities are increasingly questioning about their human rights in a majority dominated federal state. They want to know about their role in the multi-staged negotiation with the CA, suitability of federalism, concept of a republic and the vision of a New Nepal. Ordinary people also ask about the mixed election system that has been adopted and which presents a new challenge-what with the twin-ballot paper for voters and administration.

FES training series on civic education has created a synergy as demands for such activities from various quarters have increased, advocacy documents have been utilized by all sides, resource persons interviewed by the media and published in the local papers. They were even involved in non-partners' activities with the same advocacy resources. In general, our programs have strengthened the civic competence of citizens as they can debate on equal terms with their leaders and contest their view points. In many conflict-hit places, our activities provided space for dialogue among heterogeneous participants and directly contributed to building public opinion, democratic will-formation and reconciliation. We also tried to encourage participants to speak up and share their views rather than just receiving top-down dissemination of knowledge and information. In many places, they suggested to us to provide training to central level leadership and demanded more seminars in the districts and villages so that dialogues across diverse communities can build trust between conflict-torn societal groups and improve their relations with the state.

Engagement of the International Community

For an international community caught in a fluid political climate, it will be hard to enlarge the development space as agreed in the Basic Operating Guidelines (BOG), other than relief and humanitarian supplies. The presence of the international community in Nepal acts as a deterrence against excessive use of violence and abuse of human rights. Japan has put Nepal in the category of a "fragile state." By definition, a fragile state creates a situation for humanitarian intervention owing to anarchy of free wills, poor governance and failure to enforce rule of law. India has often insisted that elections to the CA must take place on time at any cost, but remained silent when the SPA failed to create a favorable security and law and order situation. The European Union and the US are insisting that the security situation in Nepal must improve for a credible, free and fair election. On January 18, the US Ambassador to Nepal, Nancy J. Powell suggesting the government and political parties to fulfil earlier commitments made in the peace accord said, "The CA polls will not guarantee sustainable peace in Nepal. What is necessary for the sustainable peace is loyalty to the nation."

On January 11, UN Secretary-General Ban Ki-Moon submitted his report to the UN Security Council proposing a six-month extension of UNMIN's mandate to support Nepal's peace process through CA elections. He has advised against downscaling the UN's presence, emphasizing that it could imperil prospects for a successful election, except in the cases of technical assistance which has already been provided. The UN too favors a credible CA election with improved security, government's engagement in a dialogue with disgruntled groups and abolition of the culture of impunity. Unlike the EU, however, India, the US and China have geopolitical priorities. India's role in bringing the SPA together against the 'monarchy' in November 2005 and their joint struggle forced King Gyanendra to hand over power to the political parties. As the SPA established their monopoly over power and resources but failed to maintain security and rule of law, it evoked the security concern of neighbours. China has voiced against "any foreign intervention in Nepal," showed interest to actively involve itself in Nepal's peace process, expressed anxiety about the events taking place in the Tarai and asked the Nepalese leaders to take independent decisions depending less on outside forces.

Aid coordination and coordination of government-donor practices have become particularly important in Nepal, especially to engage both sides in abolishing the historical practice of clientalism and paternalism, building trust on each other's role and engaging in multi-dimensional aspects of the peace-process, such as state-building, support to constitution-making, transport, communication, energy development, education, agriculture, rural development, water supply, finance, health and sanitation and sustainable development. Conflict mitigation projects should involve rehabilitation of the damaged infrastructure and internally displaced people, rural reconstruction and eradication of the root causes of mal-development which, in the first place, triggered the cycle of conflict.

Road Ahead

A credible, free and fair election depends on the ability of the political parties to create a secure environment for political actors and voters, cross-party consensus on security plans in the Tarai, engagement of movement-oriented and armed non-state actors opposed to the elections in constructive dialogues to address their outstanding grievances, dispelling the threat of pro-monarchy forces through inclusive measures and a common process of socialization and goal-orientation towards democratic peace. What happens if elections do not take place on April 10?

In case the CA election does not take place as scheduled, then this constitution, parliament and government will suffer from legitimacy deficit. The first scenario is well articulated by Minister without Portfolio Sujata Korala, "The constitution of 1991 will return." This will satisfy the traditional forces and its resistance to change. But, there will be a dangerous polarization between the radical and the conservative forces. The second scenario is the creation of a civilian government with the backing of NA. A CPN (Maoist) ideologue calls it a "democratic coup," because civilian politicians, not the King, will be utilized. A lot of things depend on the move of the international community because Nepal is an aid-dependent country and its policy, power and legitimacy flow from it. Similarly, it requires to win the confidence of India, the US and China as they are geo-strategically enmeshed in Nepal's internal developments.

A group of civil society and opposition parties are opting for a broad-based national government to hold elections. The third scenario seems optimally satisfactory if the major insurgent groups are engaged in dialogue and national consensus. Civil society groups should serve as a mediating ground for all political perspectives and mobilize national and global public opinion for it.

NEPAL POLICY A MONUMENTAL BLUNDER?

Any dispassionate analysis of the current situation in Nepal will deal with some uncomfortable questions. It seems that the

Indian government has not dealt with these questions properly. By "facilitating" the virtual Maoist-take-over of the Himalayan country, New Delhi has committed what could be, in course of time, a monumental strategic blunder. The new political era in Nepal is the result of the India-brokered peace deal in last September between the seven party democratic alliance and the Maoists who had been engaged in 10-year insurgency in which nearly 13000 people were killed. And here, all of them were anti-Monarch, since King Gyanendra was their "principal rival". That means in the heralding of the present political system in the country, the King, his loyalists, and most important, the Nepal Army, have played no role at all. Obviously, these forces are absolutely down, thanks to the great international pressure following the absolutely mindless royal take-over of the country by King Gyanendra in 2004. But to say that they are "out" for all times to come may be a little premature.

All told, Nepal is essentially a "Hindu country" and for majority of God-fearing Nepalese the King is the "Living Vishnu", the supreme God of the Hindus. They may not approve of the absolutist rule of the King, but that does not mean that they will accept the personal humiliation of the King by taking away even ceremonial role, something the present political arrangement is indulging in with fan and fare. The Institution of the monarchy or "King" has always been an important pillar in Nepalese society and polity. That is precisely the reason why countries such as India, the US, Britain and China had hitherto talked about the monarchy as an "important pillar" of Nepal. In fact, India and the US, while opposing the royal take-over, had always emphasised on the importance of Nepal remaining a "constitutional monarchy". Therefore, it is really perplexing how India is now reconciled to the Maoists' insistence on a "Republican system".

Secondly, with the King, the principal contradiction (to use the Maoists phrase) no longer the rallying point between the Nepali Congress and the Leftists, including the Maoists in the new interim Parliament, it remains to be seen how coherently this interim parliament and the interim government that will now have a Maoist deputy prime minister, is going to function and make preparations for the elections to the proposed constituent assembly. In the 330-member house, besides the 83 Maoist legislators, the Communist Party of Nepal-Unified Marxist Leninist (CPN-UML) that is also in the Koirala government has 83 MPs. Five other smaller left parties together have 16 more members. Thus against Nepali Congress's 85 members, the Left, overall, has 182 MPS. In other words, the interim Parliament is predominantly Left-oriented and that will have its impact on the Koirala's government. Therefore, in Nepal now we have a Prime Minister whose decisions will not necessarily reflect his or his Nepali Congress' views. How far this sort of alliance will lend to the stability of Nepal will always remain a question mark. One is not sure whether there will be a new "contradiction" between the Leftists on the one hand and the Nepali Congress, which represents liberal views in Nepal, on the other.

As it is, a senior Maoist central leader, Dina Nath Sharma, has been on record that there is a move now among all Left parties represented in the interim parliament to form a common front. He also said the CPN (Maoist) would lead the alliance. It is an open secret that the supreme leader of the Maoists, Pushpa Kamal Dahal, better known as Prachanda, wants to be the President, the elected head, of Nepal. That is why despite the Left's overwhelming majority in the interim Parliament, he allowed Koirala to continue as the Prime Minister.

But do Prachanda and his Maoists, represent the majority in Nepal? Let it be noted that the Maoists had performed disastrously in the parliamentary elections in early 1990s, winning just a couple of seats. It was after this that they decided to shun the democratic path and opt for the so-called revolutionary or violent path to capture power in 1996. All these years, the Maoists have used threats, extortion and killings to get their way. They have killed poor, innocent people and those who have criticised their top leaders. Their war has encouraged and spread a culture of intimidation and violence. Prachanda and others have defended these tactics, arguing that during war such incidents do occur and that they regret mistakes. However, the biggest question that remains unanswered is whether or not Prachanda and his Maoist followers have renounced violence forever in favour of multiparty democracy. Of late, Prachanda has said in various interviews that he is prepared to have peaceful competition with other political parties. But what happens if in this peaceful competition Prachanda loses? Is he prepared to sit in opposition benches as is normal in a democracy? There are no clear answers to these questions. All told, one should not forget that the Maoists still have their army and arms, which, at the moment, are in barracks and under UN supervision. And that has been made possible because Koirala as the prime Minister agreed to Parachanda's precondition that the Nepal Army, that is, the legitimate armed forces of a sovereign country, will also remain in barracks under UN supervision. All this is a temporary arrangement. What will finally happen to the Maoists Army if Prachanda sits in opposition?

In any case, before the present arrangement was agreed upon, Prachanda was of the view that "the [people's war] would not be discarded until the final construction of Communism" and that Nepal could be used "as a base area of world revolution, internationalist in content and national in form." It may be pointed out here that the Nepalese publication " The Kathmandu Post" in its issue of September 20, 2006, carried some details of the resolutions of the Fourth Conference of CCOMPOSA (Coordination Committee of Maoists Parties and Organisations of South Asia) held recently in August 2006 at an undisclosed location. These give the impression that the Maoists in Nepal, contrary to what they claim as having renounced people's war and go for competitive democracy, would continue to deepen and extend their links with the Maoists of the region and work for the seizure of power by armed force. The CPN (M)- Prachanda-led Maoists- which attended the CCMPOSA, along with eight other Maoist outfits of South Asia, was a party to the following decisions:

- The CCOMPOSA would deepen and advance the new democratic revolutions in different countries of South Asia turning into a flaming field of people's revolutionary urges and "burn to ashes imperialism (particularly US imperialism), Indian expansionism and all reaction in the region. (emphasis added)

- Called on the oppressed people of South Asian countries to join the struggle against Indian expansionism and particularly against the main enemy US imperialism.
- On Nepal, the resolution said that US hatched up conspiracies with Indian expansionism to kill the new democratic revolution in Nepal have been blocked

All this has risen to natural apprehensions that Prachanda may be following the typical Maoist path - during the second world war, Mao Tse-Tung joined the so-called United Front with the Chinese nationalists led by Chiang Kai-Shek; but once the war ended and the Japanese were defeated, he fought and drove away the nationalists to Taiwan. Now that the King has been literally overthrown, the democrats of Nepal could well be Prachanda's next targets.

As it is, the present arrangement between the seven party-alliance and the Maoists and the consequent interim constitution do not reflect the aspirations of all the Nepalese. Besides, critics have pointed out major flaws in the interim constitution. For instance, through gerrymandering, it gives disproportionately high representation to certain regions of the state while denying the people living in the Terai Region, derogatorily referred to as 'Madheshis', their rightful share in governance. They are believed to constitute more than fifty per cent of the population of Nepal. If true representative elections were to be held in Nepal, these Madheshis would surely hold the levers of power. However, whereas the hill constituencies with hardly six to eight thousand voters send one representative to the Parliament, almost seventy to eighty thousand voters elect one representative in the Terai region.

Administratively present day Nepal is divided into 75 districts. Out of these 55 districts are hilly and snow clad, and despite being larger in size, are sparsely populated. The northern border of many of these districts have borders Tibet. The 20 Southern districts have common borders with West Bengal, Bihar, Uttar Pradesh and Uttaranchal in India. The mother tongue of the sons of the soil in these 20 districts is Maithili, Bhojpuri, Avdhi, and other dialects of Hindi, but they interact with each other in Hindi and have

Hindi as their common language of communication. These people not only speak Hindi but are also culturally and ethnically closest to India.

And this is something that has not gone well with the dominant political elites of Nepal, including the Maoists. Policy makers in Nepal and India must not lose sight of imperatives of geopolitics. While the main threat that Maoists held was the siege or capture of capital Kathmandu, the Madhesis can economically strangulate Nepal as most of the supply arteries from India passes through the Terai region.

Geographically, the other neighbour of Nepal, China, is ill-placed to be an effective alternative. Incidentally, the Maoists have relatively lesser influence in the Terai region; they are more powerful in the hilly countryside. As a result, there are organisations like Madheshi People's Right Forum and (MPRF) and Janatantrik Terai Mukti Morcha, which are not happy with the "flawed" interim constitution.

They have regularly organised "bandhs" and paralysed the normal life as a matter of protest. They demand genuine devolution of power and rights to preserve their language and culture. How, then, the Leftist-dominated Nepalese polity, which obviously does not like Terai region's special affinity with India, will reconcile with these demands is going to be a major challenge as far as peace and stability in Nepal is concerned. This brings, finally, the question of the India-factor.

The relationship between India and Nepal is always unique, given the fact that the two share an open border. And this border has been used by anti-India elements to access India. India's concerns arise from the fact that eastern Nepal which borders the narrow sensitive Siliguri corridor connecting the entire north-east to the rest of India, is being used by Pakistan's ISI to sponsor insurgency in the north-east and transfer small arms and contraband.

In other parts of India too, it is reported that the large quantities of weapons and ammunition seized, including RDX, have been traced to the Nepalese route. Secondly, and this we have already noted, the Maoists of Nepal have always had close relations with their counterparts in India, particularly the dangerous Maoist Communist Centre (MCC) in Bihar and the People's War Group (PWG) in Andhra Pradesh. With the twin forces of the ISI and Maoists, who now rule the country, in its territory, Nepal will attract all the more attention in India now onwards.

Prachanda, of course, is thanking India these days for its positive role in legitimising the Maoists in Nepal. But, will he reciprocate? Given the above-mentioned resolution of the Fourth Conference of CCOMPOSA, that is doubtful. Besides, Prachanda's recent statements that "the Kashmiri people should also get their right of self determination - the right to decide their fate and this applies to the people of north-east India" (though he made it clear that self determination does not exactly mean separation) and that "Nepal should maintain equidistance from India and China" - something that would defy history - are certainly food for thought for India.

THE REFORM AGENDA

The Government of Nepal (GoN) designed PRSP during the Tenth Plan/PRSP, formulated Medium Term Expenditure Framework (MTEF), and also prepared an Immediate Action Plan (IAP). The structural reforms under implementation comprise:

1. Public Expenditure Reform;
2. Tax Reform;
3. Public Enterprise Reforms;
4. Facilitating Private Sector Development;
5. Financial Sector Reforms;
6. Decentralization;
7. Civil Service Reforms; and
8. Sector-Specific Reforms.

Nepal's recent experience with implementing economic and sectoral reforms provides some valuable lessons, which can help guide future reforms in Nepal. Particularly noteworthy is the fact that wide-ranging reforms have been successfully carried out against a background of political instability, conflict and economic backwardness. However, these adversaries have come to an end with the accomplishment of historic election of Constituent Assembly held on April 10, 2008. It has been realized that development of hydro-power and tourism sector is necessary from the standpoint of employment generation and economic growth. Government will encourage the private sector to set up power generation facilities and funding will be made available through the Power Development Fund. In pursuance of the statement made in the current year's budget, the government will work to make Nepal a regional tourist hub.

FINDINGS, DISCUSSION AND CONCLUSION

Who Controls the Lifelong Learning Policy and Practice in Nepal and How? This research indicates that the policy and practice of lifelong learning in Nepal is mainly manipulated and influenced by global donor agencies and corporates such as the World Bank, the European Union (EU), the International Monetary Fund (IMF), the Asian Development Bank (ADB), United Nations Educational, Scientific and Cultural Organization (UNESCO) and the Organisation for European Economic Co-operation and Development (OECD) countries that are facilitated by social elites, mainly Brahmins, Chhetris and Newars in Nepal.

These have occupied almost all the country's key posts and controlled Nepal's resources, marginalising the indigenous nationalities, lower castes, poor and landless class and women. These three castes control the flow of (formal) knowledge, lifelong learning and its policy and practice for their own communities (for example: Sanskrit University of Dang) and individual benefit.

The role of elites in the lifelong learning process differs significantly from place to place and from one community to the next. The elites close to the state have been controlling the knowledge system and the lifelong learning processes. This is to ensure their privileged position and to maintain their stronghold in the productive resources; this group of elites has also been controlling the lifelong learning policy and practices of the nation-state.

Why Have the Lifelong Learning Initiatives and Trials Failed? Nepalese lifelong learning policy is written with emotive slogans and wonderful goals because this is a high level-begging bowl designed by the country's high-level think-tanks. It is mainly based on the donor agencies' and social elites' interests and not on the needs of the Nepalese people. As a result, lifelong learning initiatives failed in the past and not functioning well in the present for example, National Education System Plan (NESP) 1971, the unsatisfactory achievement of adult literacy programmes and Education for All (EFA) 1990.

One of the objectives of EFA 1990 was to provide all children of the world with access to good quality basic education by 2000, but that objective was not achieved. Thus, the Dakar World Education Forum 2000 came up with a revised vision, mission, goals and strategies and added another 15 years from the year 2000 to 2015 to achieve those goals. However, I did not find this in practice; hence, the future of the current lifelong learning project of EFA 2000 – 2015, coordinated and operated by UNESCO, already looks gloomy.

The policy always remains poles apart from ground realities and most of the time plans and projects appear to conclude without achieving their aims and objectives. Policy making and planning is only a starting point. An effective practice is vital towards achieving satisfactory goals. There appears to be no effective and sustainable relationship between the learning policy and practice of Nepal.

The World Bank, IMF, the ADB, OECDs and the EU have claimed that they are primarily committed to poor countries in alleviating poverty and their learning policies are based on this principle. However, they never dissociated their political economic tool -the so-called 'Structural Adjustment Policies'- from their loan packages. In consequence, only a handful of social elites and donor countries became rich and the majority of Nepalese people have suffered from hunger and disease and currently so-called 'good education' is beyond the earning capacity of poor people. This is one of the main reasons why the country plunged into civil war.

POLITICAL CONDITIONS

1990–1996: Parliamentary Monarchy

Until 1990, Nepal was an absolute monarchy running under the executive control of the king. Faced with a people's movement against the absolute monarchy, King Birendra, in 1990, agreed to large-scale political reforms by creating a parliamentary monarchy with the king as the head of state and a prime minister as the head of the government.

Nepal's legislature was bicameral consisting of a House of Representatives and a National Council. The House of Representatives consisted of 205 members directly elected by the people. The National Council had 60 members, 10 nominated by the king, 35 elected by the House of Representatives and the remaining 15 elected by an electoral college made up of chairs of villages and towns. The legislature had a five-year term, but was dissolved by the king before its term could end. All Nepalese citizens 18 years and older became eligible to vote. The executive comprised the King and the Council of Ministers (the Cabinet). The leader of the coalition or party securing the maximum seats in an election was appointed as the Prime Minister. The Cabinet was appointed by the king on the recommendation of the Prime Minister.

Governments in Nepal have tended to be highly unstable; no government has survived for more than two years since 1991, either through internal collapse or parliamentary dissolution by the monarch. In the first free and fair elections in Nepal in 1991, the Nepali Congress was victorious. The 1994 election defeat of the Nepali Congress Party by the Communist Party of Nepal (Unified Marxist-Leninist) (CPN(UML)) made Nepal the first communist-led monarchy in Asia, with Man Mohan Adhikary prime minister. In mid-1994, parliament was dissolved due to dissension within the Nepali Congress Party. The subsequent general election, held 15 November 1994, gave no party a majority and led to several years of unstable coalition governments. As of the May 1999 general elections, the Nepali Congress Party once again headed a majority government. There have been three Nepali

Congress Party Prime Ministers since the 1999 elections: K.P. Bhattarai (31 May 1999–17 March 2000); Girija Prasad Koirala (20 March 2000–19 July 2001); and Sher Bahadur Deuba (23 July 2001–2003). The final distribution of seats in Parliament gave the Nepali Congress 113; the CPN(UML) 69; the RPP 11; the RJM 5; the NSP 5; the Workers and Peasants Party 1; and the United People's Front 1. Nepali Congress Party has divided to Nepali Congress Party led by G. P. Koirala and Nepali Congress (Democratic) led by Sher Bahadur Deuba.

Amongst the elected MPs, 39 MPs belong to Nepali Congress (Democratic). Former Prime Minister and Influential Leader Krishna Prasad Bhattarai has expressed his support for Nepali Congress (Democratic). Both Congress parties regard Krishna Prasad Bhattarai as their main leader.

King Gyanendra discharged Sher Bahadur Deuba and on 4 June 2003 appointed Surya Bahadur Thapa as Prime Minister.

1996: Maoist Insurgency

In February 1996, the Communist Party of Nepal (Maoist) began a violent insurgency in more than 50 of the country's 75 districts. About 13,000 police, civilians, and insurgents have been killed in the conflict since 1996. In July 2001 Prime Minister Deuba announced a cease-fire, which the Maoists pledged to observe, as part of a government effort to seek a negotiated solution to the conflict. Although Maoist-instigated intimidation and extortion continue, the killings have largely subsided since the cease-fire was announced. The government and Maoists held talks in August and September 2001.

Political parties agreed in 1991 that the monarchy would remain to enhance political stability and provide an important symbol of national identity for the culturally diverse Nepali people. The King exercises limited powers, including the right to declare a state of emergency in the event of war or armed revolt, with the advice and consent of the Council of Ministers and the Prime Minister. According to the constitution, the King's declaration of a state of emergency must be approved by a two-thirds majority of the lower house of the Parliament.

2001: Royal Massacre

On June 1, 2001, Crown Prince Dipendra was officially reported to have shot and killed his father, King Birendra; his mother, Queen Aishwarya; his brother; his sister, his father's younger brother, Prince Dhirendra; and several aunts, before turning the gun on himself. Although he never regained consciousness before dying, Crown Prince Dipendra was nonetheless the king under the law of Nepalese royal succession. After his death two days later, the late King's surviving brother Gyanendra was proclaimed king.

2005–2007: Suspension of parliament and Loktantra Andolan

On 1 February 2005 King Gyanendra suspended the Parliament, appointed a government led by himself, and enforced martial law. The King argued that civil politicians were unfit to handle the Maoist insurgency. Telephone lines were cut and several high-profile political leaders were detained. Other opposition leaders fled to India and regrouped there. A broad coalition called the Seven Party Alliance (SPA) was formed in opposition to the royal takeover, encompassing the seven parliamentary parties who held about 90% of the seats in the old, dissolved parliament.

The UN-OHCHR, in response to events in Nepal, set up a monitoring program in 2005 to assess and observe the human rights situation there. On 22 November 2005, the Seven Party Alliance (SPA) of parliamentary parties and the Communist Party of Nepal (Maoist) agreed on a historic and unprecedented 12-point memorandum of understanding (MOU) for peace and democracy. Nepalese from various walks of life and the international community regarded the MOU as an appropriate political response to the crisis that was developing in Nepal. Against the backdrop of the historical sufferings of the Nepalese people and the enormous human cost of the last ten years of violent conflict, the MOU, which proposes a peaceful transition through an elected constituent assembly, created an acceptable formula for a united movement for democracy. As per the 12-point MOU, the SPA called for a protest movement, and the Communist

Party of Nepal (Maoist) supported it. This led to a countrywide uprising that started in April 2006. All political forces including civil society and professional organizations actively galvanized the people. This resulted in massive and spontaneous demonstrations and rallies held across Nepal against King Gyanendra's autocratic rule.

The people's participation was so broad, momentous and pervasive that the king feared being overthrown. On 21 April 2006, King Gyanendra declared that "power would be returned to the people". This had little effect on the people, who continued to occupy the streets of Kathmandu and other towns, openly defying the daytime curfew. Finally King Gyanendra announced the reinstatement the House of Representatives, thereby conceding one of the major demands of the SPA, at midnight on 24 April 2006. Following this action the coalition of political forces decided to call off the protests.

Twenty-one people died and thousands were injured during the 19 days of protests. On 19 May 2006, the parliament assumed total legislative power and gave executive power to the Government of Nepal (previously known as His Majesty's Government). Names of many institutions (including the army) were stripped of the "royal" adjective and the Raj Parishad (a council of the King's advisers) was abolished, with his duties assigned to the Parliament itself. The activities of the King became subject to parliamentary scrutiny and the King's properties were subjected to taxation. Moreover, Nepal was declared a secular state abrogating the previous status of a Hindu Kingdom. However, most of the changes have, as yet, not been implemented. On 19 July 2006, the prime minister, G. P. Koirala, sent a letter to the United Nations announcing the intention of the Nepalese government to hold elections to a constituent assembly by April 2007.

December 2007 to May 2008: Abolition of the monarchy

On 23 December 2007, an agreement was made for the monarchy to be abolished and the country to become a federal republic with the Prime Minister becoming head of state. Defying political pundits, who had predicted it to be trounced in the April

2008 elections, the Communist Party of Nepal (Maoist) became the largest party amidst a general atmosphere of fear and intimidation from all sides. A federal republic was established in May 2008, with only four members of the 601-seat Constituent Assembly voting against the change, which ended 240 years of royal rule in Nepal. The government announced a public holiday for three days, (May 28—May 30), to celebrate the country becoming a federal republic.

Current (2008 onwards)

Major parties such as the Unified Communist Party of Nepal (Maoist), Communist Party of Nepal (Unified Marxist-Leninist) and the Nepali Congress agreed to write a constitution that replaces the interim one within the time limit of 2 years. However, incooperative and "selfish" behaviour of the political parties has been cited as the major cause behind the derailing of the peace process. The Maoists, as the largest party of the country, took power right after the elections were held and named Pushpa Kamal Dahal or Prachanda as the Prime Minister of the country.

CPN UML also joined this government but the Nepali Congress took part of the main opposition. People soon saw that the country's situation deteriorated and political turmoils were in store. Prachanda soon fell into a dispute with the then army chief Rookmangud Katwal and decided to sack him. But the President Ram Baran Yadav as the supreme head of military power in the country revoked this decision and gave the army chief additional time in office. An angry Prachanda and his party quit the government, majorly citing this reason and decided to be the main opposition to the government headed by CPN UML and co-partner Nepali Congress afterwards. Madhav Kumar Nepal was named the Prime Minister.

The Maoists have been to this date demanding superiority of civilian supremacy to army supremacy. This created turmoils in the country and showed vividly that development was a dream far away and the political leaders were just wrangling for power. The Maoists have been forcing closures or commonly known as *bandhs* in the country and have also declared autonomous states for almost all the ethnic groups in the country, seen as a part of revenge against the action that foiled their decision to sack the army chief. Political leaders are discussing plans to end this turmoil, but none of the talks have been successful. Rising inflation, economic downturn, poverty, insecurity and uncertainty are the major problems. Many analysts opine that this freedom has brought anarchy to the country. Many don't even believe the political parties will be successful on writing a constitution.

POLITICAL PARTIES SYSTEM

The Nepali Congress Party

The Nepali Congress Party, a reform-oriented centrist party, has been in continuous operation since it was founded under a slightly different name in 1947. Elected to office in 1959 in a landslide victory, the Nepali Congress Party government sought to liberalize society through a democratic process. The palace coup of 1960 led to the imprisonment of the powerful Nepali Congress Party leader, B.P. Koirala, and other party stalwarts; many other members sought sanctuary in exile in India.

Although political parties were prohibited from 1960 to 1963 and continued to be outlawed during the *panchayat* system under the aegis of the Associations and Organizations (Control) Act of 1963, the Nepali Congress Party persisted. The party placed great emphasis on eliminating the feudal economy and building a basis for socioeconomic development. It proposed nationalizing basic industries and instituting progressive taxes on land, urban housing, salaries, profits, and foreign investments. While in exile, the Nepali Congress Party served as the nucleus around which other opposition groups clustered and even instigated popular uprisings in the Hill and Tarai regions. During this time, the Nepali Congress Party refused the overtures of a radical faction of the Communist Party of Nepal for a tactical alliance.

Although the Nepali Congress Party demonstrated its ability to endure, it was weakened over time by defection, factionalism, and external pressures. Nevertheless, it continued to be the only organized party to press for democratization. In the 1980 referendum, it supported the multiparty option in opposition to the *panchayat* system. In 1981 the party boycotted the Rashtriya Panchayat elections and rejected the new government. The death in 1982 of B.P. Koirala, who had consistently advocated constitutional reforms and a broad-based policy of national reconciliation, further weakened the party.

In the 1980s, the Nepali Congress Party abandoned its socialistic economic program in favor of a mixed economy, privatization, and a market economy in certain sectors. Its foreign policy orientation was to nonalignment and good relations with India. Although the party also boycotted the 1986 elections to the Rashtriya Panchayat, its members were allowed to run in the 1987 local elections. In defiance of the ban on demonstrations, the Nepali Congress Party organized mass rallies in January 1990 that ultimately triggered the prodemocracy movement.

Following the humiliating defeat of party leader K.P. Bhattarai by the communist factions in the 1991 parliamentary elections, Girija Prasad (G.P.) Koirala was chosen by the Nepali Congress Party as leader of its Parliamentary Board. As prime minister, he formed the first elected democratic government in Nepal in thirtytwo years. G.P. Koirala was the third of the Koirala brothers to become prime minister. Along with his elder brother, B.P. Koirala, he was arrested in 1960 and was not released until 1967. After a period of exile that began in 1971, he returned to Nepal in 1979 under a general amnesty. He was elected general secretary of the party in 1976 in a convention at Patna and played a key role in the prodemocracy movement. G.P. Koirala was known for favoring reconciliation with the left, but he also wanted to pursue national unity and Western-style democracy.

The Communist Parties

Like the Nepali Congress Party, the fractured communist movement was deeply indebted to its Indian counterpart, whose initiative had helped to found the Communist Party of Nepal (Marxist) in 1949 in Calcutta. Nepalese communists looked askance at the Nepali Congress Party leadership as willing collaborators of Indian expansionism and called for broad-based alliances of all progressive forces for the establishment of a people's democracy. As many as seventeen factions, ranging from the quasiestablishment royal communists to extremely radical fringe groups, vied for leadership and control, preventing the movement from making significant gains. The proscription of political parties in 1960 affected the communists less severely than other parties because communist factions proved better at organizing and operating underground and at making the transition to covert activity. Little effort was exerted to detain communist leaders, and in the months following the palace coup d'état in 1960, the Communist Party of Nepal (Marxist) was allowed to operate with a perceptibly greater amount of freedom than any other party. The Communist Party of Nepal (Marxist-Leninist) was established in 1978, one of many splinter groups under the name Communist Party of Nepal. In spite of many vicissitudes encountered since the movement's inception, the communists maintained national attention because of continued support from the peasant and worker organizations and the fact that the country's poverty and deprivation offered a fertile ground for Marxist ideals. Support was maintained through the All Peasants Union and the Nepal Trade Union Congress.

Communist groups wielded significant influence in the universities and professional groups. The movement had a dedicated cadre of motivated youth who followed party discipline strictly. Whereas the Nepali Congress Party seemed to accommodate the old guard at the expense of the younger generation, communists more ardently sought younger members. Most of the mainstream communist groups in the 1980s believed in democracy and a multiparty system, recognized no international communist headquarters or leaders, and abjured the Maoism many had embraced earlier.

The United Left Front coalition, organized in late 1989, supported multiparty democracy. During the prodemocracy movement, it played a crucial role by joining the interim government led by the Nepali Congress Party and by submerging serious differences of opinion. Although differences in the communist camp were endemic when the movement was underground, the internal conflicts lessened as communists operated openly and began to look toward future electoral gains. The success of the communist parties in the May 12, 1991, election, came as a shock to the Nepali Congress Party, which had failed to repeat its 1959 landslide victory. Although there was some unity among the communist factions of the United Left Front, there was no agreement to share seats with the other factions or groups. The Communist Party of Nepal (United Marxist-Leninist) faction—formed as a result of a merger between the Communist Party of Nepal (Marxist) and the Communist Party of Nepal (MarxistLeninist)—came in second to the Nepali Congress Party. The head of the communist leadership echelon was Madan Bhandari, son of a Brahman priest, who was working to turn his Communist Party of Nepal (United Marxist-Leninist) into a formidable political power. He stunned the Nepali Congress Party in the 1991 elections by narrowly defeating its leader, K.P. Bhattarai, for a parliamentary seat in Kathmandu.

As a partner in the interim coalition government, the Communist Party of Nepal (United Marxist-Leninist) had endorsed, although reluctantly, the new constitution, which retained the monarchy. The communists received popular support for their allegations that the Nepali Congress Party was too close to India and was a threat to Nepal's sovereignty. Other mainstream communist leaders were Man Mohan Adhikari and Sahana Pradhan, both originally of the Communist Party of Nepal (Marxist); and Bishnu Bahadur Manandhar of the Communist Party of Nepal (Manandhar), another communist faction.

Other Political Parties

There was a phenomenal rise in the number of political parties--particularly between May and September 1990—as strategic maneuvers to participate in parliamentary elections and find a niche in postelection Nepal occurred. The Nepal Sadbhavana Party (Good Will Party), one of several regional and ethnic parties, was founded in April 1990. It aimed at promoting the interests of the Tarai Region, including the expulsion of the Hill people from Tarai and the establishment of a special relationship with India in the framework of nonalignment. A forum for people of Indian descent, the party also favored the introduction of Hindi as the second national language. Its ideology supported a democratic socialist society. Other Tarai Region parties included the Nepal Tarai Unity Forum, the Nepal Tarai Association, and the Nepal Tarai Muslim Congress Party.

Among the several ethnic parties were the National People's Liberation Front (Nepal Rashtriya Jana Mukti Morcha), the National Mongol Organization (Rashtriya Mongol Sanghatan), SETAMAGURALI (an acronym of names of different ethnic groups of eastern Nepal including the Tamang, Magar, and Gurung), the Front of the Kirat Aborigines (Nepal Kirat Adhibasi Janajiti Morch), the Freedom Front of the Limbu People (Limbuwan Mukli Morcha), and the Nepal Nationalist Gorkha Parishad, or Parishad (Nepal Rashtrabadi Gorkha Parishad). The Parishad, revived in September 1990, was founded in 1951 as part of Rana revivalist politics and had placed second in the 1959 general elections. Some of its senior leaders later joined the Nepali Congress or *pancha* camps.

Of those groups favoring the monarchy, two conservative parties received considerable attention. Hastily founded by two former prime ministers, both parties were called the National Democratic Party—suffixed with the names Thapa or Chand enclosed within brackets. Other parties of this political bent included the National Democratic Unity Panchayat Party (Rashtriya Prajatantrik Ekata Panchayat Party), Nepal Welfare Party (Nepal Janahit Party), United Democratic Party (Samyukti Prajatantra Party), and Nepal Panchayat Council (Nepal Panchayat Parishad). Besides the Nepali Congress Party, fifteen centrist parties also had emerged. Most of these parties were founded by former members of the Nepali Congress Party and defecting *pancha* who had shifted allegiance to the multiparty system. The Women's Democratic Party aimed at promoting the rights, interests, and freedoms of Nepalese women.

8

Constitutional Development

THE RANA SYSTEM

Beginning in 1856, the centre of power in Nepal rested with the Rana prime ministers, who retained sovereign power until the revolution of 1950-51. Many of the nobles who participated in the consultative court called the Assembly of Lords, or Bharadari Sabha, had been slaughtered at the Kot Massacre in 1846. Following his official visit to Britain and Europe in 1851, Jang Bahadur Kunwar (later called Jang Bahadur Rana) began to use the Bharadari Sabha as deliberative body for state affairs.

For almost 100 years, this council served as a rubber stamp for the Rana autocracy. The next major effort at institutional development was initiated in 1947 by Padma Shamsher Rana, a liberal prime minister, who appointed a Constitutional Reform Committee to draft the first constitution. Known as the Government of Nepal Constitution Act, 1948, this constitution, written with the help of Indian advisers, superficially changed the Rana system. It established a bicameral legislative body. The entire membership of one house and a majority of the other was selected by the prime minister, who could reject any measure that the legislature might pass. There was a cabinet of at least five members, of whom at least two were chosen from among the few elected members of the legislature. The act also specified that a *panchayat* system of local self-government would be inaugurated in the villages, towns, and districts. It enumerated certain fundamental rights and duties, which included freedoms of speech, the press, assembly, and worship; equality before the law; free elementary education for all; and equal and universal suffrage. Despite the appearance of reform, the alterations made in the Rana system by the constitution were slight. The more conservative Ranas perceived the constitution as a dangerous precedent, forced Padma Shamsher to resign, and suspended promulgation of the constitution. The constitution became effective in September 1950 but remained in force only until February 1951, when the Rana monopoly was broken and the creation of a new constitutional system began.

The Interim Constitution, 1951

The revolution of 1950-51 resulted in the overthrow of the Rana system. In 1951 King Tribhuvan Bir Bikram Shah announced by royal proclamation an interim government and an interim constitution until a new Constituent Assembly could be elected. The interim constitution, based on principles in India's constitution and entitled the Interim Government of Nepal Act, 1951, ratified the end of the authority of the prime minister and the system surrounding that office. It also reasserted the king's supreme executive, legislative, and judicial powers. The king exercised his executive authority through, and was aided and advised by, a Council of Ministers, which he appointed and which served at his pleasure.

The king also appointed an Advising Assembly to sit until the Constituent Assembly was elected. The king retained sovereign and plenary legislative powers. The Advising Assembly was, with certain exceptions, authorized only to discuss matters and to recommend measures to the king for enactment into law. The final authority to approve any legislative measure lay with the king. The constitution also established a Supreme Court, made the king supreme commander of the armed forces, reiterated and enlarged upon the fundamental rights included in the Rana constitution, and proclaimed numerous social and economic objectives of the government. These objectives were to promote the welfare of the people by securing a social order in which social, economic, and political justice pervaded all the institutions of national life. King Mahendra (reigned 1955-72) vigorously sought to broaden the monarch's political base, but the Nepali National Congress succeeded in gaining some democratic reforms. Although the constitution was expected to be temporary pending the election of a Constituent Assembly and the preparation of a permanent organic law, King Mahendra was unable to resist the increasingly well-orchestrated political demands by the Nepali National Congress for a more democratic and representative government, and was forced to promulgate a new constitution.

The Royal Constitution of 1959

The most significant aspect of the constitution of 1959 was that it was granted by the king rather than drawn up by elected representatives of the people as had been specified in the 1951 constitution. Although the constitution formally brought into being a democratically elected parliamentary system under a constitutional monarchy, the king retained ultimate sovereignty, even though the document itself did not explicitly grant this power. The 1959 constitution, modelled on British and Indian constitutional custom, vested executive power in the king, who was advised and assisted by a Council of State (Raj Sabha) and a Council of Ministers (cabinet). The Council of State, which consisted of officers of Parliament, ministers ex officio, former ministers, and royal appointees, advised the monarch on legislation and handled the details of regency and succession in the event of his death or disability. The general direction and control of the government were entrusted to the Council of Ministers, headed by a prime minister required to command a majority in the lower house of Parliament, to which the council was collectively responsible.

The king was an integral part of the legislative arm of the government. Parliament was defined as consisting of the king; the House of Representatives, composed of 109 popularly elected members; and the Senate, composed of 36 members of whom half were elected by the house and half were nominated by the king. All bills approved by the two houses required the assent of the king to become law. The constitution granted the king wide latitude to nullify the parliamentary system. The king could suspend the operation of the cabinet and perform its functions himself if he determined that no person could command a majority in the house as prime minister. In the event of a breakdown of the parliamentary system or of any one of a number of emergency conditions, the king could suspend either or both houses of Parliament, assume their powers, and suspend the constitution in whole or part. In December 1960, King Mahendra invoked these emergency powers to dissolve the Nepali Congress Party government. The constitutional system that had prevailed before 1959 was then returned to operation.

The Panchayat Constitution, 1962

By royal proclamation on December 16, 1962, King Mahendra announced a new constitution that radically reformed the 1959 constitution but also adopted many features of the Rana system. Known as the Panchayat Constitution, it was the fourth constitution in fifteen years.

The *panchayat* system was an institution of great antiquity. Historically, each caste group system of Nepal formed its own *panchayat,* or council of elders, a sociopolitical organization operational on a village level that could expand to include neighbouring districts, or even function on a zonal basis. Although it could be argued that the *panchayat* system was adopted from India, King Mahendra had argued for its incorporation at the national level as an exponent of Nepalese culture—a worthy and historically correct representation of cultural expression.

The 1962 constitution was based on some elements from other "guided democracy" constitutional experiments—notably "Basic Democracy" in Pakistan, "Guided Democracy" in Indonesia, and the "Dominant Party System" in Egypt. The Panchayat constitution not only codified the irrelevance of political parties, but also declared them illegal.

The 1962 constitution contained a stronger and more explicit statement of royal authority than did previous constitutions. Real power remained with the king, who was the sole source of authority and had the power not only to amend the constitution but also to suspend it by royal proclamation during emergencies. The Council of Ministers, selected from the members of the legislative (Rashtriya Panchayat, or National Panchayat), served as an advisory body to the king. Members of the Rashtriya Panchayat were elected indirectly by the members of local *panchayat* as well as by the members of professional and class organizations such as the Nepal Workers' Organization, the Nepal Ex-servicemen's Organization, and the Nepal Youth Organization. The constitution abolished all political parties.

Constitutional Amendments

The Panchayat Constitution was amended several times, primarily to increase the power and prerogatives of the monarchy against the increasing popular demand for liberalization of the political institutions and processes. In view of the mounting criticism against the Panchayat Constitution, King Birendra, who had succeeded his father in 1972, pursuant to recommendations of a specially created Constitutional Reform Commission, announced in 1975 that the constitution would be amended to include provisions governing the amending procedure itself. Previously the king could not amend the constitution unless two-thirds of the Rashtriya Panchayat ratified the proposed amendment. Under the proposed amendment, the king would have to consult a special committee of the Rastriya Panchayat before amending the constitution. In addition, the term of a delegate to the Rashtriya Panchayat was reduced from six years to four years.

The Referendum of 1980

In May 1979, concerned by the unabated political demonstrations and considerable general unrest, King Birendra called for a nationwide referendum to determine the future form of government. The referendum offered two choices: a continuation of the partyless *panchayat* system, with prospects for further reform; or a multiparty system. Although no clear definition of a multiparty system was provided, the implication was that it stood for a parliamentary system of government run on a party basis. The referendum, the first nationwide vote in twenty-two years, was held on May 2, 1980, and 67 percent of the eligible voters participated. The *panchayat* system was chosen with a majority of 54.7 percent of the votes. On May 21, 1980, the king appointed an eleven-member Constitution Reforms Commission to be chaired by the acting chief justice of the Supreme Court. On December 15, the king promulgated three constitutional amendments: direct elections to the Rashtriya Panchayat would be held every five years for 112 seats, with 28 additional seats filled by the king's personal nomination; the prime minister would be elected by the Rashtriya Panchayat; the cabinet would be appointed by the king on the recommendation of the prime minister and would be accountable to the Rashtriya Panchayat; and Nepal would commit to the Nonaligned Movement as a zone of peace. These provisions, with a few minor modifications, remained in operation until early 1990, when the prodemocracy movement successfully agitated for a multiparty democratic system.

The Constitution of 1990

Widespread prodemocracy protests toppled the *panchayat* system in April 1990. The king appointed an independent Constitution Recommendation Commission to represent the main opposition factions and to prepare a new constitution to accommodate their demands for political reform. On September 10, 1990, the commission presented King Birendra with the draft of a new constitution, which would preserve the king's status as chief of state under a constitutional monarchy but establish a multiparty democracy with separation of powers and human rights. As agreed upon earlier, the king turned the draft constitution over to Prime Minister K.P. Bhattarai and his cabinet for review and recommendations. The draft was discussed extensively and approved by the interim cabinet. A major obstacle to approval was avoided when the commission removed a disputed provision under which both the constitutional monarchy and multiparty system could have been eliminated by a three-quarters majority vote of Parliament.

On November 9, 1990, King Birendra promulgated the new constitution and abrogated the constitution of 1962. The 1990 constitution ended almost thirty years of absolute monarchy in which the palace had dominated every aspect of political life and political parties were banned. The constitution, broadly based on British practice, is the fundamental law of Nepal. It vests sovereignty in the people and declares Nepal a multiethnic, multilingual, democratic, independent, indivisible, sovereign, and constitutional monarchical kingdom. The national and official language of Nepal is Nepali in the Devanagari script. All other languages spoken as the mother tongue in the various parts of Nepal are recognized as languages of the nation. Although Nepal still is officially regarded as a Hindu kingdom, the constitution also gives religious and cultural freedom to other religious groups, such as Buddhists, Muslims, and Christians. The preamble of the constitution recognizes the desire of the Nepalese people to bring about constitutional changes with the objective of obtaining social, political, and economic justice. It envisages the guarantee of basic human rights to every citizen, a parliamentary system of government, and a multiparty democracy. It also aims to establish an independent and competent system of justice with a view to transforming the concept of the rule of law into reality. Other safeguards include the right to property; the right to conserve and promote one's language, script, and culture; the right to education in the student's mother tongue; freedom of religion; and the right to manage and protect religious places and trusts. Traffic in human slavery, serfdom, forced labour, or child labour in any form is prohibited. The right to receive information about matters of public importance and the right to secrecy and inviolability of one's person, residence, property, documents, letters, and other information also are guaranteed.

Part three of the constitution provides for the fundamental rights of citizens. Although some elements of fundamental rights guaranteed in the 1962 constitution are reflected in the 1990 constitution, the latter provides new safeguards in unequivocal language and does not encumber the fundamental rights with duties or restrictions purported to uphold public good. All citizens are equal before the law, and no discrimination can be made on the basis of religion, race, sex, caste, tribe, or ideology. No person shall, on the basis of caste, be discriminated against as an untouchable, be denied access to any public place, or be deprived from the use of public utilities. No discrimination will be allowed in regard to remuneration for men and women for the same work. No citizen can be exiled or be deprived of liberty except in accordance with the law; and capital punishment is disallowed.

In addition, sections on fundamental rights provide for freedom of thought and expression; freedom to assemble peacefully and without arms; freedom to form unions and associations; freedom to move and reside in any part of Nepal; and freedom to carry out any profession, occupation, trade, or industry. Similarly, prior censorship of publications is prohibited, and free press and printing are guaranteed.

Unfettered cultural and educational rights also are guaranteed. Articles twenty-three and eighty-eight provide for a citizen's right to constitutional remedy. Any citizen can petition the Supreme Court to declare any law or part thereof as void if it infringes on the fundamental rights conferred by the constitution.

Rights regarding criminal justice include the guarantee that no person will be punished for an act unpunishable by law or subjected to a punishment greater than that prescribed by the laws in existence at the time of commission of the offense; no person will be prosecuted more than once in any offense; and no one will be compelled to bear witness against himself or herself. Inflicting cruelty on a person in detention is prohibited, as is detaining a person without giving information about the grounds for such detention. Further, the person in detention must be produced within twenty-four hours of such arrest before the judicial authorities. Any person wrongly detained will be compensated.

The constitution lays down various directives in matters of political, economic, and social development, and foreign policy. These lofty policies are guidelines to promote conditions of welfare on the basis of the principles of an open society. One objective is to transform the national economy into an independent and self-reliant system by making arrangements for the equitable distribution of the economic gains on the basis of social justice. The constitution stresses the creation of conditions for the enjoyment of the fruits of democracy through the maximum participation of the people in governance of the country. Other aims include the pursuit of a policy in international relations that will enhance the dignity of the nation and ensure sovereignty, integrity, and national independence and the protection of the environment from further ecological damage

NEPAL CONSTITUTION: A HISTORIC STEP

The adoption of a federal, democratic and secular Constitution in Nepal is a historic occasion. The protracted struggle of the Nepalese people against feudal authoritarianism and for democracy has culminated in the establishment of a federal, democratic and secular State. Eight years after the interim Constitution, after a tortuous political process, the Constituent Assembly voted overwhelmingly (507 out of 601) to approve the Constitution. We congratulate the people of Nepal, the three major political parties – the Nepali Congress, the CPN(UML) and the UCPN(M) – and all democratic forces for this significant achievement.

India should have been the first to welcome the adoption of the Constitution. Instead, the Modi government has adopted a negative attitude and an unwarranted interventionist stance. Two days after the adoption of the Constitution in the Constituent assembly, the Modi government sent Foreign Secretary Jaishankar to Kathmandu to meet the president and the prime minister and leaders of major political parties in an attempt to stall the formal proclamation of the Constitution which took place on September 20. The plea made for this blatant interference in Nepal's sovereign matters is that that Constitution was not inclusive enough and there was serious unrest among the Madhesi people. After the formal promulgation of the Constitution, the Indian foreign ministry issued a statement expressing concern at the protests and violence and just "noted" the adoption of the Constitution. This was followed by two statements on successive days expressing concern about the situation in the Terai region and calling upon the Nepalese government to take the Madhesi people's concern on board as far as the Constitution is concerned. The Indian Ambassador was also recalled for consultations.

There has often been a big brother attitude to Nepal on the part of the Indian ruling establishment. This has however been taken to new heights now with the callous disregard shown to Nepal's sovereign right to formulate the country's Constitution as per their own democratic process. The Constitution has enunciated fundamental rights of citizens which are more wide-ranging than those provided in the Indian Constitution. The electoral system has provision for proportional representation for 45 percent of the seats in the House of Representatives. Quotas are provided for women, dalits, Madeshis and janjatis in various constitutional bodies. There are seven provinces and three levels of government – the federal, provincial and local. There are many features of the Constitution which represent an advance over existing democratic Constitutions in South Asia, though there may be some shortcomings too.

One of the clauses in the draft constitution which was opposed vehemently by some sections in Nepal was the definition of Nepal State as secular. The pro-monarchy Rashtriya Prajatantra Party and various other Hindutva outfits organised protests throughout the country demanding that Nepal be declared a Hindu State. The Constituent Assembly rejected this demand overwhelmingly. The RSS and all the Hindutva forces in India campaigned, supported and propped up the forces within Nepal who wanted a Hindu Rashtra. BJP MP Avaidyanath had written to the president of Nepal and the chairman of the Constituent Assembly calling for Nepal to be declared a Hindu Rashtra. Earlier, Rajnath Singh, the union home minister, as a BJP leader had visited Nepal to attend the funeral of then Prime Minister GP Koirala in March 2010. On that occasion he had said "We used to feel proud that Nepal was the only Hindu kingdom in the world. I will be happy when Nepal is a Hindu state again." (IANS, March 22, 2010). The Hindutva organisations from India sent their sadhus and leaders to participate in the campaign for a Hindu Rashtra in Nepal.

The rejection of the demand for a Hindu State and the assertion that Nepal will be a secular republic has outraged the Hindutva forces in India. The BJP shares this anger, though it cannot display it openly. This has probably contributed to the negative stance taken by the Modi government.

The Madhesi people who constitute 50 percent of the population of Nepal may have legitimate grievances. But the Modi government's open stance advocating their cause cannot but be construed as an interference in the internal affairs of a neighbouring country. The Modi government's stance of tacit support to the

Madhesi agitation is also motivated by the Bihar assembly elections where a large number of people in the border districts are linked to the Madhesi people across the border. Such narrow political considerations are also at play in harming relations with Nepal. The government and the political leadership in Nepal will have to consider how to accommodate the aspirations of the Madhesi people. Constitutions are not rigid static documents and changes can be made through the democratic process.

The Modi government's arrogant intervention has only vitiated the good neighbourly relations between the two countries. It will also send a cautionary message to all other countries in South Asia to be wary of India's big brotherly attitude.

NEITHER PEACE NOR CONSTITUTION IN NEPAL

The ongoing Nepalese Peace Process (PP) has been virtually postponed and the deadline for writing the constitution has somehow ended without even the coarse draft of the new constitution being submitted. The Constituent Assembly (CA) and its Government have totally failed to achieve its principle tasks. They are neither able to complete the constitution writing process nor to enforce properly the comprehensive peace accord.

Mainly, the Peace Process was simply destroyed due to the consensual confrontation between the Maoists and the Nepal Government for the integration issues of vieux jeu-Maoist combatants into Nepalese security force. It is comic to mention that both parties agreed to integrate the former Maoist guerrillas into the Nepalese security system but have always been undecided about the number of guerrillas that should integrate and why?

The United Nations Mission in Nepal (UNMIN) is supposed to provide technical support in the peace process, however the role of UNMIN has not been very useful. It has become a burden on the Nepalese Peace Process, and the UN too, because its role pushed the entire process into political polarization and left the parties in the position of confrontation and mayhem due to faulty peace diplomacy. Surprisingly, the Internal and external stakeholders in the Nepalese Peace Process have remained silent on these issues, as they say they consider it an internal matter for the nation. For this reason, the bilateral confrontation on integration affairs has become one of the major hurdles to achieving peace through a comprehensive peace accord.

Unfortunately, the Peace Process is not a true priority on the agenda of the Nepalese political parties, which we can easily see by observing the progress in implementation of the comprehensive peace accord. The Government and the Maoists have failed and wavered from their commitment and duties to carry out the comprehensive peace accord in a systematic manner. There is no political culture of self-examination on their own lapses in performing roles and responsibilities towards the peace process and constitution writing. They deliberately failed to rule and operate the CA, Cabinet and Peace Process through political consensus in a constitutional manner as agreed. Most of the political parties are on a mission to capture the cabinet and seek to extend their powers in multifarious ways as much as possible.

Sadly, the CA has become a huge national burden and just a salary provider for its members. In other words, the CA members are temporary jobholders and it was just strategically created to provide employment for political workers. So we should not have expected any great and historical things like a new constitution for New Nepal and sustainable peace from such people who have not even delivered even the minimum characters, role and performance of CA member. Many People have started to comment that CA is a just crowed of ineligible political citizens who are unaware of the interest of our nation and people. This crowd only care about their individual interests, ignoring the people's mandate and national priority.

CA members must be accountable and should start to refund immediately all received incentives, salary, privileges and facilities to the state. Nepal has no ability to afford such huge administrative and financial expenses against the uncertainty of constitution writing and peace process. They should stop playing with the future and emotions of the people and the nation. The CA members and government have worked against the peace process, mandate of CA election and second peoples' movement.

Woefully, the routine jobs of the Nepalese political parties are to demonstrate and organize strike against the ruling parties and people. The Nepalese politicians and political parties abuse their own proclamations, commitments and public promise and mandates. They feel proud to declare general strikes, transportation halts, gheraos, bandhs, stoning, and other unconstitutional and illegal activities.

Shamefully, they claim that the baleful activities are done on behalf of the people to achieve public and national interests, but ignoring their political future and ethics, they never think about their constructive role and contribution. They just act to oppose everything just because they are in opposition. The mentality and poor attitude of political parties is a major cause of the postponing the Peace Process and barring the nation from a new constitution. The complete comprehensive peace accord in new dimension and new approach through multi-partner-partnership approach since the exiting peace accord and its proper implementation have been proved faulty at many ways i.e. cantonment management, guerrilla integration, political harmonization, disarmament, transitional justice etc., and constitution of various commissions for New Nepal as agreed in CPA and mentioned in the Interim constitution of Nepal.

The existing comprehensive peace accord and the Interim Constitution of Nepal have failed to drive the nation in accordance with the mandate and spirit of CA election and mandate of Janaandolan-2. UNMIN and other national and international stakeholders were in favour of the peace process, so the United Nations, Government of Nepal and the Maoist Party itself must rethink before further extending UNMIN in Nepal.

It is highly risky to continue the expired and defective Comprehensive Peace Accord of Nepal. So, the stakeholders must concentrate on the technical parts of the peace accord especially in the areas that are obstacles in execution of the Peace Accord, while restructuring the accord. Empirical assessment of the activities of the exiting CA assembly has already concluded that the CA model of constitution building is a failure here. The Janaandolan-2 and election efforts of CA were wasted; there are no exemplary products of the existing CA. People do not see any countable respect towards the motto of janaandoalan-2 and institutionalization of its achievement.

It is a pity to see that everything is in transition except the selfishness of the political parties and leaders. The nation is in a state of confrontation, and civil war and riots could start anytime, if the political scenario does not change properly. The impunity, crime, corruption, violence appears to be beyond control. Life, liberty, property, public freedoms and the rights of people are in serious danger. Governance and judicial systems are in disorder. All people should wake up urgently against the corrupt political parties and leaders to force them to dissolve the CA and work in favour of a fresh start for the nation.

Nepalese need a fresh start to begin constitution building process that could be managed by amending provision of the Interim Constitution of Nepal. We cannot be held any longer under the captivity of constitutional uncertainty and transitional state. The people of the nation have no more patience, they cannot wait to get and practice defective pieces and provisions of constitutional and governance products.

The existing CA cannot fulfil their minimum roles and assigned responsibilities, they are just disqualified political workers. Every Nepalese wants to save the nation from political, economical, administrative, judicial and diplomatic failure, otherwise the existing political parties and leaders will collapse the nation for fulfilment of their own political and individual vested interests.

It is a huge challenge for all honest citizens to address the trivialities and contemporary transitional scenario of Nepal, which has arisen due to inefficiency and incapability of the existing CA and Government. In plain language, most of the existing political parties and leaders are great cheaters, who have committed crimes against the nation and the people of Nepal by ignoring the Peace Process and delaying the constitution. Indeed, the CA has victimized the currents generations and will cause problems for future generations too. Our nation is about to collapse politically and financially. It is being listed as failed nation.

Therefore, we must think at least about protection and prevention of our future generations from political deadlocks, they will not excuse us for our deeds if we do not play a constructive and fair role. So, every individual and institutional actor must start to raise productive voices against the criminalized political scenario in Nepal. Let's try to minimize the results of the ongoing political crimes and dilemmas; otherwise we will achieve neither peace nor constitution.

POLITICAL STANDOFF IN NEPAL OVER CONSTITUTION

Political tensions in Nepal are rising as the May 28 deadline for drawing up a new constitution approaches. The fragile ruling coalition is deadlocked in disagreement with the Maoist opposition, the Unified Communist Party of Nepal-Maoist, over a number of key constitutional questions. At the same time, no resolution has been reached over the integration of thousands of former Maoists guerrillas into the country's regular army. In a speech last Thursday in Kathmandu, UN Secretary-General for Political Affairs Lynn Pascoe warned that there was "a sense of deep concern, a fear that Nepal's opportunity for a durable and transformative peace could slip away unless actions are taken urgently to restore momentum". While carefully avoiding the suggestion that renewed civil war was imminent, he said: "Nepal remains suspended at a delicate point along the nation's journey from war to peace."

The so-called peace process followed the eruption of a mass popular movement in April 2006 that brought an end to the autocratic rule of King Gyanendra. The Maoists, who were instrumental in containing the political eruption, signed a deal with the existing establishment parties, including Nepal Congress and the Communist Party of Nepal-UML (CPN-UML), in December 2006 to end their guerrilla war and enter into the political mainstream. The agreement initiated by India was backed by the major powers and the UN, which supervised the disarmament of Maoist fighters and their confinement to camps.

The Maoists won the largest bloc of seats in elections in April 2008—a measure of popular hostility both to the monarchy and the establishment parties. The parliament, which is also functioning as a constituent assembly to draw up a new constitution, formally abolished the monarchy and declared the country to be a "federal democratic republic". The Maoist-led government, however, proved to be short-lived and collapsed last May after a constitutional standoff over its decision to sack the head of the army. The current ruling coalition of 22 parties is headed by the CPN-UML of Prime Minister Madhav Kumar.

Last year's standoff between the Maoist government and General Rookmangud Katawal highlighted the central role of the army, which was the central prop of the monarchy. The army chief repeatedly refused to integrate any of the former Maoists guerrillas. The government's attempt to sack him was overruled by the country's president, and the Maoists quit office in protest. The episode only further strengthened the army's defiance of any attempt to subordinate it to government or parliamentary control. In his comments last week, UN official Pascoe warned that the integration of Maoist guerrillas into society was a key element of the peace process. "Unfortunately, Nepal today still has two armies, and no agreed strategy for what to do about this. Thousands of former Maoist combatants remain in camps that were intended to last only a few months."

However, Pascoe's plea for a resolution was immediately rebuffed by the present army chief, General Chhatraman Singh Gurung, who declared that the former Maoists fighters would not be enlisted "en masse" because it would "divide the security agency on political lines and ultimately disintegrate the country". He said some Maoist cadres could be recruited into the police, the border security force and other non-military agencies, while remainder could be sent overseas to get jobs.

The army is increasingly flexing its political muscle. The *Nepal Telegraph* reported on Monday that the top generals from five districts were due to hold an "emergency meeting" yesterday to "discuss strategies" in the event that "Nepal's political actors fail to draft the constitution on time". The outcome of that meeting was of course to be "kept a guarded secret". The Brussels-based International Crisis Group highlighted the army's "more overt, assertive political role" in a report entitled "Nepal's Future: In Whose Hands?" published last August. Speaking of the army, the report stated: "It is encouraged and supported by many who see it as the only credible opposition to the Maoists. It not only survived the republican transition but has thrived. Helped by timorous [political] parties, it has successfully pushed for a substantial budgetary increase, protected its de facto autonomy, retained its full strength and pressed for new lethal arms imports—in breach of the ceasefire."

The resurgence of the military is also a direct product of the failure of Maoists or the present government to address the pressing social needs of the majority of the population. Amid the global economic crisis, unemployment in the country rose from 42 percent in 2008 to 46 percent in 2009. Nearly 40 percent of the population live below the official poverty line. Conditions in many rural areas are primitive, without access to electricity, clean water and basic health care and education. Far from challenging capitalist rule in Nepal, the Maoists through the 2006 agreement integrated themselves into the capitalist state and, while in government, did everything possible to reassure big business and bolster private profit. Their orientation is the outcome of their reactionary Stalinist "two-stage" theory, which confined political opposition to abolishing the monarchy and put off any struggle for socialism to the "second stage"—that is, to the indefinite future.

The result has been growing popular disaffection with the Maoists, for whom many people voted in 2008 hoping for a better future, and a revival of the political fortunes of right-wing royalists, no doubt backed by the army, who have been quick to exploit the situation. On February 22, the previously marginalised Rastriya Prajatantara Party (RPP) called a strike that paralysed much of Kathmandu to demand a referendum over bringing back the monarchy.

As the deadline for a new constitution draws closer, the political tensions will only increase. Current discussions in the constituent assembly are deadlocked over basic issues, including the type of federal framework and the relationship of the president to parliament. The Maoists have called for a federal structure based on ethnicity, whereas the government coalition supports one based on geographic regions. The Maoists favour an executive presidency, which they think they will win election to, while their opponents back a parliamentary system. The entire debate is driven purely by political expediency, not any concern for the democratic rights of working people. While there is provision in the interim constitution to extend the constituent assembly for another six months, all sides are positioning themselves for a political crisis. While the generals secretly discuss their strategies, the Maoists are warning of a "revolt" if no constitution is drawn up, and denouncing "international conspiracies" against the country—a reference to India in particular. While a renewed guerrilla struggle cannot be ruled out, the Maoist rhetoric is in large measure empty bluster—while speaking of "revolt", the party's main demand is to be included in the ruling coalition.

Political tensions in Kathmandu are only compounded by growing rivalry between the major and regional powers for influence in Nepal—particularly between India and China. Both countries are providing economic aid to Nepal and are courting various political parties and actors, including the military, in a bid to secure their economic and strategic interests. India has long regarded Nepal as being within its sphere of influence, while China is concerned to protect border areas, especially politically sensitive Tibet.

India helped initiate and backed the peace deal in 2006, but never envisaged that the Maoists would win the 2008 election. Relations with the Maoists frayed even further when they whipped up Nepali nationalism by criticising Indian "interference" and forged closer ties with Beijing. New Delhi is also concerned that Maoist political influence in Nepal will encourage various guerrilla insurgencies inside India itself.

As last August's International Crisis Group report explained: "Never able to digest the Maoist [election] victory and uncomfortable with popular demands for change, it [India] has pursued increasingly interventionist tactics through proxies in Nepali political parties while continuing its policy of ring-fencing the army as the most reliable bastion against Maoist takeover or anarchy. Its resolute opposition to all but token People's Liberation Army [Maoist guerrillas] integration has unbalanced the peace equation without offering an alternative."

China, on the other hand, has maintained ties not only with the Maoists but also with the present government and the army. Senior delegations of the Nepali Congress and CPN-UML have been invited to Beijing. It should be recalled that during the country's civil war China had no qualms about supplying the Nepalese army with arms to fight the Maoists. China is particularly sensitive to the activities of Tibetan exiles in Nepal, which could trigger renewed unrest over the border in Tibet itself.

THE CONSTITUTION OF THE KINGDOM OF NEPAL, 1990

The Constitution of the Kingdom of Nepal promulgated in 1990 has been modelled after the West-Minister style of parliamentary form of government, which is highly centralized and exclusionary. Indeed, winner takes all in such a system. Given socio-cultural diversity of the Nepalese society and culture, the Constitution discriminates and excludes minorities in many ways. The Consultative workshop organized by Nepal Federation of Nationalities (NEFEN) with support from Minority Rights Group International (MRG), has identified 26 provisions in the Constitution and 49 legal Acts that discriminates against indigenous nationalities. There are many such provisions that discriminate against other minorities. Also, caste-based untouchability has been made illegal but lack of laws has made it meaningless in practices.

There has been a strong demand for secularism not only by the non-Hindus but also by the Hindu Dalits who have been forced to face caste-based untouchability by their "upper caste" Hindu counterparts. In spite of a fact that Nepal is a multi-religious country and a historical fact that about 150,000 people demonstrated in the streets of Kathmandu, which was the largest gathering ever in the history of Nepal, demanding for secularism, the Constitution of the Kingdom of Nepal, 1990 declared Nepal as a Hindu State, prohibited to form any political parties on the basis of religion. According to the Article (4) of the Constitution, 'Nepal is a multiethnic, multilingual, democratic, independent, indivisible, sovereign, Hindu and Constitutional Monarchical Kingdom.'

Another most discriminatory provision is the distinction between "nation's language" and "national languages." The Constitution declared Nepali language as the only official language. Article 6 of the Constitution states, '(1) The Nepali language in the Devnagari script is the language of the nation of Nepal. The Nepali language shall be the official language. (2) All the languages spoken as the mother tongue in the various parts of Nepal are the national languages of Nepal.'

Article 18 (2) in the Fundamental Rights, the Constitution has restricted the right to education in one's own mother tongue with such restriction, 'Each community shall have the right to operate schools up to the primary level in its own mother tongue for imparting education to its children.' Such a provision restricts the right of education in mother tongues beyond grade five.

Many indigenous nationalities of Nepal have a culture of eating beef ("cow meat"). The National Code of Nepal (Muluki Ain) prohibits killing of cow and the offender gets life sentence. Instead of declaring national animal with full cultural sensitivity, Article 7 (2) of the Constitution declared cow, which is sacred for the Hindus only, as the national animal. Therefore, indigenous nationalities are prohibited to slaughter cow and eat its meat.

A study conducted by the Forum for Women, Law and development (FWLD) in 2000 stated, 'there are 118 Clauses/Section/Rules, two Rules in their entirety, and 67 Schedules/Annexes/Forms in 54 different laws including the Constitution which have discriminatory provisions'. The Constitution and laws discriminate women in every field including citizenship, property, education, employment, health, marriage & family, legal & court proceedings. For example, Article 9 of the Constitution discriminates women thus, '(1) A person who is born after the commencement of this Constitution and whose father is a citizen of Nepal at the birth of the child shall be a citizen of Nepal by descent. (2) Every child who is found in within the Kingdom of Nepal and the whereabouts of whose parents are not known shall, until the father of the child is traced, be deemed to be a citizen of Nepal by descent.'

Forms and Origins of Discrimination

There are several historical markers of domination and discrimination against indigenous nationalities and other minorities in Nepal. These are as follows:

The main historical marker of Hindu domination begins with caste restructuring by King Jayasthiti Malla in the Kathmandu Valley in the fourteenth century. The King invited five Brahmin priests from India to Kathmandu. Based on their advice, the King restructured the Newars, the indigenous nationalities of the Kathmandu Valley, into 64 castes based on occupational division of labour. These caste divisions were neither based on hierarchic Hindu varna model, that is, Brahmin at the top followed by Kshyatriya, Vaisya and Sudra at the bottom, nor on inscription. It indeed paved a way for intensification of the processes of Hinduization or Sanskritization of indigenous nationalities of Nepal.

The second historical marker of Hindu Bahun-Chhetri domination is the conspiratorial attack against the Magar King of Lig-Lig Kot by King Drabya Shah, who later won a war against the Khadka King of Gorkha in 1559 A.D.. This was the beginning of the downfall of independence of indigenous nationalities in Nepal.

The third historical marker of continuing Hindu Bahun-Chhetri domination is the territorial "unification" of Nepal in 1769 by King Prithvinaryan Shah. Prior to 1769, indigenous nationalities had their own rule in their respective traditional homelands. King Prithvinarayn Shah annexed small but independent kingdoms, "22 and 24 principalities," of different indigenous nationalities either through defeat in war or through mutual agreement of autonomy within the centralized state. After the defeat of Kirtipur in the Kathmandu Valley, King Prithvinaryan Shah ordered to chop off nose tips and ear of the peoples of Kirtipur that weighed 18 dharnis, i.e. about 8 kilos. Thus, one can imagine the extent of brutal physical violence and humiliation to minorities and indigenous nationalities under the sword of Prithvinarayan Shah. The King accepted that Nepal is a country 'a garden of four castes and thirty-six varna' but his mission was to make Nepal a "real India" ("*Asali Hindustan*"). The main consequence of the "territorial unification" was that all indigenous nationalities lost their independence and gradually lost their rights to land, water, forests, mines, rivers and pastures. Thus, indigenous nationalities began to loose their language, religion, culture and indigenous knowledge system.

The fourth historical marker is the Muluki Ain (National Code of Nepal) of 1854 implemented by Junga Bahadur Rana, the founder Prime Minister of 104-years of autocratic Rana rule. The National Code, the first ever codified law applicable in all parts of Nepal, restructured caste and ethnic groups and divided them into fourfold social hierarchy. The Tagadhari (sacred thread wearing or twice-born) caste was the top, followed by the Matawali ("alcohol drinking castes"). They were sub-divided into namasine (enslavable) and masine (slavable) groups. Although, indigenous nationalities never belonged to Hindu social hierarchy but the Rana ruler legally included them in the second in the hierarchy as "alcohol drinking caste." Pani nachalne chhoee chhito halnu naparne (impure but touchable castes) were third and pani nachalne chhoee chhito halnu parne (impure and untouchable castes) belonged to the bottom of the social hierarchy. The whole National Code, including the punishments was based on caste discrimination. Thus during the 104-years of Rana rule, indigenous nationalities of Nepal were Hinduized and Sanskritized. As its consequences, many indigenous nationalities began to loose their language, religion and culture. The most devastating events in this period was confiscation of traditional Kipat land tenure and re-distribution of land to state elites, i.e. Bahun, Chhetri, Rana and Thakuri, through Birta and Jagir land tenures and exploitation of Indigenous Nationalities and Dalits through forced free labour such as jahra, rakam, beth and beggar. The Rana rulers prevented Tamangs, one of the Indigenous Nationalities of Nepal, from joining British-India Army and any government jobs in Nepal, except as Pipa (porter) in Pipa Goswara office in Singha Durbar.

During the Partyless Panchayat rule from 1960-90 under the direct and active rule of King Mahendra and King Birendra, the rulers launched a campaign of "One King, One Country; One Language, One Dress." The project of "melting pot" was intensified in a country characterized by "salad bowl" of caste, ethnicity, language, religion, culture and region. Any organized effort to preserve and promote indigenous nationalities' language, religion and culture was charged as "anti-King," "anti-constitution," "anti-national," and "communal." Also, caste-based untouchability was abolished in the revised National Code of 1963 but due to lack of necessary laws, its practice continues unabated. The People's Movement of 1990, following the pro-democracy wave in the Soviet Union, eastern-European countries, and other parts of the world, jointly organized by the Nepali Congress Party and the United Left Front, including the Nepal Communist Party (Marxist-Leninist), demolished the autocratic partyless Panchayat political system and restored democracy in Nepal. It raised a lot of hope and expectation to reduce socio-cultural and political inequalities. The hope remained unfulfilled.

Finally, the Maoist "People's War" that started in February 1996 has brought the issues of indigenous nationalities, Dalits, women and other minority groups to the forefront. The government security forces tend to treat them with hostility as potential "terrorist."

Indigenous Nationalities & Minorities

Although there is commonality among different minority groups in Nepal, that is, all of them are discriminated due to the dominance of Brahmanistic ideology, policy and practices. This is, however, manifested in somewhat different forms with similar and/or different consequences among different minority groups. Common contested prime issues of all minorities are elimination of all forms of domination and discrimination, secularism, affirmative action, representation in decision-making positions, and factual census data. Nevertheless, there are some issues very specific to each of the minority groups. This section will analyse the contested prime issues of indigenous nationalities, Dalits, linguistic groups, religious groups, Madhesi and women. They all have raised their respective issues in a peaceful way through interaction programs, seminars, workshops, conferences, press release, memorandum, street demonstration, publications and so on. These all groups are never tired of making demands with His Majesty's Government of Nepal but the latter hardly hear these voices and raise frustration of these right-based activists. If HMG-N and donors do not hear these voices, Nepal will be entangled in disastrous civil war sooner or later.

Indigenous nationalities: Indigenous nationalities and other minorities are against domination, subjugation, suppression, oppression, depression, compression, exploitation, monopoly etc. by dominant castes (Bahun-Chhetri), religion (Hindu), language (Nepali) and culture (Hindu), sex (male), region (the Kathmandu Valley). They all are against all forms of discrimination. They are indeed for inclusive democracy through elimination of Bahunism (Brahminism); land rights; right-to-self determination; federalism; proportional representation; secularism; caste/ethnic; linguistic, religious, gender, regional and cultural equality; mainstreaming caste/ethnicity, language, religion, gender, and region; empowerment of caste/ethnic, linguistic, religious, gender, regional and cultural groups; and effective implementation of international instruments of human rights, including indigenous nationalities right, minority rights and women's rights.

Before 1990, demands of organized indigenous nationalities were branded as "anti-national," "anti-King," "anti-political system," "anti-constitution," "divisive," and "secessionist" by the dominant group. Although, the Tharu had formed the Tharu Kalyankari Sabha in 1950 and the Tamang and the Thakali also formed their own organizations, these organizations were confined to purely cultural activities only. It was the Newar of the Kathmandu Valley who raised their voice for language rights since the time of the autocratic Rana rule and they intensified their demand during the autocratic partyless Panchayat rule. Some indigenous nationalities made efforts during late 1970s to form a federation of different indigenous nationalities, such as the SETAMAGURALI, but the rulers suppressed any such effort. After the people's movement and the restoration of democracy in 1990, those indigenous nationalities who were already organized intensified their efforts and unorganized ones also began to organize.

Such a hopeless situation changed after the people's movement of 1990 that overthrew the autocratic partyless Panchayat political system, which was based on the active leadership of the King. The Constitution of the Kingdom of Nepal, 1990 declared, in its preamble, that human rights, freedom and equality will be guaranteed through the parliamentary form of government, constitutional monarchy and multi-party democracy. Although the Constitution accepted Nepal as a multi-caste/ethnic country but also it declared Nepal as a Hindu kingdom and Nepali language as the only official language of the country. Unfortunately, during the first half of the last twelve years, any organized efforts or their demands were labelled as "communal," "secessionist," "disintegrative" etc. by the dominant group. Despite of negative perception of the dominant group, indigenous nationalities expanded and intensified their movement for equal rights since 1990, the dominant group was forced to accept, since mid-nineties, that indigenous nationalities have been indeed discriminated by the State in the last two and a quarter centuries. Till now indigenous nationalities are against the domination of Bahun-Chhteris. They are against them in many issues. They, therefore, have been demanding for equity and equality.

Dalits: Although the term "Dalit" is still controversial, however, the Dalit leaders and their organizations have now accepted to identify their community by this term not to loose its historical, ideological, social, cultural and political contexts. In the past, Dalits were referred by several terms including "untouchables," "Sudra," "pariganit," "water unacceptable caste," and "Harijan" ("god's people"). The New National Code of 1963 abolished caste-based untouchability, but due to lack of laws, its practices continue unabated. A recent study conducted by Bhattachan *et al.* (2001) revealed at least 205 different forms of caste-based untouchability are practiced in different parts of Nepal. Another study conducted by Dahal *et al.* (2002) revealed that Dalits are marginalized in every field due to caste-based discrimination.

In spite of Dalits being Hindus and Nepal being the only Hindu kingdom in the world, Hindu "high caste" peoples continue to treat Dalits very inhumanly as untouchable peoples. Practices of untouchability exist not only between the Dalit and non-Dalit but also within the Dalits, between "high caste" and "low caste" Dalits. For example, Kami is at the top of the social hierarchy, followed by Sarki, Damai and at the bottom are the Dom. Such practices were legally enforced by the National Code of 1854. Therefore, it is not a creation of the Dalit community as such. Similarly, some Hinduized or Sanskritized indigenous nationalities also practice caste-based untouchabilty because of the same Code.

The National Code of 1854 placed Dalits in the third and last in the four-fold social hierarchy as untouchables and the whole legal system discriminated on the bases of castes, Dalits were oppressed and suppressed in every sphere. They were not able to get organized and raise their voice until mid-1940s. It was, the Kapalis of Kathmandu Valley initiated Dalit movement with a demand for entry in Hindu temples, including the temple of Pashupatinath in Kathmandu. Since then other Hill Dalits, particularly, Blacksmith and Tailor (Damai or Pariyar) intensified the Dalit movement with demands for elimination of all forms of caste-based unotuchability. By now, the Hill Dalits, particularly, Kami, Sarki and Damai are better organized and other Hill Dalits and Madhesi Dalits are yet to get organized and intensify the Dalit movement. As an exception, recent Chamar movement in Siraha was very powerful and successful in their struggle against caste-based untouchability.

Linguistic Minorities: Among the linguistic minorities, the Nepal Bhasa speaking Newars have been in the front line of equal language right movements since the time of autocratic Rana rule. The Madhesis, who have their own mother tongues, also intensified the movement for equal language rights since the dawn of democracy in 1950. HMG-N's following language policy adopted in 1956 was nothing but a predatory for mother tongues ,

'Nepali should be the medium of instruction, exclusively from the third grade on, and as much as possible in the first two grades.

No other languages should be taught, even optionally, in the primary school because: few children will have need for them, they would hinder the teaching of Nepali. ...'

This policy was pursued vigorously during the partyless Panchayat rule from 1960 to 1990. The Newars, with support of other indigenous nationalities continued to intensify the language movement but the dominant group branded such efforts as "anti-national," "communal," "anti-constitutional" and "secessionist".

The movement received legitimacy after the promulgation of the Constitution of the Kingdom of Nepal, 1990, which accepted Nepal as a multi-lingual country but unfortunately, differentiated between nation's language and national languages and declared Nepali as the only official language of Nepal. Thus, the new Constitution worked as catalysis of struggle for equal language rights. Due to mounting pressure from the equal language rights, HMG-N set up the National Languages Policy Recommendation Commission in 1993. The government did not implement the recommendations made by the Commission but as a window dressing, the government set-up a committee to identify the languages in which news could be broadcasted from the government owned Radio Nepal. Initially, five-minutes news was broadcasted in nine languages and now it is broadcasted in 16 languages, including Sanskrit. Equal language rights activists have been denouncing that the government's negative attitude towards mother tongues is exhibited by giving priority to Sanskrit, a dead language, against other live languages.

The Local Self-Government Act of 1998 gave rights to local bodies, DDCs, VDCs and Municipalities to preserve and promote national languages. In the course of its implementation, Kathmandu Municipality, Rajbiraj Municipality and Dhanusha DDC decided that Nepal Bhasa (Newari language) will be used as an additional official language and Rajbiraj Municipality and Dhanusha DDC decided that Maithil language will be used as an additional official language in their respective local bodies. Later, in a writ petition against the use of national languages as official languages, the Supreme Court of Nepal made a ruling on June 1, 1999 that none of the government bodies, including local government bodies, must use Khasa/Nepali language as the only official language. Protesting against such court decision, equal language right activists closed down the Kathmandu Valley for one day and since then

Language discrimination has deprived mother tongue speakers from education, including under Basic and Primary Education Project (BPEP) and being literate, right to information, and right to development. As a consequence, they are deprived from getting scholarship for higher education abroad and passing examination taken by Public service Commission for various gazetted and non-gazetted civil service posts.

Religious Minorities: Given the out of proportion representation of Hindus in executive, legislature and judiciary and also in media, minority religious groups, including Kirants, Buddhists, Islams and Christians, have been systematically marginalized by the dominant Hindu religious group. All these minority religious groups are against Hindu domination but some religious groups, particularly Kirants and Buddhists are vocal critics whereas other groups such as Islams and Christians are in defensive posture due to fear of backlash from the Hindus.

Although, political leaders, policy makers, planners, development practitioners etc. never get tired of saying that Nepal is characterized by religious harmony, the reality is entirely different. It is true that in the past, different religious groups have not resorted to violence and insurgency but it does not mean that there were no incidences of communal clashes at different places in different times. For example, there were several cases of Hindu-Muslim clashes in some Terai districts, including Banke, Rautahat and Kapilvastu. In such clashes, often referred as "communal clashes," the local administrators, security personnel and political leaders, who mostly belong to dominant Hindus, organize meetings involving all groups and find out solutions, which invariably favours the Hindus.

Another example of Hindu-Buddhist conflict was the so-called "Hindu-Buddhist unity conference" organized by the Hindus in Lumbini in the year 2000.

Madhesi: Madhesis have been treated as second-class citizens after the territorial integration of Nepal by King Prithvinaryan Shah in 1769. During the autocratic Rana rule, Madhesis were required to obtain visa to visit the Kathmandu Valley. Madhesi representation in Army, civil service, judiciary is negligible but their representation in cabinet, Parliament, and political parties is low. Due to marginalization of Madhesi by the dominant caste, they formed the Nepal Sadavabana Party, a region-based political party and formed coalition government time and again. In the last twelve years of democracy, all political parties, including the Sadvabana Party failed to address the fundamental problems facing the Madhesi community. Many Madhesis, therefore, formed the Madhesi Liberation Front as a wing of the Nepal Communist Party (Maoist), who is waging an insurgency for the lat seven years. Madhesi movement as a social movement is between the political party and liberation front. They are mainly against Khasa-Brahmanism. They are for regional autonomy.

Often Madhesi are wrongly stereotyped as "Indians" by the Hill people. They are as Nepalese as any other Nepalese people. Due to centuries of suppression and oppression against Madhesis, they generally shy away from speaking out loudly against such practices. However, the communal tension between the Hill peoples and Madhesis that broke out for few days in December of 2001 indicated that the bond that ties between the Hill people and Madhesi are very fragile and that Madhesi have courage to speak out against suppression and oppression against them.

Women

Women comprise a little more than a half of the total 22.3 million population of Nepal. The Nepalese women are not a homogenous group. Instead, it is characterized by diversity in terms of race, caste, ethnicity, language, religion, culture, and region. All Nepalese women are victims of gender discrimination but the nature, forms, degree and intensity differs among different caste/ethnic, religious and cultural groups. Therefore, some Nepalese women are victimized more than other women. The so-called high caste women of the Hills are single victim of gender discrimination but of the Madhes (Terai region) are victims of gender and regional discrimination. Similarly, women belonging to indigenous nationalities are multiple victims, one from gender discrimination and other from ethnic, linguistic, cultural and religious discrimination. Hill Dalit women are victims of gender and caste-based discrimination but Madhesi Dalit women are additional victims of regional, cultural and linguistic discrimination.

The extreme forms of gender discrimination are found among the Hindus whose society is characterized by patriarchy. Hindu women have no access to and control over property and have restricted mobility. They are dependent to men throughout their life, that is, daughters are dependent to fathers, wives to husbands and mothers to sons. In contrast, women belonging to indigenous nationalities have relatively more freedom, social mobility, access to and control over resources than their Hindu counterpart, but they are underrepresented not only in women's rights movement but also in public positions as the latter dominate them.

Women's rights movement has a history of about five decades. The movement has been dominated mainly by women belonging to the dominant Bahun-Chhetri castes and the Hinduized Newar women. To assert their due place in both the women's rights movement and the national development, indigenous women have formed their organizations and federated in National Indigenous Women's federation (NIWF) and Dalit women have formed Feminist Dalit Organization (FEDO). Among the minorities, international donors have been giving support, both technical and financial, to women's movement and women's empowerment since the seventies in the names of Women in Development (WID), Women and Development (WAD) and Gender and Development (GAD). In the seventies and eighties, women's movement was more focused on income generation but since the nineties its focus is on rights-based movement. The Nepalese women are against all forms of discrimination against women. They are indeed for gender equity and equality.

Violence on Indigenous Nationalities & Minorities

Till now there has been no caste or ethnic, linguistic and religious insurgency in Nepal in the past but now there is such possibility. The Nepal Communist Party (Maoist) has been waging a Maoist insurgency in the form of "People's War" since February 13, 1996 with support of different minorities—women, Dalits, indigenous nationalities and Madhesi. It has been primarily a class based internal (civil) war but interestingly class has been blended with caste/ethnic, regional and gender components. The rationale for the "People's War" given by the Maoist are twofold: one, stop imperialism and expansionism of the external forces and two, eliminate internal social and spatial contradictions of a semi-feudal political-economic system.

The immediate reason for the birth of insurgency appeared to be the failure of HMG-N led by Prime Minister Sher Bahadur Deuba of Nepali Congress Party to address 40-points demands submitted to be as a memorandum. However, the main reasons for the rise of insurgency include lack of decentralization of power and authority, rising corruption, nepotism and favouritism, lack of democratic culture in political parties, poverty, failure of foreign aid to address the burning issues of the peoples at the grassroots level, and soicocultural discrimination against Indigenous Nationalities, Dalits, Madhesi, and linguistic, religious and regional groups.

OTHER FEATURES OF THE CONSTITUTION

The constitution guarantees the citizens' unfettered rights to political pluralism and a multiparty democracy. All legitimate political organizations or parties that register with the Election Commission are allowed to publicize and broadcast for the purpose of securing support and cooperation of the general public toward their objectives and programs. Any law, arrangement, or decision that restricts any of these activities is inconsistent with the constitution and void. Any law, arrangement, or decision to impose a one-party system is also inconsistent with the constitution and void. Under the section on political organization, any political party is not eligible for registration if it discriminates, if at least 5 percent of its candidates are not women, or if it fails to obtain at least 3 percent of the total votes cast in the previous election to the House of Representatives. The constitution may be amended or repealed by a majority of two-thirds in each house of Parliament. However, such amendment or repeals may not be designed to frustrate the spirit of the preamble of the constitution, which recognizes the Nepalese people as the source of sovereign authority. After passing in both houses, any bill to repeal or amend the constitution must receive royal assent.

The Executive

Executive powers are vested in the king and the Council of Ministers—a prime minister, deputy prime minister, and other ministers as required. The direction, supervision, and conduct of the general administration of the country are the responsibility of the Council of Ministers. All transactions made in the name of the king, except those within his exclusive domain, are authenticated by the Council of Ministers. The king appoints the leader of the political party commanding a majority in the House of Representatives as prime minister. If a single party does not have a majority in the house, the member commanding a majority on the basis of two or more parties is asked to form the government. When this alternative also is not possible, the king may ask the leader of a party holding the largest number of seats in the house to form the government. In this case, the leader forming the government must obtain a vote of confidence in the house within thirty days. If a vote of no confidence is obtained, the king will dissolve the house and order new elections within six months. Other ministers are appointed by the king from members of Parliament on the recommendation of the prime minister.

The constitution declares the king the symbol of the nation and the unity of its people. Expenditures and privileges of the king and royal family are determined by law. The king is obliged to obey and protect the constitution. Although, as in previous constitutions the monarch remains the supreme commander of the Royal Nepal Army, a three-member National Defence Council, headed by the prime minister, commands the military.

Nonetheless, the king retains his power over the army because if there were a threat to sovereignty, indivisibility, or security because of war, foreign aggression, armed revolt, or extreme economic depression, he could declare a state of emergency. During the period of emergency—which would have to be approved by the House of Representatives within three months and which would remain in effect for six months from the date of its announcement, renewable for six months—fundamental rights, with the exception of the right of habeas corpus, could be suspended.

Additional prerogatives of the king include the power to grant pardons; suspend, commute, or remit any sentence passed by any court; confer titles, honours, or decorations of the kingdom; appoint all ambassadors and emissaries for the kingdom; and remove any barriers to enforcing the constitution. The king also nominates the members of the Raj Parishad (King's Council), the body that determines the accession to the throne of the heir apparent.

The Legislature

The constitution provides for a bicameral legislature, the Parliament. This body consists of the king and two houses, the House of Representatives (Pratinidhi Sabha) and the National Council (Rashtriya Sabha). The House of Representatives has 205 directly elected members.

The term for the House of Representatives is five years unless it dissolves earlier, pursuant to the provisions of the constitution. On the recommendation of the prime minister, the king may dissolve the house, but new elections must be held within six months.

Administrative districts are the election districts; and each district's allocation of seats is proportional to its population. All persons eighteen years or older are enfranchised.

The National Council has sixty members consisting of ten nominees of the king; thirty-five members, including at least three women, to be elected by the House of Representatives by means of a single transferable vote, pursuant to the system of proportional representation; and fifteen members to be elected by the electoral college comprising the voters, including the chair and deputy chair of the village and town and district committees of various development regions. The National Council is a permanent body; onethird of its members must retire every two years. Council members serve six-year terms.

With the exception of finance bills, introduced only in the House of Representatives, bills may be introduced in either house. All bills, however, must be passed by both houses before receiving royal assent. When a bill is rejected by the National Council, the House of Representatives has the overriding authority. If the joint session of Parliament receives and passes a bill that the king returned for reconsideration, it receives royal assent within thirty days. The king may, when both the Houses of Parliament are not in session, promulgate ordinances, which are not effective unless approved by both the houses when reconvened. Financial procedures are outlined in part ten of the constitution, which states that taxes cannot be levied or loans raised except in accordance with the law.

The Judiciary

An independent judiciary, unencumbered by the executive branch of the government and palace interference, was a stated goal of all political parties. Of the many changes which have taken place since the fall of the Ranas in 1951, among the most striking have been the growing autonomy of the courts and the gradual liberalization of many basic judicial principles. Despite major improvements, however, the judicial system has suffered from serious impediments in providing speedy, expeditious, and equal justice. The independence and integrity of the judiciary were repeatedly questioned in the press; intervention of political figures and government officials in the judicial process was a frequent occurrence; and caste and economic status were important determinants of the availability of justice.

The court system formerly was one of many instruments used by the prime minister to maintain the authoritarian rule of the Rana family, and the concepts of law it applied were arbitrary, punitive, and oppressive. After an initial attempt to keep the judiciary subordinate when the monarchy was restored, it was allowed to become a relatively independent branch of government. Reforms in the legal system rendered both substantive and procedural law progressively more systematic. Never clearly demarcated, the jurisdiction of the courts became further complicated with the introduction of the *panchayat* system, which at the local level exercised some quasijudicial functions. Therefore, the fundamental role of the judiciary and its position within the government became a subject of national focus during the prodemocracy movement. According to the constitution, the courts comprise three tiers: the Supreme Court, appellate courts, and district courts. In addition, courts or tribunals may be constituted for the purpose of hearing special types of cases.

The Supreme Court is the highest court. All other courts and institutions exercising judicial powers, except the military courts, are under its jurisdiction. The Supreme Court has the authority to inspect, supervise, and give directives to all subordinate courts and all other institutions that exercise judicial powers. The Supreme Court has both original and appellate jurisdiction and consists of a chief justice and fourteen other judges. The chief justice is appointed on the recommendation of the Constitutional Council. Other judges of the Supreme Court, appellate courts, and district courts are appointed on the recommendation of the Judicial Council.

All appointments are made by the king. The tenure of office of the chief justice is limited to seven years from the date of appointment. Supreme Court justices can be impeached in the House of Representatives for reasons of incapacity, misbehaviour, or malafide acts while in office. The Judicial Council, presided over by the chief justice of the Supreme Court, makes recommendations and advises on appointments, transfers, and disciplinary actions of the judges and other matters relating to judicial administration.

All appointments, promotions, transfers, and disciplinary actions of the judges of the appellate and district courts are under the jurisdiction of the Judicial Council. An independent Judicial Service Commission, appointed by the king, and with the chief justice of the Supreme Court serving as ex-officio chairman, appoints, transfers, promotes, and provides departmental punishment of the gazetted officers of the civil service.

An Abuse of Authority Investigating Commission is empowered to investigate the misuse of authority or corruption by public officials. Members of the commission have no specific party affiliation and are appointed by the king on the recommendation of the Constitutional Council.

The Supreme Court is the supreme judicial authority of the nation. All orders and decisions made by the court are binding. Any interpretation of a law or any legal principle laid down by the court is binding on all, including the king.

As a guarantor of personal liberty and fundamental rights conferred by the constitution, the Supreme Court has the authority to declare a law as void ab initio if it finds that the impugned law contravenes the provisions of the constitution. The Supreme Court also has the power to issue appropriate orders and writs, including habeas corpus, mandamus, certiorari, prohibition, and quo warranto.

The Civil Service

The Nepal Civil Service Act, passed in 1956, classified all civil employees of the government into two categories—gazetted services and nongazetted services. Gazetted services included all services prescribed by the government by notification in the *Nepal Raj Patra,* the government gazette. In 1991 categories of the gazetted services were education, judicial, health, administrative, engineering, forest, agricultural, and miscellaneous services. The gazetted posts were further grouped into classes I, II, and III. Nongazetted posts also had several class echelons. As of 1990, there were approximately 80,000 civil service employees in all ranks.

According to the 1990 constitution, all members of the civil service are recruited through an open competitive examination conducted by the Public Service Commission. Police and military officers are excluded from the jurisdiction of the commission. The chairman and other members of the commission are appointed by the king on the recommendation of the Constitutional Council. The commission must be consulted in all matters concerning laws relating to the civil service—such as appointment, promotion, transfer, or departmental punishment. Tenure, benefits, and postings were regulated by the Nepal Civil Service Act of 1956.

The Administrative System

The *panchayat* system represented "democracy at the grassroots," and until April 1990 it included four integrated levels: local or village, district, zonal, and national—the Rashtriya Panchayat. Only the village *panchayat* was directly elected by the people. Championing *panchayat* rule as a political system, king Mahendra was able to tap into nascent Nepalese nationalism and also to outmaneuver the evolving political parties which had posed a challenge to the monarchy's vested power.

The country was divided into fourteen zones and seventy-five districts in support of the complex hierarchy of the *panchayat* system. The lowest unit of government was the *gaun panchayat* (village committee or council), of which there were 3,524. A locality with a population of more than 10,000 persons was organized as a *nagar panchayat* (town committee or council). The number of *nagar panchayat* varied from zone to zone. Above the *gaun panchayat* and *nagar panchayat* was the district *panchayat*, of which there were seventyfive. At the apex of the *panchayat* system was the Rashtriya Panchayat, which served as the unicameral national legislature from 1962 until 1990.

The district *panchayat* had broad powers for supervising and coordinating the development programs of the village and carried out development projects through the district development boards and centers. Each of the seventy-five districts was headed by a chief district officer, who was an elected official, responsible for maintaining law and order, and for coordinating the work of the field agencies of the various ministries.

The zonal *panchayat* was responsible for implementing development plans forwarded by the central government, formulating and executing programs of its own, and planning, supervising, and coordinating district development programs within its jurisdiction. Zonal commissioners exercised full administrative and quasijudicial powers. Each zone was administered by a zonal commissioner and one or two assistant zonal commissioners, all directly appointed by the king. Zones and districts were further regrouped into five development zones in 1971-72, an administrative division that remained in effect in

1991. A drive for political liberalization, which had begun shortly after the 1959 constitution was abrogated and all political activities were banned in 1960, did not climax until the prodemocracy movement of 1990. At that point, ongoing debilitating interparty conflicts and halting demands for reforms of the political system ended, and national energy focused on a movement to achieve democratic rights. During the prodemocracy movement, some of the *pancha* (*panchayat* members) loyalists even were openly friendly with their former adversaries.

The interim government that was installed in April 1990 consisted of strange bedfellows, who, however, succeeded in steering the nation to its first free and fair elections in thirtytwo years. In April 1990, the *nagar panchayat* was renamed *nagar polika* (municipal development committee), and the *gaun panchayat* became *gaun bikas samiti*, or village development committee. The Ministry of Local Development posted an officer to each district to help with the various programs of the development committees. In mid-1991, a Nepali Congress Party government was in power, and a conglomerate of communist parties was playing the role of constitutional opposition. At that time, there were 4,015 village development committees and thirty-three municipal development committees. Elections for the heads of the development committees were scheduled for June 1992.

The Panchayat System

For centuries the government had been run by a number of interrelated aristocratic families. Despite the limitations of a royal ban on political parties and other impediments, political parties did exist and operated clandestinely. To escape harassment or imprisonment, many political leaders went to India, where they also received logistical and other support.

Under the *panchayat* system, there were six government-sponsored class and professional organizations for peasants, laborers, students, women, former military personnel, and college graduates. These organizations were substitutes for the prohibited political parties and provided alternate channels for the articulation of group or class—rather than national—interests. The professional and class organizations were warned repeatedly against engaging in political activity; nevertheless, they offered the only political forum open to many Nepalese, and even some Nepali Congress Party and communist partisans considered them worthy of infiltration.

The king also launched an independent national student association, the National Independent Student Council (Rashtriya Swatantra Vidyarthi Parishad), to control the political activities of the students. The association failed to gain support, and successful student agitation in 1979 forced the king not only to abolish it but also to initiate constitutional reforms leading to the national referendum of 1980. Also in 1980, a group of dissident *pancha* brought a no-confidence motion against Prime Minister Surya Bahadur Thapa on charges of bureaucratic corruption, food shortages, and lack of economic discipline. Surya Bahadur, however, was a perennial political survivor and was returned to office in 1981.

King Birendra devised the Back-to-the-Village National Campaign (BVNC) in 1975. The BVNC was intended to circumvent the possibility of opposition within the *panchayat* and to create a loyal core of elites to select and endorse candidates for political office, thereby neutralizing the influence of underground political party organizers in the rural areas. Although it was envisioned as a means to mobilize the people for the implementation of development plans and projects, the shortlived BVNC—it was suspended in 1979—was in reality an ideological campaign to reinforce the importance of the partyless system. The campaign stressed that the partyless system was appropriate to the ways of the Nepalese people; the party system was a divisive and culturally alien institution.

Each zonal committee had a BVNC structure, with a secretary nominated by the king. The BVNC network was extended to the district and village levels so as to reinforce a national communication system. However inasmuch as the government paid the BVNC central and zonal committee members and restricted chances for popular participation, the committees carried out the same activities as the *panchayat*. In actuality, the BVNC was created by the king to ensure a loyal organization and circumvent active party members from gaining seats in the *panchayat* elections. The BVNC became an organization of centrally controlled loyal *panchayat* elites and an insurance policy for palace initiatives.

The only significant opposition to the monarchy came from the Nepali Congress Party, which operated from exile in India. Other parties either accepted and operated within the *panchayat* system on a supposedly nonpartisan basis or merged with the exiled Nepali Congress Party, polarizing politics over the issue of monarchical rule. Even the Communist Party of Nepal, divided on the tactical question of whether to seek the direct and immediate overthrow of the monarchical system or to work within it, had split into factions—a radical wing operated in India and a moderate wing underground in Nepal. Some party members, to gain tactical advantage over the Nepali Congress Party, entered the *panchayat* system with the tacit approval of the palace.

Ethnic plurality, income disparity, linguistic diversity, pervading regional loyalties, underdeveloped communications, and a paucity of written and electronic media also hindered party organization. The dominant high-caste political leaders were more interested in sharing or gaining access to power than in developing lasting foundations for party politics.

Reportedly, before political organizations were banned, there were sixty-nine political parties, most of which were characteristically fluid in their membership and inconsistent in their loyalties. Personalities rather than ideologies brought individuals and groups under the nominal canopy of a party. Fragmentation, recombination, and alliances for convenience were the outstanding aspects of party behaviour.

In the polarized political climate, the monarchy looked at the *panchayat* system as its only dependable support base. The*panchayat* apparatus provided access for politically motivated individuals to form a new elite. Although the political leadership and following of the Nepali Congress Party initially stayed away from the *panchayat* system, over time, and in the absence of an outlet for political activities, some defections took place. Nevertheless, the lateral entry of some pro-Nepali Congress Party elements did not substantially change the character of the *panchayat* leadership, which was dominated by rural elites of the Hill Region rather than the urban Kathmandu and Tarai Region elites who had been in the forefront of political activities.

The system was designed so that the established parties would gradually shrink and lose their influence and control. Once the new *panchayat* leadership matured, however, some members became restive under the excessive control of the palace. This group of the *panchayat* elite opposed the system from within and overtly joined the prodemocracy movement.

In the last four decades, there was significant progress towards democracy in Nepal's traditionally authoritarian political system. The first national elections in Nepal took place in 1959— some eight years after the overthrow of the Rana system.

The Nepali Congress Party-dominated government, victorious in the 1959 parliamentary elections, was overthrown by King Mahendra within two years—resulting in the ban on political parties. The pattern that developed over the following decades was that of a monarchy reinforcing its power through the traditional institution of the *panchayat*.

The *panchayat* system, co-opted and easily manipulated by the monarchy to suit its political ends, nevertheless was slowly but steadily subjected to pressures to change.

Over time the monarchy was forced by necessity to expand the role of elections in response to the mounting discontent of a citizenry living in an age of heightened political awareness and rising expectations. This trend culminated in May 1991 with the first truly free elections in over thirty years, ushering in a new political era. The Nepali Congress Party obtained a workable majority within the framework of a constitutional monarchy and affirmed the rise of a nascent democratic force.

One of the ramifications of the prodemocracy movement was the beginning of a process of integration in national politics and decision making. With an elected Parliament and demands for an equitable allocation of resources to different regions, it was likely that all regions would compete for equality in national politics and that the monopoly of power by select families would erode, as would the excessive influence of the Kathmandu Valley Brahman, Chhetri, and Newar elites. At the beginning of 1990, the *panchayat* system still dominated Nepal.

Although the institution itself was the object of derision from opponents of the *panchayat* system, it appeared unthreatened. Within a few months, however, its position eroded and then crumbled with bewildering speed. The surge of the successful prodemocracy movement sweeping Eastern Europe, parts of the Soviet Union, and several Asian countries profoundly inspired the Nepalese people.

Also contributing to the sudden transformation were the economic woes of Nepal, exacerbated by India's refusal to renew a trade and transit agreement; widespread bureaucratic inefficiency and corruption at all levels of government; the misgivings openly expressed by the international donors over the country's inefficient use of aid; and a deplorable record on human rights. In January 1990, the Nepali Congress Party held its first national convention in thirty years in Kathmandu.

It was well attended by party delegates from all districts and observers from all political parties. Also present was a multiparty delegation from India, headed by Janata Dal (People's Party) leader Chandra Shekhar, who subsequently became Indian's prime minister. The Nepali Congress Party cooperated with the United Left Front parties, a coalition of seven communist factions, in a joint program to replace the *panchayat* system with a multiparty political system and launched the Movement for the Restoration of Democracy, or prodemocracy movement.

Beginning on February 18, 1990—the thirty-ninth anniversary of King Tribhuvan's declaration of a multiparty democracy and the thirtieth anniversary of the antidemocratic usurpation of power by the palace—a series of spontaneous and sometimes turbulent mass demonstrations rocked major cities. People took to the streets to demand the restoration of a multiparty democracy, human rights, and fundamental freedoms.

The success of the Kathmandu *bandh* (general strike) by prodemocracy forces on March 2 was repeated in other parts of the country over the course of seven weeks. By the time the movement succeeded in totally uprooting the *panchayat* system, at least fifty people were dead, and thousands were injured as a result of the force used by the authorities in suppressing the agitation. The government also had incarcerated national and district-level leaders of both the Nepali Congress Party and the United Left Front.

Unable to contain the widespread public agitation against the *panchayat* system and the mounting casualties, and fearing for the survival of his own monarchical status, King Birendra lifted the ban on political parties on April 8.

The unrest persisted. In the midst of continued violence, a royal proclamation on April 16 dissolved the Rashtriya Panchayat and invalidated provisions of the 1962 constitution inconsistent with multiparty democracy.

The next day, the king named Nepali Congress Party President K.P. Bhattarai, a moderate who had spent fourteen years as a political prisoner, as prime minister and head of the interim government. The government also freed all political prisoners, lifted control of all domestic and foreign publications, and established a commission, known as the Mullick Commission, to investigate the recent loss of life and property.

The eleven-member Bhattarai cabinet, composed of four members of the Nepali Congress Party, three members of the United Left Front, two human rights activists, and two royal nominees, was immediately entrusted with the task of preparing a new constitution and holding a general election. Pending the adoption of a new constitution, the interim government agreed that Nepal should remain under the 1962 constitution. In the interest of continuity and orderly management of public business, the interim government resisted demands from the left for a mass purge of the bureaucracy and die-hard *panchayat* elements. Bhattarai's goal was national reconciliation in a multiparty democracy.

After nine months of politicking, the constitution was proclaimed on November 9, 1990. Elections to the House of Representatives were held on May 12, 1991. The new government faced the immediate problems of restoring law and order, providing economic relief to the populace, and establishing its claim to sound administration, a somewhat difficult task because the parties of the interim government had been in the opposition for a long period of time.

Furthermore, pro-*panchayat* thugs who had tried to foment chaos and law and order problems to discredit the new government had to be brought under control. The situation improved as many former *panchayat* leaders who had previously supported moves for a multiparty democracy openly supported the political changes and offered to cooperate with the new government-taking advantage of political opportunism.

9

Nepal's Emerging Security Issues

In the past two decades, the security perception of Nepal has shown some significant deviation from typical traditional military-based threats to more diverse threats emanating from a range of nontraditional, non-military components. These emerging changes in the perception of the nature and trends of threats could be largely attributed to both internal dynamics and the external atmosphere. Internally, Nepal has seen major changes to its political structures in the last two decades.

The democratic transition in the 1990s generated enormous political consciousness and social awareness among the Nepalese people. Freedom of speech, the right to organise and the flourishing of the media have all played a significant role in empowering the general public. People have become more attentive to their rights and to issues that relate to their day-to-day lives. Problems like political instability, the failure to maintain law and order, social discrimination, disparities in development, the lacks of inclusiveness, the failure of institutional delivery and the inefficient governing system have generated enormous interest. The failure of successive governments to address these problems in past decades played an instrumental role in allowing hard left forces like the Maoists and terrorist and criminal groups to consolidate and expand their strength and activities. This caused armed conflict over the last ten years, which led the country to a state of chaos, instability and violence.

During the Maoist insurgency, more than 13,000 people lost their lives, tens of thousands were injured and an even larger number of people were displaced from their homes, precipitating an internal refugee crisis. People's desire for peace and democracy resulted in a massive uprising in April 2006 which forced the King to surrender power to the political parties and to reinstate the parliament that had been dissolved. This also led to the holding of an election to the Constituent Assembly in April 2008 and the declaration of the Federal Democratic Republic of Nepal. The government formed after the CA election is under tremendous pressure to free its people from the clutches of violence and to secure their basic needs, such as sufficient food, shelter, education, health care, human rights, political stability and security.

The ten years of conflict also triggered many other social and environmental crises in Nepal. For example, due to the escalation of violence in rural areas, forced migration has been taking place which has precipitated a large number of internal refugees, particularly in the Mid and Far West hill districts and also in the mid-Tarai regions. Similarly, out-country migration has become a common phenomenon as hundreds of thousands of young people have left the country to seek jobs. There are also about 110,000 forcibly migrated Bhutanese refugees who have been languishing in various camps in two Eastern districts (Morang and Jhapa) for almost two decades, and there are about 25,000 Tibetan refugees taking shelter in different parts of Nepal. The plight of these groups of refugees and of Nepal's own internally displaced persons is linked with a variety of social problems, such as deteriorating law and order due to their increasing involvement in criminal activities and increasing conflict between the local community and refugees over access to resources and employment opportunities.

Another major concern related to migration and security is the increase in the incidence of HIV/AIDS, since large numbers of the temporary migrant population working in India and also internal migrant groups, particularly in roadside areas, have become infected. This is associated with their high mobility and migration, but also with the trafficking of women and children, commercial sex workers, intravenous drug users, and the high rate of STI. High mobility, (both internal and external) migration, and poverty are overwhelmingly considered to be the root causes of the high incidence of HIV/AIDS both in Nepal and elsewhere.

Forced migration has become another major security issue for Nepal in recent years. The violent conflict over the past ten years and the existence of many armed groups in the Tarai region has induced internal displacement. It is estimated by various organisations working in this field, such as the Norwegian Refugee Council, the United Nations High Commission for Refugee (UNHCR) and the Informal Service Sector (INSEC), that up to 200,000 people have been internally displaced during the ten years of the Maoists' 'People's War'. Displacement was caused by both sides, i.e. both by the Maoists and by the Army's excessive use of force and the abuses it committed. Due to the increasing insecurity and threat posed by these armed groups, people fled their own native villages and sought refuge either in their district headquarters or in major cities like Kathmandu, Nepalgunj, Pokhara and Biratnagar. Though no exact figure is available, it is estimated that a large number of people, particularly from the Mid West and Far West regions also fled to India, which has for a long time been a popular migration destination for Nepalese people. They go to cities like Mumbai, Delhi, and Hyderabad and work in very unsafe and unhealthy environments, and then return with number of problems, including HIV/AIDS. The security and care of people infected with HIV/AIDS is another issue that the state now needs to focus on, particularly in Far Western Districts such as Achham, Bajhang, Kailali, Bajura, Baitadi, etc.

The use of terror tactics by extremist groups to assert political or social agendas has become common in Nepal. A number of small armed groups who split from the Maoists are involved in arbitrary killing, abduction, intimidation and harassment of common people in the mid- and East Tarai districts of Nepal. The increase in such activities poses a serious challenge to law and order in those districts and the surroundings areas. Bhutanese refugees based in Nepal have also recently formed a Communist Party of Bhutan (Maoists) and have decided to launch armed rebellion against the King's regime inside Bhutan. It has been reported that the Bhutanese Maoists are establishing links with the Maoists and other extremist groups in India. Their involvement in violent activities would have a serious impact in Nepal's border regions of Nepal and in India too.

Although the 'People's War' was ended following the signing of the Comprehensive Peace Agreement in November 2006 between the Government of Nepal and the CPN (Maoists), the issue of the return of internally displaced people (IDPs) has not been resolved. This is due to the present coalition government's lack of comprehensive policies and programmes, the continued threat of extortion and harassment, and the refusal to return property confiscated by the Maoists. Large numbers of displaced people are still living in terrible conditions in various parts of the country. The safe return of these IDPs and their resettling in their native places is another challenge for the country. The IDP issue has seriously disturbed the security environment in big cities and in various district headquarters. If the prevailing frustration and disappointment among these IDPs persists, there is a danger that they will take extreme steps such as joining extremist groups.

Another serious threat for Nepal today is environmental insecurity. The fast degradation of shared rivers, the frequent bursting of glacier lakes and increasing landslides and floods due to torrential rainfalls in the mid-mountains are just some of the issues facing Nepal today on the environmental front. Furthermore, increasing urbanisation and the growth of unplanned city centres have created serious threats to the health of urban people. A report published by the Asian Development Bank stated that the capital city Kathmandu has become the most polluted city in Asia in recent years.

Meanwhile, the changing external atmosphere around Nepal, especially the increasing rapprochement between India and China, has also changed the nature and trends of threat perception in Nepal. Over the last two decades, bilateral relations between India and China have improved remarkably. China's decision to adopt an open door policy in the early 1980s and India's economic liberalisation policy in 1991 have been a marked shift in their traditional foreign policy behaviour. Both the Indian and Chinese leaderships realised that the old, ideology-led foreign policy no longer works due to the growing processes of globalisation and inter-dependence. In line with their changing relations at the bilateral level, India and China have also started to co-operate with each other in managing their relations with neighbouring countries, including Nepal.

Both countries are trying to find new ways of managing relations in the changing context. Over the last decade, both India and China have adopted several policies in line with the changing environment. The introduction of the 'Gujral Doctrine' in the mid-1990s was one step towards changing old policies towards neighbouring countries. Likewise, India's willingness to participate in private-level relations with Nepal rather than the typical government-togovernment level of the past also indicates that it now encourages relations with Nepal based on a multiplicity of agencies and actors. Similarly, China has revitalised its neighbourhood policy over the last decades by introducing a 'Comprehensive Periphery Policy' which means having an integrated regional policy with neighbouring countries. The Chinese Government has also been cautiously expanding its political influence in the subcontinent, without harming the growing amity with India.

India and China have expressed serious concern about the recent escalation of violence and the breakdown of law and order in Nepal. They fear that the growing conflict in Nepal would have spillover impacts on bordering areas in both countries. The hijacking of an Indian Airlines New Delhi-bound flight from Kathmandu by Islamic terrorists in 1999 raised the serious possibility that Nepali land could be used against India's interests. The growing nexus between different armed groups in Nepal and India, human trafficking, and uncontrolled migratory movements are issues that India and Nepal have identified as new threats to the security and interests of both countries. New Delhi has repeatedly asked Nepal to control the activities of groups allegedly supported by Pakistani intelligence acting against India from Nepali land. Similarly, China's concern today is that insecurity and instability in Nepal might strengthen anti-China elements in the Tibet Autonomous Area, which is itself regarded as trouble spot for China.

With these changes to the situation at all levels – internal, regional and international – Nepal has found that many of its traditional security threats have been diluted but that many new, non-traditional security threats have become more pronounced. The changing nature and trends of threats perception in Nepal can be seen in some recently published studies in Nepal. Writing about the changing threat perception in Nepal, Indrajit Rai states that 'when we talk about Nepal, perception of threat in mind, Nepal has least possibilities of direct external arms attack but there are maximum chances of threat for the people of Nepal. In other words, Nepal is not secure from internal threats – insurgency, poverty, education and health problems'. He further states that the people of Nepal are not secure at all. Lokraj Baral emphasises a people-centric approach in both the theory and practice of security. He states that 'the recent pro-democracy movement in Nepal has established the fact that the military along cannot protect the rulers if the people fail to identify their interest with that of the state run by anti-people rulers. The comprehensive security idea has emerged strongly as even democracy without human empowerment and social justice cannot create a congenial atmosphere for security of the sate and people'. The conventional tendency of states to secure their position under the banner of so-called 'nationalism' has also been increasingly challenged in the changing security environment.

Baral states that 'in Nepal, for instance, King Gyanendra's coup of 1 February 2005, which drove the King to take back all powers as well as to depart from the established constitutional process, is being justified in the name of safeguarding the country and the people against 'terrorism' perpetrated by the Communist Party of Nepal (Maoists). But less than one and half year, his regime had become much more vulnerable to domestic conditions and international pressures and was overthrown by the people's popular uprising'. However, electoral democracy alone cannot ensure all aspects of security or the comprehensive security of the people and the nation if it fails to deliver people's basic needs such as food, shelter, clothes, health care facilities, improved environmental conditions, and freedom from fear. Lama argues that 'the skewed distribution of both development benefits and the development of peoples' capabilities explain to a large extent the ongoing socioeconomic dissidence of the 'Maobadi' and the caste-ethnic group resurgence in different regions of Nepal'.

A Report on Poverty stated that Nepal now stands at the crossroads amidst a morass of crisis: an economic crisis, a political crisis, a governance crisis, a security crisis, and above all a poverty crisis. R. Bhattarai points out 'in the changing concept of security and strategic considerations, Nepal has been facing a tremendous pressure in freeing its people from the clutches of violence and security for them basic needs such as sufficient food, shelters, education, health care and security. The state's failure to initiate socio-economic development has been one of the major causes of conflict, which has led the current state of chaos, instability and violence'. Jagannath Adhikari points out that changes in national economic conditions such as the decline in agricultural production and food security, and the existence of various traditional barriers against women obtaining domestic non-farm work, have been the main causes for the increased out-migration of Nepali women.

Restoring peace and maintaining political stability following the violence of the last decade is a major concern for the people of Nepal today. Leading political analysts have concluded that the conflict has evolved into the most serious internal crisis Nepal has faced since its founding in the mid-eighteenth century. Nepal's internal socio-economic, political, ethnic and environmental issues need 'securitisation' as they increasingly appear to be existential threats to society and the country itself; a response by the state is therefore required.

Improving bilateral relations between Nepal's two giant neighbours India and China has contributed to changing the nature and trends of the threat perception in Nepal. Lama writes: 'What is striking in all this is the seemingly irreversible nature of the growing economic engagement between China and South Asia. These economic ties cannot be withdrawn with the flick of a switch when tensions flare'. Olav F. Knudsen argues that the policies of great powers are seen to determine the fate of small states. In his article, 'Analysing Small-State Security: The Role of External Factors', Knudsen argues that 'in times of high tension between the great powers, even small problems loom large. The actions of other governments may more easily provoke reactions under high tensions'. In the same article he further elaborates that 'in periods of low tension, there is no apparent security problem for the small state, a perception which grows stronger as a low-tension period endures'. Both India and China's concern in Nepal is related with security and stability: both countries are emerging powers in the region and they need a peaceful environment on their borders and in neighbouring areas to grow and expand their strength and influence.

Bhattarai argues that 'India and China's paramount concern in Nepal today is related to security and stability. Any disturbances in Nepal would have spill over impacts on both countries. The changing internal dynamics and the external nature and trends of threats perception in Nepal need to be analysed in a broader framework of non-traditional security discourse. This will help to identify how humanitarian issues have constructed 'securitisation' processes while military and state interests, including external threats, have increasingly been 'desecuritised' or less prioritised in the current Nepali context.

SECURITY CONCERNS

Nepal, a landlocked country, located at an altitude varying from 70m to 8,884m is bordered by two countries—India and China. To its south, east and west is India. Indo-Nepalese borders are not separated by any natural barriers and, in fact, there is a free movement of people and goods. To the north, Nepal is bordered by the Tibetan region of China. There are 28 passes on the Sino-Nepal boundary, of which three important routes are open throughout the year. Threat perceptions to India do not directly arise from Nepal per se 3. They arise from:

- the possibility that through Nepal's northern borders any power (emphasis on China) upon entering Nepal, can easily access the Indian mainland since Indo-Nepal borders are not separated by any natural barrier and in this sense are open;

- that a Nepal which is not stable politically and economically would be more vulnerable to such an eventuality, and this would consequently result in the Indian mainland also being exposed;
- that Nepal may adopt policies (internally and externally) which would be detrimental to the security interests of India.

The geo-strategic importance of Nepal as articulated by free India was a continuation of the perceptions of British India which had concluded treaty arrangements with Nepal in this regard. The hereditary Rana autocracy ruling Nepal followed a policy of isolation and maintained these arrangements as the continuity of their regime depended on British support. However, by the time British withdrew from the subcontinent, the Indian freedom movement influenced some sections in Nepal too, to demand democracy and an end to Rana autocracy. Transition, thus, was to take place not only in India but also in Nepal. The Ranas sought the support of free India in return for being sympathetic to the latter's security concerns.

Contradictions were bound to arise. The key word for India was the need for "stability" in Nepal, so that it would not become vulnerable to outside pressures. Nehru wanted an arrangement in Nepal which would not result in a complete break from the past and which would also result in a forward movement. Those contending for power in Nepal were: the Rana autocrats who for over a hundred years had exercised absolute power; the monarchy which for over a hundred years had not exercised real power; and finally, the democrats, represented by the Nepali Congress, who were not a cohesive group and had serious personality clashes. In these circumstances, India's involvement and attempt to find a solution was bound to satisfy some at the expense of the others because it would be seen as aligning with one party. This would also reduce the chances of manoeuvring in case the need arose to support one party against the other, in India's national interest.

The result was the Delhi Settlement, according to which King Tribhuvan would continue to be the king of Nepal and an interim Cabinet of 14 members would be formed, half of whom would be popular representatives and the rest would be supporters of the Ranas. This, it was hoped, would provide progress without a complete break with the past. Success, however, was elusive, first due to the differences between the Ranas and the Nepali Congress, and later, when the Nepali Congress also failed to provide a viable alternative. The attempts continued till 1955, when the Cabinet was dissolved and the direct rule of the crown was promulgated under King Tribhuvan who was keen to establish a democratic government in due course. India's security concerns with Nepal had intensified following China's proclamation on September 10, 1949, that Tibet was part of Chinese territory and that no foreign intervention would be tolerated. On October 7, 1950, the Chinese occupied Eastern Tibet, resulting in Nepal having contiguous borders with China. With danger to Nepal's territorial integrity being detrimental to India's security, stability in Nepal became a top priority for India.

Building Convergences

To meet India's security concerns (and those of Nepal too), India and Nepal concluded in 1950 the Treaty of Peace and Friendship. The treaty, considered the bedrock on which Indo-Nepal relations are built, has clauses addressing both security and economic aspects. The letters exchanged along with the treaty also form an important part of the understanding leading to mutual security. The treaty was to remain in force till either party gave notice of one year. Some of the important clauses of the treaty and the letter spell out that the two countries would inform each other of any misunderstanding with any neighbouring state likely to cause a breach in the friendly relations between the two countries; that the two countries would not employ a foreigner whose activities would be prejudicial to the security of the other; that arms or warlike material which Nepal imports through the territory of India shall be with the assistance and agreement of India. This particular clause could be incorporated not only because Nepal is a landlocked country but more important because it is for all practical purposes India-locked. It is this one factor which reduces Nepal's choices and manoeuvrability in both security and economic aspects.

The economic clauses in the Treaty of Peace and Friendship of 1950 refer to the national treatment which will be given to the nationals of the other regarding participation in industrial and economic development, residence, ownership of property, etc. As a result of this treaty, the people of Nepal are free to take up employment, buy property (like Indians can in Nepal) and even be part of the government services in India except in the limited seats of the Indian Administrative Service (IAS), Indian Police Service (IPS) and Indian Foreign Service (IFS). This clause is important to Nepal because of the low level of economic development in Nepal.

The treaty of 1950 should always be looked at as a whole package and not in parts, as is normally done. The economic and security provisions of the treaty are two sides of the same coin. While officially Nepal has not asked India for a review of the treaty, in other fora, from time to time, criticism on the security clauses is aired to the exclusion of the benefits which accrue to it in the economic sphere. It is due to the uniqueness of these provisions—economic and political—that India terms the bilateral relationship as a special one.

Along with the Treaty of Peace and Friendship was concluded the Treaty of Trade and Commerce. It covered the very crucial issue of facilities provided to Nepal for transit regarding trade not only with third countries, but also movement of goods from one place to another within Nepal through the Indian territory. During this period, more than 90 per cent of Nepal's trade was with India. Apart from trade and transit, India assisted Nepal in the construction of airports, canals, water supply, irrigation, roads, etc. Of the total aid of Nepalese Rupees (NR) 9,49,69,000 received by Nepal in 1951-56, India's contribution amounted to NR 7,00,18,000.[12]

In 1951, the two countries decided to establish border checkposts along Nepal's border with Tibet, manned jointly by the Nepalese Army personnel and Indian wireless operators. This enabled the Government of India to receive intelligence reports regarding military activities in the north. In 1952, keeping in view the internal and external threats to Nepal, the modernisation of the disorganised and ill-equipped Nepalese Army was considered necessary. Following Nepal's request, an India Military Mission (IMM) was deputed to Nepal in 1952 to train and modernise the Nepalese Army.

However, these measures failed to evoke any enthusiasm from Nepal, which resented such direct involvement, particularly after maintaining a policy of isolation for over a hundred years during which it even did not allow the British entry beyond a certain point. Secondly, there were the discontented political elements who were unhappy at India's involvement in the political events and decisions, and all this led to a lot of bitterness. A major reason for the convergences had been the personality of King Tribhuvan. With his death, this link was also broken.

Managing Contradictions

A new phase in the relations began with the death of King Tribhuvan in 1955. Till 1990, when the democratic revolution took place, a singular contradiction running through Indo-Nepal relations was the desire of the monarchy to wield power and the belief in India that only a democratic government would give Nepal stability. This contradiction led Nepal to dilute the spirit behind the treaty of 1950, and build new linkages. Thus, the convergences witnessed in the first phase were gradually withdrawn. Even though after some time India supported the monarchy and the Panchayati regime that Nepal introduced, the suspicions continued.

In this direction, in 1958, the IMM was downgraded and reorganised as the Indian Military Training and Advisory Group (IMTAG). However, with elections being held and the Nepali Congress coming to power, convergences were once again visible not only in the political arena but also in the economic field. In 1960, the Treaty of Trade and Transit was concluded, whose provisions indicated towards a free trade area and also additional facilities for transit. However, the dismissal of the democratic government by King Mahendra drew sharp criticism from India; this was resented by Nepal, and a threat was perceived from India itself. The regime's security was equated with state security. Thus, a divergence was witnessed, which only increased with Nepal developing ties with China and Pakistan.

Nepal soon established close cordial relations with China and later with Pakistan. King Mahendra successfully used the China card to extract concessions from India. From a historical perspective, the use of the China card by Nepal was not completely a new move. Even while dealing with British India, the rulers of Nepal had kept the China card open. As for China, its relations with Nepal assumed importance historically as well in the per cent times in the context of the former's interests in Tibet. Further, with China's differences arising with India, close relations with Nepal were welcome. China gave aid to Nepal as part of its policy. Later, it built the Kathmandu-Kodari read whose construction started in 1963 and was completed in 1965. The road provided a direct strategic connection between China and Nepal via the difficult Tibetan route. If Nepal could not resist an attack through this road, the Indian heartland would be easily accessible through the open Indo-Nepal borders. For India, these developments were a cause of grave concern.

The changing security concerns with Indo-Sino differences and the War 1962, led India to reassess its policy towards Nepal. The 1962, War disproved the long-held belief that the Himalayas were impregnable. In the change of stand, India approved of Nepal's Panchayati system, and in 1965, the arms agreement between the two countries regarding supply of arms was concluded. One of the clauses spelt out that in the event of any shortfalls in the supply of arms and equipment by the Government of India to Nepal, the Governments of the USA and UK would furnish some defence assistance in order to supplement the assistance from India. In this sense, India's role as a supplier of arms to Nepal was emphasised. In other words, it meant restating the link in the mutual security concerns of the two countries. In the economic field, India conceded concessions on transit procedures which Nepal had been asking for. Thus, India sought convergence on the security front by strengthening ties in the economic area. These moves, however, were not successful.

Problems again arose in August 1970, when Nepal further diluted mutual security concerns when it asked India to withdraw personnel at the Nepal-Tibet checkposts and the IMTAG. The divergence in security issues coincided with divergences in the economic arena too. Problems arose over the renewal of the Treaty of Trade and Transit, which expired on October 31.20 Later, Nepal accused India of a blockade, which the latter denied. India held that the differences were due to Nepal's persistent demand for a land route to trade with Pakistan, and certain policies which caused harm to Indian trade; and the Nepalese demanded two separate treaties on trade and transit, maintaining that while transit was of a permanent nature, trade interests differed from time to time. India did not agree to this. A single treaty was finally concluded on August 31, 1971, after a year of serious differences.

In 1972, King Birendra succeeded to the throne, and in 1975, he propounded the Zone of Peace proposal which was again an attempt to dilute mutual security convergences. The Janata Party government attempted to develop a close relationship and it agreed to two separate treaties—one on trade and the other on transit, in 1978. An agreement to control unauthorised trade was also concluded. Nepal had always wanted two separate treaties—one on trade and the other on transit, saying that while transit was of permanent importance, trade interests changed from time to time. However, Nepal's attitude towards India did not change.

In 1988, a complete dilution of the spirit of the 1950 Treaty took place, when Nepal bought arms from China which included anti-aircraft guns and medium range SSM besides AK-49 assault rifles, etc that entered Nepal through the Kathmandu-Kodari road. Immediately, problems over renewal of the Trade and Transit Treaties arose. There were other problems also and India conveyed to Nepal that it would discuss a single treaty of trade and transit. Differences which began over the trade issue, slowly covered the entire gamut of bilateral relations. Trade was carried on a most favoured nation (MFN) basis, and the trade and transit points which numbered 15 and 22 respectively were reduced to two.

There was, however, no sign of a solution to the problems, and Indo-Nepal relations touched the nadir. During the crisis, Nepal realised the limitations of the Chinese help.

Positive Bilateralism

Thus, problems got resolved only after the ushering in of democracy in April 1990. In a joint communique in June 1990, both the sides touched on important security and economic issues. In April 1990, India welcomed the success of the mass movement for multi-party democracy in Nepal which led to the installation of an interim government headed by Prime Minister Krishna Prasad Bhattarai. In June 1990, Prime Minister Bhattarai's visit to India ended with the signing of a joint communique which restored status quo ante in bilateral relations to April 1, 1987—the period before the emergence of bilateral tensions. During the visit, both sides undertook to fully respect each other's security concerns, not to allow activities in the territory of the one prejudicial to the security of the other, and to have consultations with a view to reaching mutual agreement on such defence related matters which, in the view of either country, could pose a threat to its security. Having done so, they seriously moved to cooperation in the spheres of industrial and human resource development and for harnessing of the common rivers for the benefit of the peoples of the two countries, and for protection and management of the environment. Various possibilities of widening bilateral economic cooperation were also considered. Later, many new agreements were signed.

The positive bilateral process continued with the visit of the Indian prime minister to Nepal from February 13 to 15, 1991, which was the first such visit in 14 years. In the coming years, such high level visits were to be a normal feature.

Later, in 1991, an Indo-Nepal High Level Task Force was up—chaired by the Cabinet secretary or equivalent on both sides and including the foreign secretary, finance secretary and commerce secretary—which prepared a comprehensive programme for bilateral cooperation. Further in 1991, as many as five important treaties and agreements were signed. These include a new trade treaty, a new transit treaty, an agreement for cooperation in controlling unauthorised trade, etc. An appreciation of each other's security interests also led to close convergence on security interests.

Other significant steps include the state visit of the King of Nepal, His Majesty King Birendra Shah, in May 1993. India's economic cooperation programme with Nepal continued with the commissioning of an industrial estate at Rajbiraj and a telephone exchange at Rangeli in Nepal. Under the new trade regime that came into force in April 1993, access to the Indian market free of customs duty for manufactured articles was improved to include articles containing not less than 50 per cent of Nepalese materials and labour.

In 1996, India and Nepal renewed the Indo-Nepal Trade Treaty for a period of five years, up to 2001. As a result, articles of Nepalese manufacture could enter the Indian market free of customs duty and quantity restrictions. It was also agreed to accord parity to Nepalese products in the levy of countervailing duty, which would be equal to the treatment provided to Indian products, on the basis of a certificate issued by the Government of Nepal.

The 1991 Transit Treaty was renewed on January 5, 1999, in Kathmandu. The renewed treaty contains liberalised procedures for the transit of Nepalese goods. Nepal's request for "automatic renewal" for further seven-year periods was accepted by India. It, however, needs to be noted that the protocal and memorandum to the treaty, containing modalities and other arrangements, would be subject to review and modification every seven years or earlier, if warranted. Thus, it is seen that though the treaty is to be automatically renewed, India would always be able to influence the important provisions in the protocol and memorandum to the treaty.

In future, another effective mechanism of cooperation will be through sub-regional cooperation, more specifically, the Bangladesh-Bhutan-India-Nepal Growth Quadrangle (BBIN-GQ). This will follow a project-led approach to cooperation in the core economic areas of multimodal transportation and communications; energy, trade and investment facilitation and promotion; tourism; optimal utilisation of natural resource endowments and environment. These projects are to be supportive of, and complementary to, the national plans of the four concerned countries. They will make best use of neighbourhood synergies and would be such that they can most productively be dealt with on sub-regional basis. Nepal is actively involved in this and will coordinate the overall sub-regional cooperation efforts. A positive aspect of this mechanism would be that it will eliminate the anti-India factor generally witnessed in development projects which are of a bilateral nature.

Do all these positive steps imply that mutual trust has been established and there is now a complete absence of mistrust and anti-India sentiments in Nepal? It is observed that as the legacy of mistrust is a long one, bilateral relations do evoke a degree of doubt. Further, in a democratic set-up, with regular elections being held, anti-India sentiments are used by many political parties to garner support. But it has been seen that with the establishment of democracy in Nepal, when in power, political parties do adopt a constructive cooperative approach towards India. Some of the issues which are yet to be resolved include the Mahakali Treaty, the Kalapani issue, the Bhutanese refugees issue (though this is between Nepal and Bhutan, Nepal feels that since it is through India that the refugees enter Nepal, India has a role to play), and the revision of certain provisions of the 1950 Treaty.

It is observed that democracy in Nepal has not meant that there are no bilateral differences, but the basic contradictions have been removed. While earlier India was accused of supporting the democratic elements, this does not happen now. Thus, while earlier the threat to the regime from these democratic elements was equated with a threat to the state, with India being the main factor, the same does not arise now. Anti-India feelings are still present but India is consciously trying to build on a cooperative model, and emphasising on economic relations, more so in the face of new security challenges.

Jaswant Singh's Visit to Nepal

India's External Affairs Minister Jaswant Singh's four-day (September 8-11) visit to Nepal has given a positive thrust and direction to Indo-Nepal relations. It builds on the approach of positive bilateralism which began in the 1990s following the establishment of democracy in Nepal. But its significance arises from the joint approach both countries will take to tackle the new challenges on the security front. The agenda for bilateral cooperation has, since a few years, been broad-based, focussing on the economy and energy. Jaswant Singh's visit enabled the developments in these areas to be reviewed and new thrust areas to be identified.

New Security Challenges

Security has always been a vital if not the core aspect of Indo-Nepal relations. However, these concerns have not remained static. With changing times, it is observed that new challenges have arisen. While traditional security concerns mentioned at the outset, arising from the geo-strategic positions remain, presently the security threats arise from the use of Nepalese territory by Pakistan's ISI (Inter-Services Intelligence Directorate) as a springboard to launch anti-India activities. India shares a 1,751-km-long open border with Nepal. The Indian states along this border are Sikkim, West Bengal, Bihar and Uttar Pradesh. The open Indo-Nepal borders (to facilitate free movement of people from both countries) are being used by anti-India elements to access India. India's concerns arise from the fact that eastern Nepal which borders the narrow sensitive Siliguri corridor connecting the entire north-east to the rest of India, is being used by Pakistan's ISI to sponsor insurgency in the north-east and transfer small arms and contraband. In other parts of India too, it is reported that the large quantities of weapons and ammunition seized, including RDX, have been traced to the Nepalese route. Presently, as the Indian external affairs minister stated, the presence of foreign intelligence agencies in Nepal is part of India's security concerns.

On the other hand, Nepal is also facing left-wing Maoist extremists within its territory. Nepal is concerned that these Maoists might develop links with similar groups in India. It is suspected that they have developed links with the Maoist Communist Centre (MCC) in Bihar and the People's War Group (PWG) in Andhra

Pradesh. With the twin forces of the ISI and Maoists in its territory, Nepal would be particularly anxious to keep the left-wing extremists and Islamic radicals separated. Presently, the Maoists are poorly armed but their destructive power can grow manifold if they have access to arms and explosives available to the ISI. India has denied reports that the Maoist rebels active in Nepal were functioning from Indian soil.

Thus, both the countries have new security concerns, which are qualitatively different from what confronted them initially, and which are more difficult to respond to in certain aspects. The threat is more diffused in nature; it is not aimed directly at the territorial integrity of either country, but the aim is to cause grave harm. The threat is from non-state actors in both countries developing linkages. This makes it more difficult to combat, unlike the earlier perceptions of threat to the territorial integrity from a particular country.

It is clear that these new security challenges have to be met through joint actions by both the countries and this is exactly what the two countries have decided to do. Both sides have decided to undertake, "integrated border management". This essentially involves infrastructural development in the border areas, including the construction of cross-border roads which connect with Nepal's main highways. This lateral construction of roads will not only encourage cross-border trade, but will have major security implications since it will help in effective monitoring of cross-border terrorism. In fact, in June 1997, the two countries decided to work closely to fight terrorism. Towards this direction, the Joint Working Group on border management has already held meetings. Both countries have also agreed to review their extradition treaty and are also considering concluding an understanding on mutual legal assistance in criminal matters.

Another important issue from the security point of view is the question of demarcation of the Indo-Nepal boundary, including the Kalapani area. The Kalapani enclave lies on the tri-junction of India, Nepal and China. Nepal has stated that this area is located within its territory, which has been disputed by India. India maintains a post of the para-military Indo-Tibetan Border Police

(ITBP) there. India holds the view that a committee was set up to examine the issue when Prime Minister I.K. Gujral visited Nepal and that India would wait for the report of the committee.

Economic Issues

Many positive steps have been taken in the economic field. India and Nepal have decided to revive the India-Nepal Joint Commission to focus on economic ties. In a bid to push trade, both countries will also work out an agreement which will facilitate the cross-border movement of motor vehicles in the next four months. An Indo-Nepal Inter-Governmental Committee will meet to promote trade, facilitate transit and control unauthorised trade between the two countries. Creation of export promotion zones at Birgunj, Biratnagar and Nepalgunj is also being envisaged. Earlier (pre-1990s), Indo-Nepal relations were primarily covered by the Indo-Nepal Treaties of Trade and Transit which had to be periodically renewed and would at times cause concern to both sides. Presently, both countries have moved beyond these issues to cooperate in other areas.

Both countries have decided to focus on the development of hydro- power in Nepal. In this direction, it has been decided that a Joint Office (JPO) will be set up to prepare a detailed project report for the 6,000 MW Pancheshwar project by November 1999. It has also been decided that the necessary steps for the preparation of the detailed project report on the 2,000 MW Saptakoshi project will be undertaken.

Both countries have also decided to encourage the involvement of the private sector in developing small and medium sized power plants in Nepal since the larger projects will have a gestation period of eight to 10 years. India is giving top priority to energy imports from Nepal which it sees as part of its larger effort to achieve national energy security. This would also help in bringing down the trade deficit which is in India's favour.

India has called for the need to go beyond the South Asian Free Trade Agreement (SAFTA) and South Asian Preferential Trade Agreement (SAPTA) so that a South Asian Economic Zone could be established which would provide enormous benefits to the region. India has further stated that it supports the South Asian growth quadrangle (BBIN-GQ) concept initiated by Nepal.

Other Issues

A major highlight of the foreign minister's visit was the inauguration of the B.P. Koirala Institute of Health Sciences at Dharan, and the Neo-Natal and Maternal Intensive Care Units at the Maternity Hospital in Kathmandu. India and Nepal have agreed to set up a Joint Task Force (JTF) to study the problems of flood control and forecasting in Nepal and adjoining areas of India in a comprehensive manner; it is to submit its reports in six months. The two countries also decided to give a new thrust to the development of agriculture in the Terai region which borders Indian states. On the issue of refugees—Nepalese-speaking people—from Bhutan to Nepal, India has stated that it favours direct talks between Thimpu and Kathmandu to resolve the issue.

NEPAL'S SECURITY

Located right between the two largest countries in Asia – India and China – and being a landlocked state, national security issues have always been a major concern for Nepal, ever since its unification by King Prithvi Narayan Shah in 1769. Nepal's foreign and security policy evolved against the backdrop of the concurrent but separate threats posed by the British East India Company to the South and by the steadily expanding Chinese presence in Tibet to the North. Even after the emergence of India as an independent country and China as a People's Republic, Nepal's security threats perception has not altered significantly over the past seven decades. Though there are various factors, including its location, size, and public psyche, which help to explain Nepal's maintenance of traditional analysis of the threats to the country, the single most important factor determining its threats perception was the conflictual relationship between India and China after the 1962 war. This was made more complex by the India and China policies which competed to expand their area of influence in the region.

Being right in the middle of the two largest Asian countries and having an open border with India has had enormous impact on Nepal's security and strategic perceptions ever since its birth. The great strategist of that time, King Prithivi Narayan Shah, described Nepal's geo-strategic position as a 'yam between two boulders', showing that he was very much aware of Nepal's geographical location, its size and its two immediate neighbours. He further elaborated that Nepal should keep good neighbourly relations with both of its neighbours and should not ally with one against the other. Prithivi Narayan Shah's analysis has been reflected by many writers both in Nepal and in India, all of whom have said that if anything dictates Nepal's security policy, it is its geographical location.

Nepal's policy of equidistance and its attempts to isolate itself from increasing democratic influences from India triggered a range of activities that brought an element of competition into the Chinese and Indian presence in Nepal. This could be witnessed in foreign aid, where these countries built a number of infrastructural projects of high strategic significance. For instance, India's building of the Tribhuwan Highway to link the plains of India with Kathmandu and China's building of the Kodari Highway linking the border region of Tibet with Kathmandu injected new security dynamics into Nepal. Similar actions could be seen on the trade and the investment front. India extended a liberal trade exchange that provided unilateral access for Nepalese products to Indian markets. Meanwhile, China provided adequate space for the widening of traditional economic exchanges in border areas with Nepal.

The British colonial rulers of India sought to keep Nepal within the Indian sphere of influence and regarded the Himalaya as a second frontier under the widely practiced 'Himalayan frontier policy'. Due to its strategic importance for defence against China, the British did everything they could to transform Nepal into a friendly buffer state between China and the British possessions in India. After the end of British rule in India, the post-colonial government of India also took note of Nepal's strategic importance and quickly signed a Treaty of Peace and Friendship in 1950 covering all aspects of Nepal-India relations, including defence and security related issues, followed by a letter of exchange. It is interesting that the post-independence Indian government signed such a comprehensive Treaty with the oligarchic Rana regime at a time when this regime was facing mounting pressure from pro-democratic forces and was itself about to collapse. Likewise, Nepal and India concluded an Arms Assistance Agreement in 1965, under which India undertook to supply arms, ammunition, and equipment for the entire Nepalese Army.

China was also concerned about the security and stability of Nepal and took several measures to extend its own sphere of influence. Diplomatic relations between the two countries was established in 1955, and five years later, in April 1960, a bilateral treaty known as a Treaty of Peace and Friendship was signed during the visit to China of the first democratically elected Prime Minister, B. P. Koirala. It was this treaty which resolved the two countries' long-standing border disputes, including the question of Mount Everest.

Following the overthrow of the first elected government and the imposition of authoritarian rule in 1960, King Mahendra smartly used Nepal's geopolitical vulnerability to consolidate his domestic power. In particular, the border war between India and China in 1962 and the subsequent deterioration of their bilateral relations provided further ground for him to assert the issue of national security and to quell the popular uprising against his undemocratic rule. The regime projected the King and the whole institution of the monarchy as a symbol of national unity, and any threat to the institution would ultimately mean a threat to the security of the nation.

This does not mean that Nepal faced no threats to its security in modern times. In the early 1970s Nepal faced two serious concerns for its national security. The first was when a US-backed armed group of Tibetan refugees known as the 'Khampa rebels' launched an armed insurgency on the northern border of Nepal in 1971. Another event that raised serious security concerns was when India forcibly annexed the independent Himalayan country of Sikkim in 1974, which had also been a neighbouring country to Nepal. Both of these events raised concern for the national security environment, though it was not a direct attack on the country's territorial integrity and national sovereignty.

Nepal has not faced any direct attacks from external powers, including from its immediate neighbours, India and China. However, the country has become more vulnerable and its sustainability has been questioned in recent years. This is because of its failure to manage its internal order and its inability to promote much-needed social, cultural and economic development. Its failure to provide good governance, protect citizens' basic rights and fulfil their basic needs has led the country towards chaos and instability.

The people's increasing aspirations and successive governments' failure to meet the general masses' expectations has precipitated violent conflicts, internal displacement, and an environmental crisis. The experience of many other countries indicates that ethnicity, language and religion could represent other sources of insecurity. Nepal is fast falling victim to this problem, and unless appropriate interventions are made to assure adequate space to all disadvantaged communities, this insecurity could grow. Therefore, the security threat perception of Nepal has been changing due to growing vulnerability and internal disorder rather than insecurity from external factors.

CONCLUSION

Security is very important not only for a state to survive and develop but for all human beings to live and grow. However, there is no agreement among academics and analysts as to how to define the concept of security.

Generally, security is defined as the freedom of threats, but there is no common understanding of what these threats are – threats could be different from person to person and region to region. It can therefore be said that the meaning of security is in fact in the eye of the beholder.

This article has looked at security in the context of various theoretical frameworks, while arguing that the concept of security has always been changing in response to changing contexts. Threat perceptions have never been static. Perceptions of security and insecurity arise for each state and individual according to the existing context and developments in surrounding environments.

As both the internal and external context of Nepal has gone through significant changes since the Nepali state was founded in the mid-18 century, perceptions of threats to the existence and sustainability of this state have also changed. From the time of its unification until late last century, the dominant security perceptions in Nepal have been military-centric.

This traditional security perception has the central view that security is to protect the territory and that as long as the geographical territory is secure, everything is secure within the boundary. In the Nepali context, such a national security concept was defined as early as the unification period by its founding father, King Prithivi Narayan Shaha. This way of understanding security has been the central focus of ruling elites and is still regarded as relevant, also because of Nepal's geographical location.

However, although the issue of national security is still important, its attainment is increasingly linked to human security. The idea that as long as the territorial border is secure, everything within it is secure, is now becoming an anachronism. In today's world, the security of the border is not sufficient to guarantee the security and welfare of the people.

The Human Development Report for South Asia says that national security cannot be achieved in a situation where people starve and arms accumulate, where social expenditure falls and military expenditure rises. South Asia today is the most militarised region of the world, but that does not make the region any more secure.

Such a situation has precipitated various security dynamics that have emerged in today's Nepal. Due to growing conflict and a virtual non-existence of employment opportunity, a large number of people, particularly from hill regions, have been migrating from rural to urban and rural to rural areas, particularly in the Tarai. At the same time, significant numbers of young Nepali workers have been leaving the country and going to India, the Gulf countries, Malaysia and South Korea to secure employment. Most people who leave the country face numerous problems. The securitisation of migrant workers and their rights has become a formidable challenge for Nepal.

The current crisis in Nepal has eroded social capital and community relationships, undermining indigenous forms of social networks. The state has not been able to reduce poverty, control the exploitation of disadvantaged communities by those in power, prevent environmental degradation or generate employment opportunities for large numbers of people. Nepal's vulnerabilities and its weakening position today did not come from external factors, even if to a certain degree external roles cannot be denied. However, these research findings show that the threats that Nepal faces today are more internally grown than caused by external factors.

The failure of our internal political, social and economic order are essentially the root causes for many pressing security problems: the loss of 14,000 lives; tens of thousands of injuries; hundreds of thousands homeless; the destruction of billions of rupees' worth of infrastructure; hundreds of thousands of Nepali youths leaving the country each year to seek jobs in alien lands, and their growing insecurity and vulnerability of infection from dangerous diseases; the destruction of forests and the rapid disappearance of endangered species; the scarcity of basic resources such as drinkable water, electricity, sanitation; growing ethnic and social conflict; and the prevailing situation of abject poverty.

For the first time in its history, the Army was mobilised to quell domestic rebels. Joint security forces were formed and mobilised against these domestic threats. With the intensification of conflict, the number of people serving in the Nepal Army and the Armed Police Force increased significantly, and the defence budget also increased alarmingly during that period. Even after the signing of CPA with the CPN (Maoist), the completion of the CA election and the formation of a new government under the leadership of the former rebel leader Mr. Pushpa Kamal Dahal, maintaining law and order and providing a secure environment is still recognised as the biggest challenge to this newly formed coalition government. The deteriorating security environment and the increase in violent activities are some of the main threats to the state today. More than this, however, it is necessary to identify the root causes of these mounting problems, which are not confined within the parameters of 'security' – they are related to the prevailing poverty, bad governance, a discriminative social system, the mounting gap between the 'haves' and the 'have nots', the deteriorating environmental situation and migratory movements.

In conclusion, while maintaining an underlying function of state-centric security, a traditional security approach to safeguard territorial integrity and the nation state's independence, security threat perceptions are changing. This is due to many factors: the broadening and deepening of security studies over the last two decades; Nepal's increasing vulnerabilities on the domestic front; changing bilateral relations between its two closest neighbours, India and China, from competition to co-operation; and the shift of the global political order from confrontation to co-operation since the end of Cold War. Human security issues have become more prominent, posing more serious challenges to the stability, progress and prosperity of Nepal than traditional, state-centric threats.

Bibliography

Adhikari, J. : *"Poverty, Globalization and Gendered Labour Migration in Nepal"*, New Delhi/Thousand Oaks/London: SAGE Publications, 2006.

Ashok K. : *The Royal Nepal Army : Meeting the Maoist Challenge*, Rupa, Delhi, 2005.

Bandita Sijapati: *A Kingdom Under Siege : Nepal's Maoist Insurgency, 1996 to 2003*, The Printhouse, Delhi, 2003.

Baral, Lok Raj: *Nepal: Problems of Governance.* Delhi: Konark Publishers, 1993.

Bottomore, Tom: *A Dictionary of Marxist Thought*, New Delhi, Maya Blackwell, 2000.

Cheek, Timothy: *Mao Zedong and China's Revolutions: A Brief History with Documents.* Boston: Bedford/St. Martin's, 2002.

Dasgupta, B.: *The Naxalite Movement*, Bombay: Allied Publishers, 1974.

Dhanalaxmi, Ravuri. *British Attitude to Nepal's Relations with Tibet and China, 1814-1914*. Chandigarh, India: Bahri, 1981.

Ellis, F. *Rural Livelihoods and Diversity in Developing Countries*. New York: Oxford University Press, 2000.

Frederick H. *Regionalism and National Unity in Nepal*. Berkeley: University of California Press, 1975.

Gao, Mobo: *The Battle for China's Past: Mao and the Cultural Revolution*, London, Pluto Press, 2008.

Geremie R. *Shades of Mao: The Posthumous Cult of the Great Leader.* Armonk, N.Y.: M. E. Sharpe, 1996.

Ghosh, Suniti : *The Historic Turning-Point: A Liberation Anthology*, Calcutta, 1992.

Gurung, G. 2002. *"Foreign Labour Migration and the Remittance Economy of Nepal."* Critical Asian Studies.

Höfer, András: *The Caste Hierarchy and the State in Nepal: A Study of the Muluki Ain of 1854.* Innsbruck: Universitätsverlag Wagner, 1979.

Kansakar, V. B. S.: *"International Migration and Citizenship in Nepal"*. Kathmandu: Central Bureau of Statistics/UNFPA, 2003.

Kant, Adhikari, Krishna . *Nepal under Jang Bahadur, 1846-1877.* Kathmandu: Buku, 1984.

Kumar, Satish. *Rana Polity in Nepal: Origin and Growth.* New York: Asia, 1967.

Leo E. *Nepal: Strategy for Survival.* Berkeley:University of California Press, 1971.

Lindell Jonathan: *Nepal and The Gospel of God,* New Delhi: United Mission to Nepal, 1979.

Marie Lecomte : *Hindu Kingship, Ethnic Revival, and Maoist Rebellion in Nepal,* Oxford University Press, Delhi, 2009.

Messerschmidt, Donald A.: *The Moran of Kathmandu,* Bangkok: White Orchid Press, 1997.

Muni, S.D. : *Maoist Insurgency in Nepal : The Challenge and the Response,* Rupa, Delhi, 2004.

Parmanand. *The Nepali Congress since Its Inception: A Critical Assessment.* Delhi: B.R. Publishing, 1982.

Regmi, D. R.: *Medieval Nepal,* Vol. II, Calcutta: Firma K. L. Mukhopadhyay, 1966.

Schurmann, Franz: *Ideology and Organization in Communist Nepal.* Berkeley: University of California Press, 1971.

Sever, Adrien: *Nepal under the Ranas,* New Delhi: Oxford and IBH Publishing Co. Pvt. Ltd., 1993.

Sharma, P. 1989. *Urbanization in Nepal.* Hawaii: East-West Population Institute.

Sijapati, Li, : *A Kingdom Under Siege : Nepal's Maoist Insurgency, 1996 to 2003,* The Printhouse, Delhi, 2003.

Skeldon, R.: *Migration and Development: a global perspective.* Harlow: Longman, 1997.

Stuart R. Schram: *The Political Thought of Mao Tse-Tung.* New York: Praeger, 1969.

Thapa, Deepak : *Understanding the Maoist Movement of Nepal,* Centre for Social Research and Development, Delhi, 2003.

Uddhab P : *Maoist Movement in Nepal: A Sociological Perspective,* Adroit, Delhi, 2007.

Upreti, B C : *Maoists in Nepal : From Insurgency to Political Mainstream,* Kalpaz Pub, Delhi, 2008.

Vannini, Fulgentius: *Christian Settlements in Nepal Duringthe Eighteenth Century,* New Delhi: Messers Devarsons, 1977.

Index

M

N

P

R

S

❑❑❑